Svenska Litteratursällskapets skrifter, vol. 37

Strindbergian Drama

THEMES AND STRUCTURE

by Egil Törnqvist

ALMQVIST & WIKSELL INTERNATIONAL
STOCKHOLM, SWEDEN

HUMANITIES PRESS
ATLANTIC HIGHLANDS, N.J., USA

ISBN 91-22-00441-6

First published in Sweden 1982 by
Almqvist & Wiksell International, Stockholm
in collaboration with
Humanities Press Inc., Atlantic Highlands, N.J. 07716, USA
ISBN 0-391-02463-9

Published with support from
Humanistisk-samhällsvetenskapliga Forskningsrådet
as Svenska Litteratursällskapets skrifter no. 37

Printed in Sweden by
Almqvist & Wiksell, Uppsala 1982

No predetermined form is to limit the author, because the theme determines the form.

Strindberg

Contents

1. Introduction

Masters of drama from Aeschylus to Beckett are few. Strindberg is one of them. His importance for the development of modern drama, now generally recognized, is enormous.

In view of this, one would expect to find an extensive literature on Strindberg as a craftsman—especially since the literature on this writer now comprises thousands of items. For although we may certainly take an interest in "the playwright as thinker" (Bentley), it is not only, or even primarily, his ideas that matter but the way in which these ideas are expressed.

Surprisingly enough relatively little has been done so far to throw light on the formal characteristics of the Strindbergian play, on its remarkable power to hold audiences for a hundred years. We need only turn to a comparable figure like Ibsen to find a different picture.

There are various reasons for this. Most important, perhaps, is the fact that Strindberg wrote in a minor language. This goes for Ibsen too of course. But unlike Strindberg, Ibsen has been blessed both with an ambitious, if not perfect, Norwegian edition (Bull/Koht/Seip), and with a very impressive English one (McFarlane). With regard to Strindberg we are still waiting for an adequate critical Swedish edition of the collected works,[1] and there is no selective standard edition in English. Rather, translations of Strindberg's plays, of very varying quality, have been published here and there, in a somewhat haphazard fashion (cf. the list of translations, p. 252 ff.). It is obvious that Ibsen under these circumstances must appear to be a much more attractive object of research than Strindberg in the Anglo-American part of the world.

A second reason may be found in the fact that Strindberg, unlike Ibsen, cannot easily be included in the tradition of Aristotelian drama. Since most commentators on dramatic technique have been, and still are, more familiar with this tradition than with what we may loosely term modernistic trends, the result is that Ibsen is a *sine qua non* in numerous works on playmaking, while Strindberg usually receives no more than passing attention.

A third reason may be found in the Swedish scholarly tradition. One rightly expects major contributions to come from Strindberg's own countrymen, who are themselves steeped in Swedish culture and who are able to discern overtones in Strindberg's language to which non-Swedes would not be sensitive. For some reason, Swedish scholars have not paid as much attention to the dramas as one would expect—in view of the fact that we here deal with the most significant part of Strindberg's *oeuvre* and the most obvious Swedish contribution to world literature.

Moreover, those Swedes who *have* dealt with the plays, have usually done so from an extrinsic rather than an intrinsic point of view. Thus much of the biographical and literary background for the dramas has been mapped out, while the dramas themselves have been discussed more in passing and rarely from a strictly dramaturgic point of view. That this has been so is no doubt partly due to the somewhat unfortunate academic division of disciplines: while literary scholars tend to study the plays as literature, theatre scholars tend to examine them in their staged versions; the former ignore the fact that we deal with *plays* by Strindberg, the latter that we deal with plays by *Strindberg.* Attention to both aspects has mostly come from non-Swedish scholars—with all the obligatory disadvantages just indicated.

A brief exposé of the major works devoted to Strindberg's plays will confirm the foregoing statements.[2] The first significant Swedish contribution, Lamm's two-volume study of Strindberg's total dramatic *oeuvre* (1924–26), unfortunately available only in Swedish, is still the basic study. Lamm provides a wealth of valuable information in his analyses and shows a marked intuitive sense for what is essential in the plays. Unlike many of his contemporaries, he is also aware of the significance of the post-Inferno plays. Impressive though it is as a pioneering work, Lamm's somewhat essayistic treatment of the dramas does not stand up to modern scholarly criteria. Thus Lamm, although certainly aware of the fundamental difference between the dramas as texts and as productions, does not draw the consequences of this awareness. Nor does he clearly distinguish between 'objective' plot account and subjective interpretation.[3] Highly speculative are his descriptions of the creative process, the road from original idea to published play (G. Lindström, 1963*a*, H. Lindström, 1976, 63).

Convinced that Strindberg's writings cannot be separated from his life, and that a true understanding of the plays must be based on knowledge about the man who wrote them, Lamm is primarily interested in the biographical-literary-ideological background. This explains why he devotes as much or more space to circumstances around the plays as to the plays themselves. In this respect Lamm has laid a firm foundation for later, largely positivistic Swedish research on Strindberg as a dramatist.

This appears perhaps most clearly in Ollén's useful survey (1948, augm. ed. 1961) stressing on the one hand the biographical background of the plays, on the other their stage history. In the last chapter of his dissertation, Brandell (1950) examines themes and symbols in *To Damascus I* in the light of Strindberg's psychic constitution. Hagsten's investigation (1951) of Strindberg's first important historical drama carries the significant title "The Author of *Master Olof*"; the emphasis is on the genesis of the play and on its autobiographical aspects. A similar approach is found in Smedmark (1952), who extensively deals with the ms. material. A more obvious concern with dramaturgic (theatrical) problems is found in Josephson's study (1965) of *Miss Julie,* which is examined both from an extrinsic and from an intrinsic point of view. The same double approach characterizes Brandell's (1971) illuminating "model analysis" of *The Father.* Good observations on themes and symbols in some of the post-Inferno plays are found in Stockenström (1972).

More in line with Strindberg's own view—"But my person? What can you do with that? You have my works!" (letter to Emil Schering, December 22, 1904, *ASB,* XIV, 88)—are the non-Swedish scholars who almost unanimously have let the intrinsic approach prevail. Highly speculative and verbose but not without stimulating ideas is the Dane Børge (1942), who deals with all the plays, except the historical ones, from 1898 onwards. The central thesis of his dissertation gives an idea of his general outlook:

> We are once more faced with the fact, overlooked by scholars up to the present time and not comprehended because of a lack of dramaturgic appreciation of modern drama, namely that *The Great Highway* takes place in the consciousness of the Huntsman just as *To Damascus* does in the thoughts of the Stranger and *A Dream Play* in those of Indra's Daughter. (356)

Even more speculative than Børge, and with far less foundation in the play text, is Fraenkl in his Norwegian monograph (1966) on *The Ghost Sonata*.

Already in 1931 French readers could partake of Jolivet's overall study, in which the plays are discussed in relation to the French drama tradition. By contrast, Gravier (1949) pays special attention to those elements in the plays which have proved influential on later drama. A playwright's view is expressed in Adamov (1955), while in Vogelweith's (1972) psychoanalytically oriented study Strindberg is seen as a playwright "à la recherche d'un autre moi. Et c'est de ce *désir de métamorphose* que jaillit précisement le courant le plus profond du théâtre de Strindberg" (8).

A marked interest in the dramaturgic aspects of the plays is found in various German works beginning with C. D. Marcus' study (1920) of all the plays, followed by Diebold's (1928) influential discussion of the post-Inferno dramas. Exceedingly important is the Strindberg chapter in Szondi's (1956) pioneering work on modern drama, in which the formal aspect stands central. Szondi demonstrates convincingly the subjectivism of Strindbergian drama as well as the introduction of epic elements in the post-Inferno plays. 1962 brought a major contribution by the German-Swede Berendsohn, who examines the structure and style of a great number of the plays with great precision—while at other times he limits himself to a presentation of carefully arranged material suitable for analysis. A balanced and rewarding dramaturgic approach is employed in Lunin (1962), where the formal characteristics of five dramas, one per subgenre, are extensively dealt with; the five selected plays function as paradigmas of respectively "das naturalistische Drama, das Märchendrama, das historische Drama, das Traumdrama und das Kammerspiel" (4). A monograph on *Ein Traumspiel,* by Müssener, appeared in 1965; the very precise, somewhat formalistic examination has its greatest strength in the presentation of the ms. material and the discussion of the genesis of the play. Special attention is paid to the chamber plays in Pilick's (1969) investigation. A recent brief but informative survey is Paul (1979).

The marked disinterest in Strindberg in Great Britain is reflected in the meagre output of book-length studies of the plays. Apart from Lucas' (1962) highly subjective and unreliable study, there is Ward's (1980) examination of themes in a great number of the non-historical plays.

More attention has been shown by the Americans. Already in 1930 Dahlström brought out a pioneering work, in which he anticipated the recent tendency to see expressionist elements also in the so-called naturalistic dramas. In his thorough examination Madsen (1962), by contrast, sticks to the traditional view of these plays. Special attention is given to the historical dramas in Johnson (1963), a balanced presentation of a subgenre little known outside Sweden. Stimulating observations are found in the introductory studies by Valency (1963), Steene (1973) and Johnson (1976). A fruitful approach to the mythopoeic elements inherent in most of the plays is indicated in Carlson (1979). A marked feeling for the medium characterizes the articles by Sprinchorn.

If the situation regarding the formal aspect of Strindberg's plays today appears rather different from the one only ten or fifteen years ago, it is because there are now obvious signs that the dramatic genre is beginning to attract the same serious attention as those of the epic and lyric have long received (Van Kesteren, 41 ff.). Until fairly recently, it was a startling fact that critics belonging to those literary 'schools' favoring an intrinsic approach (the Russian formalists, the American New Critics, the French structuralists) were very little concerned with drama.[4] Most of them settled for poetry, a growing number for (short) narrative texts. Books dealing with the formal aspects of drama were certainly not lacking but the bulk of them were either pedestrian academic dissertations or conventional manuals intended for playwriting courses at drama departments.

Not surprisingly the recent interest in narrative structures has of late had its repercussions also within the field of drama, be it still on a rather modest scale. And naturally it is the play structure—the relationship of the parts to one another and to the whole—which has become the central object of investigation.

By structure in drama we usually mean plot structure, the arrangement of the (major) events of the play.[5] This is, however, a rather narrow interpretation of the term, determined by the fact that Aristotelian drama—the dominant form until this century—is highly plot-centered. In post-Aristotelian drama, it seems more relevant to relate 'structure' to the arrangement of the themes. Since Strindberg obviously belongs to both traditions—his plays constitute a fascinating one-man show in the gradual transgression from the one to the other—it is evident that a wider definition is called for. As Levitt (11 f.) indicates, 'structure' can in fact be applied to any play element; thus in addition to plot structure and thematic structure (or texture), we may speak of "the structure of the characters, the structure of time and space, and the structure of the dramatic language" (ibid.). However, we must be aware that a structural relation—whether on macro or micro level—may be of different kinds. Thus a play element (a character, a theme, etc.) may be related either to elements of the *same* kind—this is, for example, what happens when we trace a theme throughout a play—or it may be related to elements of a *different* kind, as when a character is linked with a particular theme or symbol.

With regard to the analytical approach, we may distinguish two radically different procedures. Either we may stick to the order in which the play is composed and employ a 'dynamic' step-by-step analysis—in the attempt to recreate the experience of the first-time recipient (reader or spectator). Or else we employ a 'static' method, based on our after-knowledge of the whole play, in which case we discuss the various elements—usually separately—as parts of the total drama. Jansen (81) calls the former method "la succession" and the latter "l'ensemble". From a directorial point of view, Beckerman (36 f.) similarly refers on one hand to a "vertical method of analysis" focussing on "the contextual frames within which the drama evolves", and on the other to the "horizontal approach", i.e. the study of a play by striation: plot, character description, themes, etc.

It is obvious that whereas the 'static' approach is well established, the 'dynamic' method is a novelty within drama analysis. The weakness of this latter approach is, of course, that we cannot, as analysts, completely put ourselves in the place of someone who experiences a play for the first time and consequently does not know more of it than he has already seen/heard/read. Unlike the 'static' analyst, the 'dynamic' one, in other words, finds himself in a somewhat uncomfortable double position, pretending not to know what he does know, the outcome of the play, for example. This does not mean that the method is unfruitful. On the contrary, a growing concern with what the recipient at any particular point in the play is able to grasp (or not grasp) is of utmost importance for a penetrating description of dramatic structure.[6] Rather than strictly adhere to one method or the other, I have attempted a combination in the subsequent analyses; thus emphasis is sometimes placed on the way in which a play element is developed, sometimes on how it relates to similar or different elements in other parts irrespective of their position in the play.

Useful for any structural analysis of drama is a division of the play to be examined into analyzable units.[7] Traditionally, plays are divided into acts and scenes—usually by the playwrights themselves. The act is obviously primarily a temporal and/or spatial unit. With Tomaševskij (168) we may further describe it as a psychological unit (the intervals between acts serving as periods of relaxation), a mechanical unit (for drastic changes of scenery intervals are necessary), and a thematic unit (the act may be kept together through a unity of theme).

While the term 'act' appears rather unproblematic,[8] 'scene' is confusing, since it signifies two different kinds of units. In the Anglo-American tradition, the difference between 'act' and 'scene' is not spectacular; different in size, they are both based on an adherence to the unity of place and/or time.[9] In the French tradition, by contrast, a scene is based on what we might term unity of character constellation. Also for this latter category, the term 'scene' (Fr. 'scène', Germ. 'Auftritt') is still employed by certain scholars (Van Laan, Levitt), while others, bothered by the terminological confusion homonyms may give rise to, prefer to reserve 'scene' for the Anglo-American category; for the French type they use 'mouvement' (Scherer), 'situation' (Sourieau, Jansen, Larthomas), 'segment' (Beckerman, Hogendoorn) or 'Konfiguration' (S. Marcus, Link, Pfister).

The matter is further complicated by the fact that these various terms do not refer to exactly the same phenomenon. Thus Levitt, in accordance with the French tradition, defines 'scene' as "a portion of the total play in which the stage is occupied by an unchanging group of players" (15),[10] while Van Laan provides a much vaguer explication of the same term: "any narrative unit that, having its own beginning, middle and end, stands out in the over-all pattern of action as a self-contained sequence of incidents" (229). And while Scherer's 'mouvement' in addition to the unity of character constellation, requires "l'unité du problème" (15), Larthomas, by contrast, excludes mute scenes by limiting his 'situation' to "cette ensemble qui actualise la parole" (125). Similarly, in addition to Levitt's single criterium of character constellation, Jansen's 'situation' is determined also by change of scenery: "nous instaurerons la limite entre deux situations là où un personnage entre ou sort ou bien encore là où il y a un changement de lieu dans le décor" (77).

Quite different is the reality behind Beckerman's and Hogendoorn's term 'segment'. To Beckerman a segment is "any coherent unit of theatrical time that nests within a formal dramatic unit, such as act or scene" (44). The segments are further divided into "subsegments" and these again into "subordinate units". Within each subordinate unit Beckerman distinguishes a "crux", roughly what we traditionally call a climax or crisis. As Beckerman himself points out, the establishment of coherent units is necessarily a subjective undertaking and his hierarchic tripartition is obviously not unproblematic.

While Beckerman's division into segments is determined by dramaturgic, notably rhythmic factors, Hogendoorn is more concerned with semiotic aspects. In the opening segment of *Rosmersholm*—the conversation between Rebecca and Madame Helseth, amounting to a little more than a page—he distinguishes no less than seven "subsegments", delimited by significant stage business such as changes in the positions of the characters. Both Beckerman and Hogendoorn 'direct' the text: among several possible interpretations they select one.

In conformance with Strindberg's practice, I shall use the term 'scene' both for the Anglo-American and the French type. For a refined version of the French type—the basic unit in the subsequent analyses—I shall use the term 'sequence', an internationally intelligible term which seems preferable to 'situation' precisely because it lacks a vague everyday meaning.[11] By 'sequence' is meant a unit whose beginning and end from the recipient's point of view is determined by

1. one or more entrances/exits (change of character constellation)
2. change of place
3. curtain or lights/blackout (change of time).

A special category is formed by

4. the stage directions at the beginning of each act/scene.

We here deal with sequences which subsume all the other sequences in the act/scene, since they describe the environment in which the total action of the act/scene takes place. While the 'normal' sequences (i.e. those including characters) are indicated by figures, these initial sequences are indicated by letters.

It will be seen that this definition is more accurate than the traditional French one, based merely on the stage presence of the characters.[12] It is also more precise than the division suggested by Jansen, who limits himself to the first two categories and does not distinguish between what is experienced from the stage and what from the auditorium.

Although a division of a play into sequences provides a good survey of the drama structure and has the advantage of being very exact, it presents rather rudimentary and one-sided quantitative information. In a fullscale analysis it needs to be supplemented by a qualitative examination based on a division of the play into (small) units determined by a factor other than character constellation. Within each sequence I shall therefore distinguish one or more 'segments'.[13] The governing principle for my division into segments is neither

Beckerman's concern with rhythmic components ("beats"), nor Hogendoorn's emphasis of the theatrical/visual aspects. Basic for my segmentation is instead the idea that a play consists of a series of 'topical units' and that the transition from one segment to another corresponds to a 'shift of topic' in a superficial scene. Such a division has the advantage of focussing on an aspect which is of central importance for all plays, be they closet dramas or pantomimes. (For a further discussion of segmentation, see Chapter 8.)

In the following analyses, our starting point will frequently be a 'sequence scheme'.[14] Like a crossword puzzle such a scheme can be read either horizontally or vertically. In agreement with this, we may speak of a 'horizontal' and a 'vertical' analysis, hereby using these terms in a sense differing from that of Beckerman. By a horizontal analysis I mean an examination of how a particular part of a play—an act, a scene, a sequence, a segment—is organized. By a vertical analysis I mean an examination of how acts, scenes, sequences and segments are related to one another and how plot, characters and themes develop.

From the sequence scheme the following data can be gathered:

1. The number of acts/scenes/sequences within the play/act/scene.
2. The number of characters within each sequence/scene/act.
3. The distribution of speaking/mute characters within each sequence/scene/act. (Speaking parts are indicated by italics.)
4. The number of sequences/scenes/acts within which the characters appear (stage presence).
5. The duration of each sequence/scene/act (indicated by page/line references to beginning/end of each sequence).

The sequence scheme further facilitates an analysis of the play structure in accordance with Jansen's (87) relational criteria, owing to which (1) a sequence is dependent on an earlier one if the two cannot change places without affecting the play as a whole ("relation d'antéposition"),[15] and (2) a sequence is dependent on another one if it cannot be understood without it ("relation de sélection"). Both relations can be tested, the former by reversing the sequences, the latter by excluding the sequence on which the other sequence depends. Less fundamental than the structural concepts just discussed are a number of other dramaturgic terms. These will be defined in the subsequent chapters as they first appear.

The two scholarly traditions here outlined should have given the reader a reasonable idea of what to expect from the present work, intended as a contribution both to the study of the formal characteristics of Strindbergian drama—its structure and texture—and to the methodology of drama analysis. Its title should not, of course, be taken to mean that Strindberg's dramas are thematically all alike or structured in much the same fashion; it merely suggests that it is meaningful to speak of Strindbergian drama as a corpus characterized by a certain formal and thematic identity. However vague and intuitive the adjective 'Strindbergian' used in this sense may seem, it fulfills a function as a suggestive abbreviation—as do the already commonly used qualifiers 'Shakespearean', 'Ibsenite', 'Shavian'. To put it differently: hopefully my analyses of eleven Strindberg plays will give the reader a fair impression of what the plays have in common and in what respects they differ, so that by the time he arrives at the end of the book, 'Strindbergian' has become a meaningful and pregnant qualification.

Unlike Lunin, I have not selected the eleven plays with regard to their genre characteristics. The guiding principle has been that of selecting dramas which from a structural point of view seem especially interesting; that nearly all the plays examined belong to Strindberg's best-known dramas, should surprise no-one: a great deal of their fame undoubtedly rests on the fashion in which they are structured. The notable exception is *The First Warning,* which has a relatively low status in the Strindberg canon. The reason why this play has been included is twofold: on the one hand its brevity—it is a one-acter—allows me within a limited space, to provide a relatively full analysis serving as an introduction to various problems more specifically dealt with in the subsequent analyses; on the other hand it enables me to demonstrate how even in this relatively insignificant drama, Strindberg is able to create effective theatre, be it largely with conventional means.

While the structural problem, on various unit levels, stands central in the subsequent analyses, I have tried to vary my approach by applying it to different play elements or areas. After the initial, overall analysis in Chapter 2, attention is devoted in Chapter 3 to the interplay between verbal and visual imagery, specific to the dramatic genre. Chapter 4 tackles the problem of how to deal with dramatic dialogue by focussing on the importance of the concrete situation in which a speech is uttered. Chapter 5 considers the special presentational problems related to the monodramatic form. A wider range is found in Chapter 6, where attention is paid to the function of the characters within the structure of a highly theme-centered drama, as well as to the constant employment of a double vision technique. In Chapter 7 a relatively comprehensive and *qua* plot, complex drama has been selected to demonstrate how Strindberg intertwines various threads of action to secure a sense of coherence, causality and thematic unity. Chapter 8, which is a close reading of a play opening, concentrates on the problem related to segmentation. In Chapter 9 unifying elements in a supposedly loose play structure are examined. In Chapters 10–12 three of the four chamber plays are analyzed both with regard to their structure and texture; from the analyses it appears that the plot in these dramas is of much less significance than the theme. The appendix, finally, is a warning to the innocent reader never to regard a translation of a (Strindberg) play as more or less identical with the original text; since it demonstrates how symbols, themes, significant stylistic characteristics are often lost/changed in translation, it logically relates to the main part of the book.

For obvious reasons all quotations from the plays are rendered in English translation. For most of the plays I have made thankful use of Walter Johnson's renderings; for the quotations from *To Damascus I* I depend on Evert Sprinchorn's translation, for those of *The First Warning* and *The Dance of Death I* on Arvid Paulson's somewhat verbose versions. But in all cases, and especially in the last two, I have felt free to make alterations whenever I have felt that a nuance of the original not rendered in the translation, would be of significance for my analysis. It goes without saying that the faithfulness of my renderings in such cases has often been bought at the prize of stylistic elegance. For the English version of other Scandinavian sources I myself am responsible, unless otherwise indicated. Page references are to the Swedish standard editions, that is, for dramas up to 1898 *August Strindbergs dramer* (*ASD*), for most of the remaining dramas and other published works *Samlade skrifter av August Strindberg* (*SS*), for the letters *August Strindbergs brev* (*ASB*), further his diary *Ockulta dagboken* (*OD*) and *Samlade otryckta skrifter* (*SOS*); most of the (hitherto unpublished) ms. material is found in Nordiska museets Strindbergsarkivalia, deposited at the Royal Library in Stockholm.

A fairly complete list of Strindberg's plays in English translation has been included to inform the interested reader and to encourage further research on the formal and thematic characteristics of the translations as compared to the original versions. The bibliography comprises only works cited or referred to.

All the chapters except 1, 9, 10, 12 and 13 have been published earlier, the majority in Swedish (see the bibliography); for the present study they have all, in varying degrees, been revised.

2. *Första varningen/The First Warning*—an Effective Drama

The one-acter *The First Warning* is undoubtedly one of the least appreciated dramas by Strindberg. Lamm (1924, 393) calls it "an exceedingly tasteless piece", to Jolivet (202) it is "une des œuvres les plus insignifiants de Strindberg", and Madsen has precisely the same opinion: "one of Strindberg's least important dramatic productions". Rinman (86) calls it "a trifle", and Smedmark (1970, 293 f.), similarly, regards it as "a dramatic trifle rather than a psychological study of any depth"; it is both superficial and artificial. Jacobs (1969, xxviii), on the other hand, takes a positive view of the play, finding it "more witty and playful than anything Strindberg wrote in the preceding period", i.e. from 1886 to 1889.

However, certain aspects of the playlet have been praised. Ollén (194) speaks of the elegant French style, and Rinman finds the dialogue "masterly". Of the characters, the young girl, Rosa, has attracted the greatest interest. Only Lamm finds the portrayal of her "most incredible". Rinman, by contrast, speaks of "a dashingly drawn premature teenager". Ollén is even more positive: "a brilliant character study, the very modern 15-year-old Rosa". And Smedmark interestingly points out: "our first modern study in female puberty".

Theme and plot

Lamm (1924, 394) has excellently characterized the theme of the play: "the basic idea seems to be that love cannot exist without jealousy and that the charm of a marriage consists in the constant fear of the partners that they will lose one another". Jolivet (202) calls the piece "une variation sans conséquence sur la jalousie", and Jacobs (1969, xxviii) characterizes it as "a little play about jealousy".

The interhuman relations can best be illustrated by a diagram:

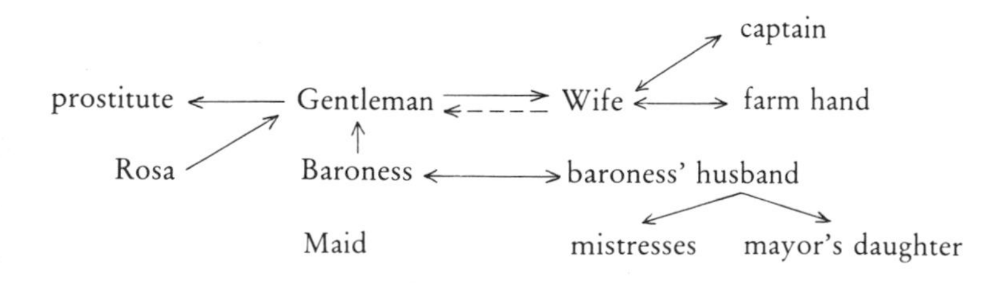

The characters lacking capitals are only mentioned in the dialogue. The arrows indicate erotic interest. The line of short dashes signifies the Wife's kindled passion for the Gentleman at the end of the play. The fact that only the Maid falls outside the erotic pattern says something about the tightness of the plot.

When the piece begins the Wife is triumphant. She completely dominates her husband. He has tried to free himself of his love for her, but without success. At the party the night before *she* has been surrounded by admirers, while *he* has appeared as the ridiculous cuckold *in spe*. The bouquet from the captain is proof that the Wife can still attract a real man, that she is still 'young'. Filled with self-assurance, she openly shows her contempt for the Gentleman and demonstrates no jealousy against the Baroness or the young Rosa, although both are clearly in love with her husband.

Gradually the situation is changed. The Gentleman reveals that he has been unfaithful to his wife with a prostitute in Genua. Rosa tells the Wife that the Gentleman has promised to help her make rose wreaths for the feast the following day—a hint that he is perhaps not so indifferent to the young girl as the Wife believes. She then witnesses the kiss between Rosa and her husband. By now she already knows that the Gentleman has kissed the hand of the Baroness. Then the fateful loss of her tooth occurs, a sign that the Wife is growing "old and ugly" and far more dependent on her husband than before. At the end the three women are equally anxious to treat the Gentleman to coffee; a switch of power has taken place. It is now the Gentleman who is surrounded by admirers. The fact that he can also attract a young girl is a sign of his preserved virility, of his 'youth'. Although *he* is now the stronger, his feelings for his wife remain constant. The situation has changed but he has not. The reason, it is implied, is that his wife never lulls him into security, always keeps his jealousy alive.

Sequences and segments

The sequence scheme for *The First Warning* is as follows:

Scene	*Seq.*	*Page/ line in ASD* IV	*On stage*			
1	A	277/1				
	1	277/6	W			
	2	277/8	*W*	*G*		
2	3	281/5	W			
	4	281/6	*W*		*R*	
3	5	283/22	*W*		*R*	*B*
	6	284/11	*W*			*B*
	7	284/17	W	G		B
4	8	284/21		*G*		*B*

	9	287/5		*G*	(R)	*B*	
	10	287/38		*G*		*B*	
5	11	289/16		G			
	12	289/17		*G*	*R*		
	13	289/29		G	*R*		*M*
	14	290/6		*G*	*R*		
	15	291/2	(W)	G	R		
	16	291/4		*G*	*R*		
6	17	292/11	*W*	*G*	*R*		
7	18	293/29	*W*	*G*			
8	19	296/1	W	*G*		*B*	
	20	296/8–12	W	*G*	R	B	

Abbreviations

W = The Wife
G = The Gentleman
R = Rosa
B = The Baroness
M = The Maid

Italics = speaking parts

While Strindberg divides the play into eight (French) scenes, our more precise division results in no less than twenty sequences, of varying length. Five sequences are mute and three of these are solo sequences. The inclusion of these sequences has a trivial, theatrical reason. Between the exit of one character and the entrance of another there must be a short lapse of time—for esthetic-rhythmic reasons. As a result we get a solo sequence. In these there is no intention to isolate a character on the stage for a special purpose.

The longest sequences consist of conversations between the Gentleman and the Wife, at the beginning and the end of the play. In seq. 2 the need for exposition motivates the length, while in seq. 18 the need to recapitulate what has just occurred and its importance for the marriage is the main reason for the extension of the sequence.

In seq. 9 and 15 we find a type of situation common in intrigue comedy: 'screen scenes', that is, sequences in which a character, who can be seen by the audience but not by the other characters, witnesses what occurs on the stage. In seq. 9 Rosa, unseen by the others, listens to part of the conversation between the Gentleman and the Baroness and witnesses his kissing of her hand. In seq. 15, similarly, the Wife witnesses the kiss that is exchanged between the Gentleman and Rosa without their seeing her. Both sequences have been included to give rise to misunderstandings which account for certain complications and thus form part of the plot.

The sequences, we have already noted, can further be divided into topical units or 'segments'. If we look closely at a fragment of dramatic dialogue, we discover that while certain clauses/sentences/speeches connect very closely, others do not. Instead of an associative flow, we experience discontinuance. The associative link may well be there but it is not immediately recognizable. As a result we get the feeling that the topic—it need not be a verbal one—is taking a new turn. We find an illustrative example in the beginning of *The First Warning:*

THE WIFE. I seem to recall that you said the same thing repeatedly last night . . .
THE GENTLEMAN (*fingering the bouquet*). Do you really recall that?
THE WIFE. I also recall that you objected to my singing so many songs . . . Don't spoil my flowers!

There is here an obvious unity of topic, underlined by the reiterated 'recall'—up to the last sentence, where a switch takes place and a new segment (segm. 2.2, i.e. segment 2 of sequence 2) begins; the topic is now no longer what happened the night before, but rather its consequence: the bouquet which the Wife has just received from the captain. Of course, the bouquet has been introduced already in seq. 1 and the Gentleman's fingering of it in segm. 2.1 further draws attention to it. But it is still not here in the focus of interest; rather, the appearance of the flowers in these parts serves to motivate the switch of topic in segm. 2.2. To put it differently: the flowers constitute a stimulus needed to effect a plausible change of subject.

Each segment should comprise a central or dominant topic; it may well include other closely related minor topics. Along these lines we may divide seq. 2 into the following segments:

Segm.	*Page/ line in ASD* IV	*Central topic*
1	277/8	G and W about yesterday's party
2	277/22	W has received bouquet from captain
3	278/4	G has been uncomfortable at party
4	278/18	G and W aging
5	279/9	W has been interested in farm hand, G jealous
6	279/21	W blushing
7	279/29	W contemptuous of men
8	280/4	G tries in vain to leave W
9	280/15	G has visited prostitute
10	280/25	W wants divorce
11	280/30	R and B in love with G
12	280/38	G about to leave

As is natural in an opening sequence like this, a great many topics are quickly introduced. Several of them are related to the past; here the question arises whether these references are brought into the dialogue in a natural way. A great many characters are also introduced: the captain, the farm hand, the prostitute, Rosa, the Baroness. Why? Evidently because they help to illustrate the unstable relationship between the married couple: both receive attention from the opposite sex; both show signs of unfaithfulness.

Although a division into segments is problematic and subjective, it is useful since it compels us to see what happens also in the micro-parts of the play, notably how transitions between segments are made; a discussion of this will be postponed till Chapter 8.

Entrances and exits

La pièce bien faite and the naturalistic drama—both relevant in this connection—are characterized by an effort to make the action seem logical, plausible. The stage presence/absence of the characters is a case in point. In *The First Warning* Strindberg adheres to this dramaturgic tradition.

All five characters obviously belong to the boarding-house, where the action takes place. The Baroness is the landlady, Rosa is her daughter, the Maid her maid, the Gentleman and the Wife guests. Since the whole play is set in the dining room, i.e. in a room to which everyone has access, the entrances are comparatively easy to account for.

It may seem as though a study of entrances and exits is merely a mechanical concern. As a matter of fact such a study leads to questions which are directly related to plot and character description. Frequently there are several possible reasons for the entrance/exit of a character and our preferences of explanation color our general view of him or her.

The motivations can be either explicit or implicit; both types abound in the play. Thus the Baroness explicitly exits in seq. 10 in order to make coffee for the Gentleman, and in seq. 19 she returns with the coffee on a tray. The Maid's single entrance in seq. 13 is prepared in seq. 10 by the Baroness' line: "And then I'll send the maid to help you pack?" Her exit is very emphatically motivated: Rosa simply tells her to leave (seq. 13). In the same way Rosa herself is sent away in seq. 17 by the Wife. The reason for Rosa's last entrance (seq. 20) is that she has come to say farewell to the couple. The Gentleman enters twice (seq. 2 and 7) to pack his suitcase, which has been placed in the dining room. The Baroness' first entrance (seq. 4) is accounted for in two different ways: (*a*) she often goes on an errand to the large cupboard in the dining room but, the Gentleman informs us, (*b*) these errands are actually merely a pretext to see him. Clearly, both the suitcase and the cupboard are in the room primarily to motivate the entrances of these characters.

More interesting are the implicit motivations. Like the Baroness, Rosa keeps coming to the dining room in the hope of meeting the Gentleman there. Her second entrance means that the time she has devoted to picking flowers is exceedingly short, but since she has just learned that the Gentleman is going to leave, it is not implausible that she hastens back to take leave of him. Her showing up on the veranda, as we have noted, takes place precisely when the Gentleman kisses the hand of the Baroness, her disappearance, shortly after he has indicated that he is going to leave the room. Apparently Rosa is at this moment afraid that the two will discover that she has been spying on them. When the Wife turns up in a similar fashion, we may imagine that she has followed Rosa in order to watch her. Her jealousy has now been aroused—as appears from her anxiety to take the place of the Gentleman when it comes to helping Rosa with the flowers.

To the explicit motivations for the Maid's entrance and exit we may add implicit ones. Thus her entrance can be seen as an illustration of how anxious the Baroness is to make a good impression on the Gentleman, her exit of how anxious Rosa is to be left alone with him. The Maid functions as an effective substitute for the Baroness, who cannot herself help the Gentleman with his luggage and who could not have been sent away by Rosa. The rivalry between mother and daughter is thus dramatized in the little episode with the Maid.

When the Wife in seq. 17 enters, the explicit reason is that she wants to treat her husband to coffee before he departs. The true reason is that she wants to regain him by (*a*) interrupting the conversation between him and Rosa and by (*b*) appearing as his submissive servant. Her re-entrance with the coffee tray is surprising—and comic. We have just learned that the Baroness has left the room to make coffee for the Gentleman. Now the Wife enters with coffee. Significantly Rosa wants to take over the tray. When the Baroness finally enters with *her* tray the comic situation culminates. With the help of the tray it is demonstrated how the three ladies try to conquer the man in exactly the same way.

Summarizing we can state that all entrances and exits can be accounted for either explicitly or implicitly and that none appears unnatural.

Prescenic and scenic action

By 'prescenic action' we mean those events which have occurred when the play opens, by 'scenic action' those which occur in the course of the play.[1] With regard to space, the scenic action can further be divided into 'stage action' and 'offstage action'.

The information related to the prescenic action is limited to two of the sequences. In the introductory conversation between the Gentleman and the Wife (seq. 2) we are informed of their matrimonial past. In the conversation between the Gentleman and the Baroness (seq. 8) we are informed of her matrimonial past and the later fate of her husband. A chronological list of the prescenic data is clarifying. The references in the lefthand column denote time before the opening of the play; vague references are indicated by question marks.

47 years	Birth of the Baroness.
37 years	Birth of the Gentleman.
36 years	Birth of the Wife.
?	The Baroness married to an officer whom she loves and who loves her and yet commits adultery.
15 years	Birth of Rosa. The Gentleman and the Wife marry.
7 years	The Gentleman and the Wife travel around.
?	The Gentleman escapes six times from his wife but always returns. During one of his escapes he visits a prostitute.
?	The Baroness' husband goes off to the war, falls in love with the mayor's daughter, is abandoned by her.
5 years	The Gentleman meets the Baroness' husband at a party in London.
4 years	In accordance with their agreement, the Gentleman now considers the Baroness' husband dead; through a kiss on hand and forehead he is now to deliver the last greeting of the deceased to his widow and daughter.
Preceding summer	The Gentleman and the Wife live on an almost uninhabited island. The Wife shows an interest in the farm hand, which makes the Gentleman jealous.
4 months	The Gentleman (and probably the Wife, too) arrive at the Baroness' boarding-house.
?	The Baroness and Rosa fall in love with the Gentleman.
A couple of days	The Gentleman wants to kiss his wife but she does not permit him to do so.
Preceding night	The Gentleman and the Wife take part in a gay party. A captain courts the Wife with success. The Gentleman, who feels ridiculed, wants to leave but the Wife prefers to stay. She entertains the company by singing.
The same morning	The captain sends a bouquet to the Wife.

A list of this kind shows rather clearly how the different events are linked—or not linked!—to one another. Why, we may ask, does it take four years for the Gentleman to fulfill his promise to the Baroness' husband. Apparently because he has forgotten or neglected it. He does not know that the Baroness has been married to the man he has met in London. This cannot be the reason why he has chosen to stay at her boarding-house. It is not until she begins to tell him about her past that he understands that the Londoner is identical with her husband. By a mere chance the Gentleman has come to stay with the very woman for whom he has an important message. By "a strange chance", the Baroness herself says, the Gentleman resembles her husband and it is this resemblance which ultimately causes her to tell the Gentleman about her husband. The arrangement seems highly artificial, yet implausibilities with regard to the prescenic action do not easily disturb us. The arrangement also throws an unfavorable light on the Gentleman; after all, he has broken his promise. But since this is never emphasized—on the contrary, the Baroness praises his character—only a close reader of the play would be aware of this weakness of his.

The scenic action is, quite simply, equivalent to those acting directions and parts of the dialogue which suggest activities. Deeds speak louder than words—this is as true on the stage as in life. Even seemingly unessential activities are often important. Let us, for example, consider those of Rosa in seq. 12–17; the directions read:

1 *in from rear.*
2 *tears off the kerchief and puts it in her pocket.*
3 *She takes his hat and brushes it.*
4 *She puts her fingers into the hole in her sleeve and tears it wide open.*
5 *He advances toward her, takes her face in his hands, and is about to kiss her forehead, when* ROSA *throws back her head and presses her lips against his.*
6 *She opens the wallpapered door, behind which the stairs are visible.*
7 *bursting into tears of anger.*
8 *tries to take the tray from* THE WIFE.
9 *puts her fingers in her mouth, embarrassed, angry.*
10 *as before.*
11 *with a curtsy.*
12 *takes her flowers.*
13 *runs out.*

None of these activities are meaningless; they all tell us something about what is going on inside Rosa. When related to the surrounding dialogue they suggest something like the following:

1 Rosa enters because she wants to talk to the Gentleman in private. We have earlier seen how she has been spying on her mother, and it is reasonable to assume that she has waited for her to leave.
2 She wants to be attractive to the Gentleman.
3 She wants to gain his favor.
4 When she does not succeed she tries to tie him to herself by providing him with a bad conscience. As we shall see, her action also has sexual connotations.
5 Whether or not she has misinterpreted the Gentleman's purpose, it is obvious that she cannot, at this point, resist her passion for him.
6 Her opening the door indicates that she wants to bring the Gentleman to the attic to show him her father's "letters to his mistresses". The kiss has awakened her passion and her aim seems to be precisely what she herself indicates: to "seduce" the Gentleman.
7 She demonstrates the impotent anger of a girl in puberty at the fact that the Gentleman does not wish to be seduced, that he considers her too young.
8 She attempts to conquer the Wife in their rivalry for the Gentleman.
9 She is still a child.
10 *Idem.* The anger is in both cases primarily directed against the Wife who treats Rosa in a condescending way.
11 She again accepts the child role.
12 She obeys the Wife's order. Rosa has definitely lost the competition for the Gentleman's favor. (The erotic significance of the flowers will be discussed later.)
13 The loser flees.

As far as the offstage action is concerned, Strindberg is necessarily very sparing. We learn little about what the characters are doing when they are away from the dining room and we do not care much about it. However, certain indications are given. Thus during seq. 2–7 the Gentleman gets dressed. Rosa is picking flowers during seq. 6–9 and changes her clothes during seq. 18–19. The Baroness makes coffee for the Gentleman during seq. 11–18. The Wife is the busiest character. During seq. 8–14 she is picking flowers, during seq. 16 (we may assume) she makes coffee for the Gentleman. Possibly she takes the tray from the Baroness just as Rosa tries to take it from the Wife—from a temporal point of view this is the best solution. The breaking of the front tooth—the only important offstage event—presumably takes place during seq. 16.

An effective drama

Under the title "an effective drama" Strindberg has himself listed the dramaturgic devices which he considers essential; such a drama, we learn,

should operate with intimations,
contain a secret which is revealed to the spectator either at the beginning or toward the end.—If the spectator knows the secret and the characters do not, the spectator enjoys their blind man's buff. If the spectator does not know the secret, his curiosity is aroused and he remains interested,
an outburst—of emotion, anger, indignation,
a reversal, well prepared,
a discovery,
a punishment (nemesis), a humiliation,
a careful resolution, with or without reconciliation,
a *quid pro quo,*
a parallellism,
a reversal (*revirement*), a rebuff, a well prepared surprise (*SOS,* II, 172)

All these devices, so characteristic of *la pièce bien faite,* can be found in *The First Warning.* Examples of intimations are found right at the beginning where the dialogue between the Gentleman and the Wife suggests that she was drunk and flirting with other men at the party the preceding night. And an intimation it is when Rosa tells the Gentleman that she "has been a woman for three years", hereby suggesting that she has had sexual intercourse already at the age of twelve and is now an experienced woman; she is not telling a lie, however, since the expression may also be taken to mean that she has had her first menstruation at the age of twelve. It is obviously the latter interpretation which agrees with the real situation.

We may speak of a blind man's buff in connection with the two *quid pro quos* which occur. When the Gentleman kisses the Baroness' hand and Rosa kisses the Gentleman on the mouth, the spectator is well informed about the true state of things, but the spying women are not. The most striking example of a secret which remains a secret to the spectator up to the end is the misadventure with the tooth. The revelation of this misadventure may also be termed "a discovery", "a surprise", "a rebuff" (for the Wife), "a reversal" (of the distribution of power between the Gentleman and the Wife), even "a punishment". For is it not the Wife's hubris in the beginning which is now punished? Since this misadventure occurs late in the play, the spectator cannot be prepared explicitly for this event—or it would no longer be a secret. Instead Strindberg resorts to implicit preparation by having Rosa, too, suffer from a problematic tooth. Examples of outbursts are found in many places, especially with regard to Rosa. Humiliations are also common. At the beginning the Wife humiliates the Gentleman, later Rosa, but in the end she herself is humiliated—by nemesis.

Of special interest is the demand for "a parallelism". This applies to the long story about the Baroness' husband. Only in this way can it be saved from Madsen's (133) negative evaluation, where he calls the fourth scene "irrelevant" and the Baroness' husband "a character completely without significance". Actually this officer, who surrounds himself with mistresses and who abandons his wife for a younger woman, has a counterpart in the Wife, who flirts with other men and who —to begin with—behaves as though she would not mind abandoning her husband for a captain. The Baroness and the Gentleman, on the other hand, share qualities like faithfulness and jealousy. They also react quite similarly: "the only woman who charmed me resembles you, or grew to resemble you", says the Gentleman early on. When the Baroness finds that the Gentleman resembles her husband, she seems to develop the same inclination to see something of the beloved one in the person to whom she feels attracted. The resemblance between the Gentleman and the Baroness' husband concerns not so much their disposition as their situation. The Wife's desperate words to the Gentleman at the end—"Well, you'll soon be free to choose a younger and more attractive wife! /—/ Now that I am old and ugly"—recall the triangle the Baroness–her husband–the mayor's daughter. But unlike the Baroness' husband the Gentleman chooses to stay with his aging wife. The pattern is now rather clear. In the *prescenic* action we deal with a man who abandons his wife for a younger woman, who in turn abandons him. In the *scenic* action we get the opposite situation: a man who does not abandon his wife for a younger woman. And yet, it is implied at the end, the Gentleman, too, runs the risk of being abandoned by his wife. The Baroness' husband has obviously never been confronted with this eventuality. That is why he abandoned his wife!

We can now answer the question: What function does the Baroness parallel have? It could of course be argued that, once included in the play in the interest of the plot, the Baroness must be provided with certain characteristics which can secure an interest in her as an autonomous person. It is then rather natural that Strindberg constructs a love story on her behalf which he ties to that of the Gentleman and his wife. However, this does not explain why he emphasizes the fate of the Baroness' husband rather than that of the Baroness herself. A better explanation would be that Strindberg places the Baroness' husband and the Gentleman in identical situations with the sole intention of demonstrating how differently they react. In this way he can outline two antithetical man–wife relations and emphasize the Gentleman's dependency on his wife.

Even more important is the significance of this parallel for the theme of the play. If we agree with Lamm that Strindberg wants to demonstrate that jealousy is indispensable for love, it is obvious that this thesis becomes much more vigorous if it is supported by two cases, not just one. With the help of the parallel situation Strindberg can, as it were, turn his pronouncement into a law of nature in accordance with the formula: the emotional stability of the (loving) subject is determined by the emotional instability of the object (of love). Since Strindberg prefers the anonymous designations Gentleman, Wife, Baroness, Maid to individual names, he again seems to stress the general significance of the action, its quality of natural law. Also the characters mentioned in the dialogue are nameless. The notable exception is Rosa, but even in her case the (symbolic) name, as we shall see, has a general significance.

An effective drama should have "a careful resolution". The play ends, in traditional comedy manner, with all the four main characters assembled for the first time on the stage, in token of their reconciliation. The Gentleman and the Wife are about to depart, together. By having him assure that they are going to Augsburg "to get us a gold tooth", Strindberg indicates, to the point of ridiculousness, that the two are now one—at least as far as he is concerned: for at the same time it is implied that due to the Wife's unreliability the couple may soon find themselves back in the situation with which the play began. Such is matrimonial life, Strindberg seems to say. Jealousy is inevitably indispensably linked to love.

The protagonist

We still lack a clear definition of the concept 'main character' ('hero', 'protagonist'). Scholars appear to employ different, rarely explicated criteria with regard to this concept.

With the help of the sequence scheme we can quantitatively rank the five characters. We then find that the Gentleman is on the stage during 14 sequences, the Wife during 12, Rosa during 10, the Baroness during 8 and the Maid during 1. As for the number of speeches and lines, we find exactly the same distribution: the Gentleman has 84 speeches (187 lines), the Wife 62 (93 lines), Rosa 34 (88 lines), the Baroness 30 (65 lines), the Maid 1 (1 line). If we limit ourselves to a quantitative argument, it is easy to see that the Gentleman is the protagonist of the play.

Yet such a limitation is clearly unsatisfactory. Apart from the quantitative factors we must take the qualitative into account; in the words of a much frequented handbook of literary terms (Shipley, 52):

> The minor figures /—/ are presented in only one aspect, as 'flat', 'thin', 'disc' characters. Sometimes /—/ even the main figures are 'stationary', static, the same at the finish as at the start; but they may be more fully shown, 'thick', 'round'. /—/ But the main figures of a work are likely to be 'developing', dynamic characters; the conflict within the story, within their spirit, wreaks its effect upon their souls.

If we apply this description to the characters in *The First Warning,* we can state that the Gentleman is rather static and passive. The activity is found among the courting ladies. In all three of them we may speak of an inner change. As soon as the Baroness learns that her husband is dead, she starts her invitations: "But now—with nothing left for me ... (*She takes hold of* THE GENTLEMAN'S *hand*)". The Wife's inner change we have already discussed—just as we have Rosa's. While we have limited possibilities of taking part in what goes on inside the Baroness and the Wife, Rosa's problems of puberty are more clearly demonstrated both in speech—Rosa's speeches are usually much more extensive than the Wife's—and in action.

Returning to the question 'Who is the protagonist of the drama?', the following arguments can be handled for the three characters who in this respect are relevant:

The Gentleman. Quantitatively, he is the dominant figure. Outwardly, the plot revolves around him. When the play opens, it is clear that he is about to leave his wife; when it ends he is reconciled to her. As the only male figure he also takes a central position in the erotic plot, courted as he is by three women.

The Wife. The action has for her much more far-reaching consequences than for him. The discovery that she has grown "old and ugly" makes her situation precarious. In accordance with this she undergoes an inner change. As we have noted, a classical hubris–nemesis pattern can be applied to the Wife. If we regard *The First Warning* as a miniature drama of fate, it is reasonable to regard the Wife as the protagonist. The play title also supports such a view.

Rosa. With regard to the plot Rosa is decidedly a subordinate character. Yet judging both by Strindberg's own comments (*ASB,* IX, 22, 93, 98, 104, 156) and those of others (Ollén, 1961, 195 f.) Rosa is the most vital character of the play. Openly revealing her varying emotions, she appears to be a 'rounder' character than the others.

The question 'Who is the protagonist of the play?' can hardly be answered unless we specify what we mean by 'protagonist'. If we stress the action of the drama—as Aristotle does—both the Gentleman and the Wife qualify, the former if we pay particular attention to the outward action (the plot), the latter if we consider an inner development more important (the hubris–nemesis pattern, the mental change). If we consider the psychological characterization of primary importance, it is natural to consider Rosa the protagonist of the play. Rather than make a definite choice between these three alternatives, we may speak of the three protagonists of the play. We must not, however, from this conclude that the question is merely academic; a director must make a choice as to which character he wants to concentrate on; in an actual production any one of the three characters may qualify as the central figure.

Character description

The relationship between plot and characters is reciprocal. On the one hand the characters are modelled in a particular way in the interest of a functional plot; on the other the plot (in its less basic aspects) may be shaped according to the nature of the characters. As has already appeared, it is almost impossible to discuss the plot of a play without touching on the depiction of the characters. The five onstage characters of *The First Warning* may be described as follows:

The Gentleman. He is 37 and is beginning to turn gray. We never learn what his profession is but we are told that at least now and then he lives an out-of-door life, fishing and hunting. He is very jealous of his wife but his jealousy is not unfounded. Emotionally attached to her, he is now trying to abandon her for the seventh time, in vain. He behaves like a gentleman toward all the women.

The Wife. She is 36, not young and not old. Her middle age explains her cynically condescending attitude to her surroundings, notably to the Gentleman and Rosa. She sometimes drinks too much and likes to flirt with other (virile) men, ignoring social barriers (the farm hand). Her characterization of her husband—"your love cools off the moment you think you have no reason to be jealous"—applies even more to herself. Although she is not a very likeable person, the Gentleman finds her adorable.

The Baroness. She is 47, widow, a good woman according to the Gentleman—though we look in vain for any signs of her goodness. Lacking in mother love, she is in love with the Gentleman or in that quality in him which reminds her of her husband. She is not a very honest person: although she knows that her husband is dead, she pretends to be ignorant of his fate. A deplorable but not very likeable character.

Rosa. She is 15, school girl. Unlike her mother, Rosa openly shows her affection for the Gentleman. Her jealousy is significantly directed not against the Wife but against the Baroness, an indication of her need to revolt against maternal authority. Erotically innocent, she tries to compete with her rivals by pretending sexual experience. To this effect she also identifies herself with the Wife and seeks to imitate her. Newly awakened sexual appetite and genuine feelings for the Gentleman account for her calculated strategy. Spitefulness and softness, ripeness and childishness mingle in her in a manner characteristic of her age. At the end she exchanges her 'sinful' dress for a white one of innocence.

The Maid. At most one trait can be attributed to her: a certain respect for the young Rosa, since she obeys her when Rosa asks her to leave, although the Baroness has asked her to help the Gentleman to pack.

This manner of describing characters, based on what Beckerman (213) terms "the character-made", i.e. an after-image, is of course very traditional. A different way of approaching the subject is to stick to the order in which the various traits of the characters are presented in the play. Such a structural or *dynamic* procedure throws light on how the different characters gradually take shape in the course of the play—much as a piece of clay gradually takes the form of a jug or a bowl; in this latter case we are concerned with what Beckerman (213) terms "character-in-the-making". In the subsequent analyses both procedures will be followed.

Time and place

With regard to time in drama we must distinguish between 'duration' (prescenic and scenic time, playing time) and 'temporal setting' (period, season, time of day in which the scenic action takes place).

While the prescenic action, as we have seen, covers a period of 47 years, the scenic action is exceedingly short. It corresponds, in fact, exactly to the playing time of the one-acter (around 30 minutes). Strindberg alludes to this when, in the beginning, he has the Gentleman state that he is to leave "in half an hour". The unity of time is in other words strictly adhered to.

As for the temporal setting, the information is very implicit. The dialogue is almost totally lacking in clear references to historical conditions. Only by combining various pieces of information—such as the fact that the play is set in Germany and that the Baroness' husband went to fight in the war and was taken prisoner, can we infer that the war referred to must be the French-German one of 1870–71. Yet since we do not know how long the Baroness' husband has been away, even this does not provide us with a very definite idea of the time of action.

More exact is the information concerning season and time of day. We learn that the following day there will be a Corpus Christi procession. Since this traditionally takes place on the Thursday after Trinity Sunday, we can conclude that the action is set on a Wednesday in late spring or early summer. As for the time of day, we may note that the Gentleman already in his first speech states that "it is noontime", and in the middle of the play the church bell strikes one.

Also the unity of place is strictly adhered to: the onstage action is set in "*a German dining room*", the offstage one in its immediate vicinity. Why Strindberg has chosen a German setting is difficult to explain on intrinsic grounds: the "*vineyards*" in the background, the references to the French-German war and to the Corpus Christi procession connote a central European country but not necessarily Germany.[2]

Despite its universal theme and lack of *couleur locale,* the action of *The First Warning,* we may conclude, is rather firmly tied to time and place. The reason for this may well be a naturalistic endeavor on Strindberg's part to indicate the slice-of-life character of the play.

Symbolism

At the beginning of the play, the Gentleman tells the Wife: "Oh, how often haven't I longed to see you old and ugly—wished that you had /—/ lost your teeth—only so that I would be able to keep you for myself and put an end to this anxiety which never leaves me!" At the end, the Wife tells the Gentleman: "/—/ I am old and ugly! /—/ I have bitten off—a piece of a front tooth! Don't look at me!" It will be seen that the two speeches correspond to one another. The significance of the mishap with the tooth at the end has been well prepared for at the beginning, and the Gentleman's positive reaction to it does not come as a surprise to us. The connection between the tooth mishap, the revelation of which constitutes the peripety of the play, and the play title is underscored by the Gentleman's line: "With pain the first tooth came and with grief the first one goes!" The loss of the tooth is "the first warning" that the Wife is getting old and must accept the consequences of this. The expression "with pain the first tooth came" may, of course, be taken literally; it is significantly preceded by the address: "Oh, you child!"

However, as we have already noted, there is another character in the play with tooth problems, a character who furthermore is constantly addressed as "child": Rosa. When we first see her, she "*wears a kerchief around her head, tied under the chin, as though she were suffering from toothache*". She also complains of toothache. The Wife looks into her mouth to see if she has a cavity but soon declares: "Why, my dear, your teeth are like pearls! (*She kisses* ROSA *on the lips.*)" Since the girl is 15 and since the Wife finds her teeth excellent, it would seem as though Rosa is bothered by a wisdom tooth.

Teeth are a symbol of sensuality to Swedenborg; whether or not Strindberg was aware of this at the time he composed *The First Warning,* this connection is relevant in the play. The Wife's asking Rosa to "open her mouth wide" has an obvious sexual connotation. And Rosa herself speaks more or less at one breath of toothache and of picking roses together with the Gentleman, of "throbbing" teeth and of a desire to be "attacked by insolent men". At the same time her pretty white teeth—corresponding to the white dress she wears at the end—reveal that she is still an unspoilt, innocent young girl. When the Wife, whose teeth are obviously in a state of decay, kisses her on the lips, her action may therefore be seen as an expression of her longing to return to the stage of purity in which Rosa still finds herself.

Jacobs (1969, xxviii) has pertinently summarized the importance of the tooth theme. The play, he points out, contains two first warnings: "just as Rosa's coming wisdom tooth signalizes the beginning of a passionate career, Olga's broken front tooth symbolizes the close of another". The play title is in other words ambiguous.

However, more blatantly, the Wife's kissing Rosa on the lips seems to be a lesbian gesture, an idea which was not foreign to Strindberg around this time.[3] Yet it is obvious that the playwright has not developed this aspect. The reason may be biographical.[4] But a dramaturgic explanation is just as possible. The Gentleman's adoration of a lesbian woman would have put both him and the reconciliation between husband and wife at the end in a ridiculous light. Emphasizing the Wife's tribadism would also have endangered her status of Middle-aged Wife, a typification which Strindberg presumably intended, since he poses against her, on the one hand the Young Girl, and on the other the Aging Woman. The lesbian component might also have led to undesirable complications of the plot.

Besides the teeth, the Wife is linked to Rosa by their common concern for flowers. When the play opens, we have already noted, the Wife has just received a bouquet from the captain. As the Gentleman keeps *"fingering the bouquet"*, she irritatedly bursts out: "Will you stop spoiling my flowers!" After which he *"flings away the bouquet"*. A little later he warns her that the time will soon arrive when she will no longer be "dancing along on roses" but when she has to count her steps. After these words, we tend to see the bouquet which the Wife has just received as a symbol of the carefree, youthful life she has led and still leads and which rests upon her preserved power of attraction. Her care for the flowers seems to express her care for this kind of life.

Suddenly a woman enters who does not receive flowers but who *is* a flower: "ROSA *enters. /—/ She carries a big basket, filled with flowers."* From her we learn that the Gentleman has promised to help her make wreaths of roses for the Corpus Christi celebration (Sw. "Helga Lekamensfest", lit. Feast of the Holy Body) the following day. This action, indicating Rosa's interest in the Gentleman, may well be taken to imply that he feels attracted by her purity, by her still virginal, 'holy' body, to that in Rosa which reminds him of his wife such-as-she-once-was. It is hardly a coincidence that the Wife is named Olga, the Russian variant of Old Norse 'Helga' (the holy one).

Yet in Rosa's eyes the purity is rather a hindrance, a disadvantage in her competition for the Gentleman's favor. Precisely that which he admires in her, she believes she must disguise to him. When we first see her, she wears "*a half-long dress*" with "*a hole torn in the left sleeve*". When the Gentleman does not notice how she exposes herself to him, she turns his attention to it: "Now see what you have done! You have torn my dress! (*She puts her fingers into the hole in her sleeve and tears it wide open.*)"

The symbolism is rather obvious. Rosa asks the Gentleman to help her bind the wreaths after having picked flowers (cf. Lat. *defloratio*) with him. When he does not do this, she goes one step further in demonstrating her longing for defloration or, as she has earlier put it, desire to be attacked by insolent men. When the Wife admonishes Rosa to "take the flowers along, in case there will be flinging of flowers" when the Gentleman departs, she cynically indicates that Rosa has picked her flowers with an earthly rather than a heavenly bridegroom in mind. That the expression "flinging of flowers" has an erotic connotation seems obvious from the context.

A symbolic meaning can also be ascribed to the two feasts framing the action: the gay party the preceding evening and the religious celebration the following day. In the former case we deal with a feast literally characterized by *Wein, Weib und Gesang,* by revelry and Dionysiac intoxication, a feast of the senses; in the latter case with a celebration commemorating the transformation of the bread at the Holy Supper, a feast of the holy body.

This antithesis is discreetly indicated in the scenery, where we find, on one hand "*vineyards*", on the other "*the spire of a church*". Similarly, in Rosa's change of dress we witness a development from sensuality to purity, a kind of transubstantiation, which in the last instance symbolizes the inner change the Wife undergoes—at least in the Gentleman's wishful thinking.

Dialogue

The switch of power that takes place in the course of the play is subtly indicated in the dialogue. The technique employed is that of letting one character use a word or expression as a weapon and then have another take over this weapon. Thus the Wife in the beginning declares that she pities the Gentleman. A little later she is willing to include herself: "Poor you and poor me!"—though her remark at this point seems self-ironical. She addresses Rosa as "You poor child!" Later it is the Gentleman who pityingly speaks of "Poor Olga!"

Even more striking is the use of the word "child". The Wife constantly addresses Rosa with this word, often preceded by "little". Her attitude is friendly but condescending. When she later feels threatened by Rosa, she prefers the more pejorative "little schoolgirl" (Sw. "skolunge"). The Gentleman's way of addressing Rosa is lovingly protective. He calls her "my child", "a very young woman, or what you call a girl", "a real big girl". Both of them thus emphasize the fact that Rosa is still a child. It is therefore a bit of a surprise when the Gentleman, just as the Wife has revealed the mishap with her tooth, says: "Oh, you child! ... With pain the first tooth came and with grief the first one goes!" The word of address at this point indicates that the Gentleman now takes the same protective attitude to the Wife as he has earlier done to Rosa. In the word "child" Rosa and the Wife unite, just as the speech as a whole, as we have noted, summarizes their fates. Since "child" moreover in this line gets an extended meaning—the Wife becomes a representative of the human child with its inevitable sorrows—it is not surprising if precisely this speech seems the most pregnant one in the play.

There are no marked individualizing elements in the dialogue. The characters all speak in much the same fashion. At most the Gentleman indicates his wittinness through a couple of expressive metaphors, while Rosa's speeches are spontaneously down-to-earth.

Remarkable (though a commonplace in Strindberg's dramas) is the frequent use of *points suspensifs* (...), indicating either pause, *ritardando* or aposiopesis. Certain psychological nuances are indicated by this punctuation mark; this is, for example, the case in the dramaturgically central line: "I have bitten off ... a piece of a front tooth!" Here *points suspensifs* indicate a pause which both adds pregnance to the line and reveals the Wife's fear to disclose to her husband what has happened.

Our analysis has demonstrated that *The First Warning* is a drama which cuts both ways. Lamm's totally negative estimation is clearly unjust; his view that the one-acter is only of interest from an autobiographical point of view tells us more of Lamm's bias than of Strindberg's drama. The accusation that the play contains a long digression and thus suffers from structural incoherence (Madsen) is also exaggerated; as we have seen the story of the Baroness' husband is related to the main plot and reasonably well integrated in the drama.

Smedmark's view that the play is flawed by a certain superficiality and artificiality cannot be as easily rejected. Behind this evaluation there seems to be an implicit comparison: *The First Warning* appears superficial compared to most of Strindberg's other dramas, including the contemporary one-acters. This may be true, but it in no way justifies our rejecting the piece as empty and altogether conventional. When Smedmark finds the beginning more satisfactory than the rest, then the reason is presumably that the initial sequences appear the most natural; when the plot machinery gets going, the improbabilities begin to turn up.

Our final judgement, then, based on the preceding analysis, may be formulated thus: *The First Warning* is a carefully but conventionally composed piece, technically dependent both on *la pièce bien faite* and on the naturalistic drama. Regarding genre, it is what Strindberg himself (*SS,* XIX, 148) called a play "from cynical life", a comedy of sorts, with an interesting theme, theatrically effective. The characters are types rather than individuals, yet drawn with a certain psychological *rondeur*; this goes especially for Rosa. A modest use of symbolism gives the play an extra dimension. The dialogue is swift and functional.

Despite a number of assets, *The First Warning* has never been a great success in the theatre. The reason is presumably that while there are good incitements here and there, insufficiency is equally prevalent. None of the characters is a markedly original creation, the theme of jealousy, in itself interesting, never becomes truly engaging, the plot is not always convincing, the dialogue rarely more than skin-deep.

With *The First Warning* Strindberg has written "an effective drama", a trifle—which, however, in a number of ways indicates that its author is not a trivial playwright.

3. Imagery in *Fadren* / *The Father*

No Swedish author has so frequently and so spontaneously resorted to the use of imagery as Strindberg. As Kärnell has demonstrated in his examination of imagery in the epic works, the image is Strindberg's most important stylistic figure. A study of the plays from this point of view can only corroborate this observation. Even in the so-called naturalistic dramas imagery abounds. *The Father* is a case in point. The play contains a great number of similes and metaphors, the latter amounting to some two thirds of the total number of images.

It is of course not always easy to determine when a word or expression is used figuratively. Often we come across words/expressions whose figurative power is exceedingly strong. But at other times we are confronted with words/expressions which have lost their figurative meaning (dead metaphors) or whose figurative meaning does not become clear until they are combined with other verbal or visual elements in the play.[1] To establish and delimit what is imagery is no easy task. An exact measuring of image frequency is, in fact, not possible. We have to be satisfied with approximate figures.

What we can clearly state with regard to *The Father* is that the flow of images is remarkably uneven; thus certain sequences are completely devoid of imagery, or nearly so, while others are very rich in this respect. This uneven distribution is directly related to the presence/absence of the protagonist, the Captain; for he alone makes use of about twice as many images as all the other characters together. Imagery is an important aspect of the characterization; and since the spiritual struggle of the Captain forms the nucleus of the play, it is not surprising that he is responsible for the major part of the images.

As for the distribution with regard to the other *dramatis personae,* we may note that the character who makes the least use of imagery is the subaltern Nöjd. Subdued and dominated by the women, Nöjd whose very name is a metaphor (meaning 'satisfied') limits himself to a couple of similes. When the Captain asks him to throw the Nurse out, because she wants to "choke" him "to death with her hymn-book", Nöjd declines: "Yes, but I can't, Captain! It's just as if you were asking me to beat up the pastor. It's like religion, it's in your bones. I can't!" The Captain's reference to the hymn-book here seems to determine Nöjd's choice of similes. The comparison with the Pastor underlines the fact that it is by virtue of religion—the connecting link between the Pastor and the women—that Nöjd is emotionally subordinated to both him and them. Nöjd represents a regressive part of the Captain in his relationship to the environment: while the officer-atheist revolts against the representatives of faith and feminism, the subaltern succumbs to them.

If Nöjd's similes are homely, Bertha's are slightly rhetorical:

> Oh yes, how I'd like to get to town, away from here, anywhere at all! Just so I'll get to see you occasionally, often. It's always so heavy, so terrible in there as if it were a winter night, but when you come, Father, it's as if we were taking out the double windows on a spring morning!

As an example of how a young girl naturally expresses herself, Bertha's similes are hardly satisfactory—even if we admit that it is difficult to recreate a language milieu of almost a hundred years ago. On the other hand they are organic in the sense that they are entirely within her sphere of experience; this is especially true of the comparison to a winter night, since this corresponds to the time in which the action takes place.

The whole play is actually set in twilight and darkness. The room in which we find ourselves has no windows and only one proper door, the second one being an invisible wallpaper door. By this arrangement, Brandell (1971, 166f.) argues, Strindberg visualizes how the characters are virtually "imprisoned in a congealed world"—as he was later to do in *The Dance of Death I.* Bertha's similes harmonize with this visual symbolism; also in this sense they are well integrated in the play.[2]

Bertha's imagery, we may conclude, is thematically organic, presentationally inorganic. It has obviously seemed more interesting to Strindberg to relate her images to the theme of the play than to make them psychologically wholly convincing, in accordance with the naturalistic formula.

The only metaphor used by the Nurse again calls attention to the weather. In Act I.7 she tells the Captain:

> You ought to be ashamed! Still, old Margret likes her great big boy, and he'll come back to her, sure enough, like a good child when the storm breaks.

For "storm" the Swedish original has "urväder", an oldfashioned word meaning 'stormy weather, whirling snow'. The metaphor prepares for the storm breaking out in Act II, a storm which according to well-known Shakespearean models (*Julius Caesar, King Lear*) mirrors the restlessness inside the Captain once his paternity has become a burning issue. The Nurse's speech also prepares for the end, when the Captain like a good child returns to her: he here blesses the Nurse-cum-mother in positions which clearly indicate that he is now her child, his head resting first against her bosom, later against her womb.

Since the Pastor represents a higher level of education, we may expect a more sophisticated kind of imagery from him. When he sides with his sister Laura in Act III, he does it with the argument that "blood is thicker than water", a proverbial cliché indicating his conventionality. As we may expect, the Pastor sticks to his biblical domain also in his choice of images, as in the following comparison from the Sermon on the Mount (Matt. 13: 24 ff.):

And I'll be the guardian of that freethinker. You know I've always considered him a tare among our wheat.

More surprising but not implausible is his reference to hunting:

You are strong, Laura. Unbelievably strong! Like a fox in a trap: you'd rather bite off your own leg than be caught!

The simile illustrates the Pastor's conviction that Laura possesses the power and recklessness of a beast. In that respect his imagery rhymes well with that of the Captain, who also compares the women to beasts, notably tigers; Laura has "gnawed and gnawed" at his will—like a rat; and the Nurse is "croaking" for his corpse like an "old crow".

We do not normally ascribe a conscience to animals, and the Pastor does indeed regard Laura as almost devoid of this human quality:

Like a master thief: no accomplice, not even your own conscience! /—/ Let me see your hand!—Not one spot of blood to give you away, not a trace of the treacherous poison! An innocent little murder that the law cannot touch.

Laura is guilty of what Strindberg calls "soul-murder".[3] She has destroyed her husband mentally by making him doubt his paternity. By having the Pastor express himself as though Laura was guilty of a real murder, Strindberg manipulates the recipient in a certain direction: Laura appears even more destructive in our eyes than she would without this imagery. At the same time the Pastor's accusation prepares us for the end of the play where the Captain virtually dies.

The impression that Laura's soul-murder is wholly comparable to a real murder is also strengthened by the fact that the Pastor's way of expressing himself calls to mind another murderess: Lady Macbeth. Earlier the Captain has accused his wife of having "dropped them [the suspicions] like henbane" in his ear—an obvious allusion to Claudius' treacherous murder of his brother in *Hamlet,* another crime determined by the will to power.

A rather transparent allusion to *Macbeth* we find at the end of Act I:

CAPTAIN (*rising*). Get out, woman! Go to hell, you witches! (*At the hall door.*) Svärd! Svärd!

The immediate reason why Svärd is called in is that the Captain wants to leave in his sleigh; it is the task of the orderly to get it ready for departure. But this is clearly a very trivial reason for having Svärd enter; from a realistic point of view the passage might easily have been omitted. However, the calling for the orderly has a deeper meaning. Just as in the case of Nöjd, the name has a significance in relation to the protagonist. The entrance of Svärd (meaning 'sword') is, in fact, a sign that the Captain is now ready to protect himself against the women–the witches; he does it by means of a decidedly masculine name (cf. the Swedish expression 'svärdssida', 'male side'). It is in this context interesting to note that Strindberg in the acting direction following shortly upon the entrance of the orderly states that the Captain "*puts on his cap and gets ready* [Sw. *rustar*] *to go out*"; the word "*rustar*" (lit. 'arms himself') indicates that before us we have not only a man who wants to escape from the satanic women but also a man who takes up arms against them.[4]

Although the Doctor is the representative of empirical knowledge and rationality, he does not altogether refrain from figurative speech:

It's the will, you see, that is the backbone of the soul; if the will is injured, the soul goes to pieces.

If he finds out you've been interfering secretly in his activities, his suspicions will have a foundation and will grow like a landslide. Besides, by doing that you've curbed his will and stirred up his impatience still more.

The Doctor's imagery is partly professionally determined (the backbone metaphor). That Strindberg favors the word 'soul' undoubtedly has to do with the fact that the Captain eventually turns soul-sick as a result of Laura's murder of his soul.

Quite apart from the question whether the images 'belong' to the characters or not—and we may note, in passing, that individualistic imagery does not agree very well with the idea of thematic coherence—stands the question whether the images are expressive and profound or merely decorative. Strindberg's skillful handling of the language appears not the least through his power to let pale or dead metaphors regain their freshness. We find an example in Act I.4:

CAPTAIN. /—/ It's a deadlock.
LAURA. Then the lock must be forced.

An even more striking example of this type is found when Laura asks: "Is this a snare!" The (corresponding Swedish) expression is so common that we hardly think of it as a metaphor. Strindberg reminds us that it is by having the Captain answer: "Of course. It's up to you to walk around it or stick your head in it." A third example is the Captain's "the child bound us together"—a colorless verb-metaphor which becomes expressive when he continues: "but the bond became a chain". The phrase "there's a crime buried here" is an inconspicuous expression which becomes dramatic when it continues: "that's beginning to smell".[5]

Laura's single striking images are found in her speech of defense at the end of the play:

I have never reflected about my actions, but they have glided along on rails you yourself have laid down /—/. Your existence has been like a stone, pressing on my heart, which has pressed and pressed until my heart has wanted to shake off the frustrating weight.

Laura's view is supported by the text. It is the Captain himself who, in a benevolent attempt to acquit Nöjd, first voices the idea that paternity cannot be proved. Yet it is difficult to regard Laura's behavior vis-à-vis the Doctor as completely uncalculating. The question whether her actions are unconscious or not, capricious or carefully planned, is intricate and falls outside our scope. What concerns us here is to what extent Laura's imagery is meaningful and adequate. The first metaphor ("glided along on rails") reminds us that the building of railways was a relevant topic in the 1880's. Even so, it seems surprising that Laura, who cannot distinguish between a microscope and a spectroscope, resorts to such a masculine and technical image—however effective it may be in its compressed restatement of the fundamental irony of the play. Closer to Laura's natural associative sphere is the stone simile. Here we suddenly get a hint that Laura's wish for power is determined by her feelings of social inferiority, the discrimination of woman in a male society.

It is important to note this, since it indicates that the conflict between the Captain and Laura is not primarily a conflict between two individuals but between two (arche)types: man vs woman. Strindberg clarifies this in at least three different ways: (1) by providing the opponents with definite sexual roles: the cavalry officer and scientist versus the housewife and embroideress, etc.; (2) by constantly resorting to generalizing expressions, e.g.: "Do you think a mother lets her child go ...", "a man can't live without honor", etc.; (3) by alluding to archetypal sex relations (Hercules–Omphale, Samson–Delilah) thereby giving historical scope to the idea that woman is by definition unreliable.

"Love between the sexes is struggle", says Laura; her metaphor belongs to the most frequent type of imagery in the play—not surprisingly since the protagonist is an officer. The first image relating to the military sphere we find as early as in Act I.3, where the Captain describes his relations to the women in the house as follows:

It's like going into a cage with tigers in it. If I didn't hold my irons red hot under their noses, they'd tear me down any time.

The imagery here seems to suggest that the Captain functions as a breadwinner to a number of cruel women. Both the antithesis man–beast and the (somewhat awkward) expression "tear me down" gives a picture of the superiority of the man over the women, who do not exactly, the Captain later assures the Pastor, put up a noble fight.

Laura, on her part, complains to the Doctor of the life she has "struggled through" by the Captain's side for many years. The verb-metaphor seems ironical in its discrepancy between what Laura wants the Doctor to believe (that she has shown the loyalty of a comrade-in-arms) and the true situation (that she has actually been her husband's enemy).

When the Captain feels that the Nurse takes Laura's side, he complains that she is going "over to the enemy". In the major settlement between the Captain and Laura in Act II.5 this imagery is developed further:

CAPTAIN. /—/ Do you think a man can live when he has nothing and nobody to live for?
LAURA. So you surrender?
CAPTAIN. No, I propose peace.
LAURA. The conditions?
CAPTAIN. That I may keep my sanity. Free me from my suspicions and I'll give up the struggle.

But Laura does not want peace, she wants victory. And she knows that she can win by keeping the Captain's doubts alive. With his remarkable 'shorthand technique' Strindberg soon shows how the Captain begs for certainty—whatever the consequences may be:

I beg you as someone wounded for the merciful blow: tell me everything. /—/ Won't you forget I'm a man, that I'm a soldier who with the word can tame people and animals? /—/ I lay down the tokens of my power, and I cry out for mercy, for my life.

Note how Strindberg combines the Captain's profession with the animal imagery. But the fight goes on:

CAPTAIN. I feel that in this struggle one of us must go under.
LAURA. Who?
CAPTAIN. The weaker, naturally.
LAURA. And the stronger is right?
CAPTAIN. Always right since he has the power.

The Darwinian idea of the struggle for existence has here been applied to the relationship between the sexes. Note how the imagery is supported by the brevity of the speeches, indicating that a duel is being fought.

When the Captain in Act III.6 is confronted with Bertha, we are again reminded of the Darwinian law of nature:

You see, I'm a cannibal, and I want to eat you up. Your mother wanted to eat me, but I didn't let her. I'm Saturn who ate his children, because they had prophesied that otherwise they would eat him. To eat or to be eaten! That's the question! If I don't eat you, you'll eat me, you've already shown your teeth.

In this naturalistic equivalent of Hamlet's meditative "to be or not to be", the earlier idea of a 'civilized', regulated war has given way to the thought of unrestrained, atavistic blood thirst. Figuratively shorn of his uniform—his mask—the Captain now voices the basic human law, that of *homo homini lupus*.

The change from regulated war to cannibalism is a measure of the Captain's increasing soul-sickness. This change agrees completely with the development of his imagery, which demonstrates an increasing tension between vehicle and tenor. This does not mean that the imagery grows less significant. On the contrary. When Strindberg at the end has the Captain resort to bold and grotesque images, it is a way of expressing a number of unpleasant truths without disturbing our sense of psychological verisimilitude. One could also put it in this way: toward the end the Captain appears as a visionary and soothsayer, akin to Shakespeare's wise fools. Just as Oedipus becomes a seer when he has put out his eyes, so the Captain becomes clearsighted when he turns insane.

One of the most interesting aspects of the imagery in *The Father* is its relation to the dramatic genre. Unlike a novel, a play contains not only verbal but also (potentially) visual and aural imagery, and it allows for subtle correspondences between these different types. We have already noted this when pointing to Bertha's references to the season. A more complex example we find in the web metaphors of the play. Already at an early point the Captain notes that "they're spinning about me". The rather vague expression gives us associations in various directions. We may think of a spider catching its victim in its web.[6] Since the Captain's antagonists are all women, we may also think of spinning as a decidedly female occupation (cf. the word 'spindle-side', Sw. 'spinnsida'); we are reminded of this aspect at the end of the play when the Captain, referring to the unnatural change of sexes brought about by Laura, exclaims: "Omphale! Omphale! Now you're playing with the club while Hercules spins your wool!" The step from Omphale to the Moirai, who spin and sever the thread of life, is a short one. Finally, we may think of the satisfied spinning of a feline animal. As we have already noted, the women are at an early point compared to tigers. When Laura at the end spreads her shawl over the Captain, he is at first reminded of her love during their early years together but after a while he bursts out: "Take the cat away that's lying on me!" The shawl clearly corresponds to the net which Clytemnestra throws over her husband in Aeschylus' *Agamemnon*. "Throw something over me", Strindberg has the Captain ask Laura.[7]

We can now see how the early verb-metaphor "spins" precisely through its vagueness can give rise to a cluster of relevant associations: spider's web, beastly sound, female occupation, male slavery (the Omphale episode), Fate (the Moirai). In the combination shawl–'net'–cat the metaphoric threads come together. A piece of theatrical property has become symbolically pregnant.

As the three Moirai demonstrate, the idea of spinning is related to severing as life is to death. Strindberg seems to allude to this when he has the Captain say:

> For me, since I don't believe in a life to come, this child was my life hereafter. That was my concept of eternal life, the only one, perhaps, that has any basis in reality. If you take that away, you cut my life short.

The reason why the question of paternity is so important to the Captain is that as a freethinker he can only think of the immortality of the soul in an indirect, immanent sense. The child becomes a substitute for the lost faith in his own immortality. The question of paternity, in other words, is not only a moral but also a religious issue.

The connection is implied precisely in the words "cut short" (Sw. "av-klippt"), which make one think both of the moment of death and of birth: the severing of the navel string. It may seem surprising that the spiritual tie between father and child is illustrated by an image related to the physical mother–child relationship. Yet this is completely in line with one of the fundamental ideas of the play, the idea that the Captain, whether he is the biological father of Bertha or not, spiritually—in his attachment to her—is her father much more than Laura is her mother.

There is a direct connection between this "cut short" and the "clipped" (Sw. "kortklippt") of the final act. When the Captain discovers that the Nurse has tricked him into the straitjacket, he exclaims: "Caught, clipped, outwitted and not able to die!" Since the child can no longer function as a "concept of eternal life", his life is cut short and he now merely desires that spiritual death may follow upon the physical one. The whole situation in Act III.6 and especially the word "clipped" lead our thoughts to Samson, whose hair was cut short and who was handed over to the Philistines by Delilah, once he had revealed to her that his strength was in his hair (Judges 16: 17–21). Like Samson, the Captain is partly responsible for his own collapse.[8]

A special type of image found in *The Father* are those which are at once central and inconspicuous. I refer to such words as "child", "mother", "father"—words which are sometimes used in a figurative sense. From a certain point of view the whole drama may be considered a play of masks or roles. The characters are playing parts to one another and the action may be described in terms of role-changes. Thus the Pastor is in turn (1) the Captain's single friend, (2) Laura's brother, and (3) the representative of the church; naturally these psychological roles are mingled but on the whole he develops in the course of the action from (1) to (3). In his relation to Bertha the Captain plays the role of (real or imaginary) father, in his relation to the Nurse and, at times, to Laura he adopts the role of child. Right at the beginning of the play he complains that his old nurse treats him as though he still "wore a bib". At the end of Act I the Nurse predicts, as we have noted, that the Captain—"her great big boy"—will come back to her "like a good child". If the Nurse typifies woman in her primeval role as nurturing mother, the Captain typifies man in *his* primeval role:

CAPTAIN. /—/ Can you tell me how you can treat a grown-up man as if he were a child?

NURSE. I don't understand, but I suppose it's because all men, big and small, are women's children . . .
CAPTAIN. But no woman is born of man.

The last line seems to be an allusion to the prophecy of the witches in *Macbeth* that "none of woman born / shall harm Macbeth"; at the end, we recall, Macbeth is killed by Macduff, "from his mother's womb / untimely ripp'd", hence not "of woman born". Similarly, the woman in *The Father,* Laura, not being "born of man" in the same sense that the Captain is born of woman, has by definition the upper hand in the struggle between the sexes. It is significant that when the Captain is tricked into his straightjacket, the Nurse plays up her mother role to his child role.

Already earlier in the play the Captain–Laura relationship has been characterized as a mother–son relationship:

CAPTAIN. /—/ Don't you see I'm as helpless as a child? Don't you hear I'm asking for pity as from a mother? Won't you forget I'm a man . . .
LAURA. Weep, my child; then you'll have your mother with you again. Do you remember it was as your second mother I first came into your life? Your big strong body lacked nerves, and you were a gigantic child, who had come too early into the world or probably hadn't been wanted. /—/ The mother was your friend, you see, but the woman was your enemy, and love between the sexes is struggle.

The relationship between the Captain and Laura has apparently been characterized by a constant shift between the husband–wife relation—which gives him an upper hand in a male society (cf. the beginning of the play where he still behaves as an authoritarian *pater familias*)—and the mother–son relation, which makes Laura the stronger of the two. None of the relationships gives them a chance to be attracted to one another as two equals. Even in bed the struggle for power is being fought out:

LAURA. /—/ But, you know, every time /—/ you came as my lover, I was ashamed, and your embrace was a joy, that was followed by pangs of conscience as if I had committed incest. The mother became the mistress, ugh!
CAPTAIN. I saw it, but didn't understand. And when I thought you were contemptuous of my lack of manliness, I wanted to win you as a woman by being a man.

A purely sexual meaning is here attributed to the concept of manliness, and the act of love itself is seen as a sexual struggle, in which the stronger, the more potent conquers the weaker. Laura's feelings of incest are hardly a reflection of a Victorian attitude to sexuality; momentarily she can accept it. Her pangs of conscience are rather a result of her experiencing sexual intercourse as woman's submission to man, as a defeat in the continuous struggle between the sexes; she is in this respect very similar to Miss Julie.

The stress on sexual roles returns in the following speech, packed with images:

CAPTAIN. /—/ But we and other people lived our lives, unconscious as children, full of notions, ideals, and illusions, and then we awakened; that would do, but we awakened with our feet on the pillows, and the one who awakened us was a sleep-walker, too. When women get old and have ceased to be women, they get beards on their chins. I wonder what men get when they become old and have ceased being men? Those who had crowed were no longer males but capons, and the pullets answered the call so that when the sun was going to rise we found ourselves sitting in full moonlight with ruins, just as in the good old days. It had been only a little morning nap with wild dreams, and it wasn't any awakening.

The Captain's poetical tirade consists of a series of paradoxes or departures from nature. The one who awakes is a sleepwalker; the one who is awakened finds himself upside down. Women grow beards; cocks and hens are castrated. There is talk of continued idealistic-romantic sleepwalking (moonlight and ruins), while it should be time for daybreak and awakening.

At the same time we note how this speech relates to the play as a whole. The reference to capons, for example, points forward to the end, where the Captain demonstrates that he is not the only cuckold. The Pastor, the Doctor and the man who once seduced the Doctor's wife—all of them share his fate; something similar may be said of Nöjd, who plays the part of a cuckold in his relationship to Emma and Ludvig. In fact, all the men in the play (except Svärd) are betrayed by women. Add to this the allusions to Samson–Delilah, Hercules–Omphale and Joseph–Potiphar's wife and the conclusion is obvious; in the words of the Captain: "Recent research says there's only one kind [of women]"—the treacherous kind.

The imagery we have so far examined can be identified in the immediate context. Besides this type, we find in *The Father* another kind, more difficult to discover: words/passages which in the immediate context seem to have merely a literal meaning but which take on a figurative significance when they are combined with words/passages in other parts of the play. We find an example in the following speech; says the Captain to Bertha:

You know what meteors are! Stones that fall down from other heavenly bodies. I can study those and tell if they contain the same elements as our earth. That's all I can see.

This speech anticipates what is to happen. Just as the Captain tries to establish a relationship between the meteors and our earth, in the same way he will soon attempt to establish a relationship between himself and the one he now addresses: Bertha. The question whether the meteors belong to our earth or to other heavenly bodies is analogous to the question of Bertha's origin. But just as the discovery that the meteors contain the same elements as our earth is no absolute proof that they emanate from here, so the resemblance between the Captain and Bertha—cf. his scrutinizing of the photographs in Act II.3—is no proof that he is her biological father. The similarity can be established, not the extraction. There is something deeply tragic in the Captain's statement about the limitation of knowledge: "That's all I can see."

But is this really an example of imagery? The answer depends on whether we take the word in a wide or narrow sense. According to traditional terminology the reference to meteors is rather a case of symbolism. But as this example shows, the boundaries between the two categories is far from clear-cut.

Let us summarize. As we have seen, Strindberg makes ample use of imagery in *The Father,* especially in the form of metaphors. The distribution of the images is rather unbalanced both with regard to the different parts of the play and to the different characters. Far more than the rest, the Captain is inclined to speak figuratively. It is not in the last instance for this reason that we agree with Laura when she says: "You should have become a writer." His imagery spans a very wide register—warfare, economy, technology, law, politics, horticulture, classical mythology—and is characterized by preciseness and boldness. It is very much through his imagery that we get the impression that the Captain is a bit of a *homo universalis,* a spiritual giant surrounded by petty souls, mostly female ones. In this way the imagery serves the subjective purpose of the playwright.

On the other hand we cannot claim that the imagery is a trustworthy gauge of the contrast between the Captain and the rest. We have seen how Laura can make use of an image which would have seemed more natural in the Captain's mouth—the same goes occasionally for the Pastor and the Doctor. The reason Strindberg has not strictly kept the imagery of one character apart from that of another is, from a dramaturgic point of view, that a certain flow of images is necessary to secure thematic unity.

The imagery of *The Father* is often imaginative and poetical—this goes at least for the Captain's images. But sometimes the rhetorical tone is disturbing. One could compare with Ibsen's (social) plays which are far more ascetic in their use of *verbal* imagery; as for the visual imagery the opposite holds good. Strindberg, like Shakespeare, had a natural inclination to think in terms of images. We have seen how the imagery in *The Father* can be related to plays like *Hamlet* and *Macbeth,* and how the weather symbolism may recall that of *King Lear.* Add to this the obvious Shylock paraphrase in Act II.5 and the resemblance to *Othello* (the dramatization of a soul-murder) and the affinity with Shakespearean drama is evident.[9]

From Shakespeare Strindberg could learn how poetical imagery can function dramatically and how similes and metaphors can serve as implicit messages to the audience of circumstances which later become manifest.

What above all must have seemed urgent to the writer of *The Father* was the possibility of widening the narrow peep-show frame of realistic drama by means of imagery.[10] Whether the attempt has succeeded may be a matter of dispute. What we can state is that the playwright in this prose drama, set in a contemporary bourgeois environment and considered by himself the prototype of modern tragedy, makes ample use of an essentially Shakespearean kind of imagery, adjusted to the milieu of the play. It is an illustrative example of how Strindberg, within the limits of bourgeois drama, attempts to preserve, or reconquer, the wide perspective of Shakespearean tragedy.

4. Speech Situations in *Fröken Julie* / *Miss Julie*

'Dialogue' (from Greek διαλογος) means 'conversation between two people'. This very precise meaning rarely applies nowadays. When speaking of dialogue in drama, we usually mean either (1) everything that is verbalized in a stage production—what Ingarden calls *Haupttext*—or, with a narrower definition, (2) all conversations; in this latter case soliloquies and asides are not considered part of the dialogue. I shall here use 'dialogue' in the first sense.

Within the dialogue I distinguish between the following speech situations:

(1) pantomime (nobody speaks)
(2) monologue (speech by one character)
(3) duologue (conversation between two people)
(4) triologue (conversation between three people)

Although irrelevant with regard to *Miss Julie*, the list may easily be extended; we may speak of quattrologues, quintologues, etc.—and of multilogues (conversation between an unspecified number of people). A special type falling under category (2) is the 'soliloquy' (speech by someone who is or believes himself to be alone). A special type falling under category multilogue is the 'solo chorus' (speeches spoken in unison by all characters), in a sense comparable to the soliloquy.

It is obvious that several speech situations are possible within one and the same sequence. Thus a mono-sequence permits types (1–2), a duo-sequence types (1–3), a trio-sequence types (1–4), etc. Often the speech situation within a sequence changes; thus 'triologue' may well be a rough designation for a trio-sequence in which several speech situations occur and in which the speeches are very unevenly distributed.

With regard to communication, three alternatives are possible. The speaker may direct himself (1) exclusively to the recipient (soliloquy, aside, solo chorus), (2) exclusively to one or more characters (silent speech), or (3) both to the recipient and to one or more characters (monologue, duologue, multilogue). It is evident that of these alternatives, (3) is the rule, while (1) appears sporadically and (2) is rare.

Since in *Miss Julie* we deal only with three proper speaking parts, the possibilities to vary the speech situations are limited. Even so, it is surprising to what extent Strindberg, within the narrow limits allowed him, is able to create variation. The sequence scheme gives a clear picture of how the play is constructed also in this respect:

Seq.	*Page/ line in ASD* III	*On stage*			
A	312/1				
1	313/1	K			
2	313/3	*K*	*J*		
3	316/5	*K*	*J*	*Ju*	
4	317/24	K			
5	318/4	*K*	*J*		
6	318/19	*K*	*J*	*Ju*	
7	322/37		*J*	*Ju*	(*P*)
8	332/1				*P*
9	332/8			Ju	
10	332/10		*J*	*Ju*	
11	347/35		J		
12	347/37	*K*	*J*		
13	351/15		J		
14	351/18		*J*	*Ju*	
15	354/19	*K*	*J*	*Ju*	
16	354/34	*K*		*Ju*	
17	356/3	*K*	*J*	*Ju*	
18	359/1–362/16		*J*	*Ju*	(*C*)

Abbreviations

K = Kristin
J = Jean
Ju = Julie
P = The people
C = The Count

As appears from the scheme, we have five pantomimic sequences in the play; of these only two (seq. 4 and 13) are long enough to permit of extensive pantomimic acting; we here deal with 'cover sequences', inserted to give the impression that the time spent on onstage occupations corresponds to the time used for offstage activities: while Jean and Julie are dancing in the barn, Kristin is curling her hair in the kitchen (Dyfverman, 143). Strindberg here seems concerned with naturalistic verisimilitude.[1]

The speech situations consist of one solo chorus, eight duologues and four triologues. It should be observed that the people in seq. 8 have two offstage listeners (Jean and Julie); and that seq. 7 and 18 are considered duologues, although we also find here offstage characters (placed within parentheses), in the last instance even a character unheard by the recipient.

It is significant that the first two duologues are given to Jean and Kristin. Here we are confronted with traditional exposition in the form of gossip among servants about their superiors. After two triologues, which underline the triangular situation—Jean's position between the two women, erotically and socially—and create suspense, two long duologues between Jean and Julie follow, one before and one after their sexual intercourse. By this arrangement the psychological change of roles is stressed: Jean has ascended, Julie descended, socially speaking.

The following duologue between Jean and Kristin is determined by the fact that the recipient must be informed about Kristin's knowledge of what has happened and of Julie's awareness of this knowledge. Part of the suspense now concerns the question: Will Julie get to know that Kristin knows? Kristin must then disappear again, so that she cannot (yet) prevent Jean's and Julie's escaping together. Again we get a duologue between Jean and Julie, culminating in the murder of the greenfinch, an event which gives Julie a reason to seek support from Kristin who now re-enters. After a short triologue—a cover sequence—we get the first and only duologue between Julie and Kristin, amounting to an attempt to get the cook to join her mistress and recent lover on their escape trip to Switzerland. It is an ironic variation of the conventional *confidente* situation, the function of which is primarily to clarify to Kristin what is in the make—so that she soon, in seq. 17 (formally a triologue), can prevent the escape. As I have already pointed out, the final sequence is a duologue of sorts. Jean and Julie are now left alone on the stage. The simplest explanation for this arrangement is that both are in favor of the idea that she take her life. They promote in other words an action culminating in Julie's suicide.

Next to the 'normal' speech situation we find, as already indicated, a number of variants. Thus Jean partly disappears in seq. 6 in order to change coats. A little later Kristin falls asleep in her chair. In seq. 17 Julie seems for a while totally unaware of what is going on around her. And in seq. 18 the Count announces his homecoming through the speaking-tube. In all these cases we may speak of at least a potential change of speech situation.

So far we have been concerned chiefly with the sender in the communicative process, asking: Who speak(s)? While this question is easy to answer unequivocally, it is often difficult to state for certain who listen(s). Yet this question is of utmost importance for our interpretation of the inner processes governing the actions of the characters.

With regard to the variants just mentioned we may further ask: Why do the characters not always enter/leave the stage properly? Why does Jean not leave the kitchen altogether when he wants to change coats? Why does not the sleepy Kristin go to her room immediately? Why does the Count not appear in the doorway? In short: Why does Strindberg in all these cases choose to have a third character partly present? A similar problem is found in seq. 16–17.

In order to answer this question we must examine each situation separately.

Let us consider them in order of presentation. Toward the end of seq. 6 we find the following exchange of speeches:

JULIE. /—/ But why are you wearing livery on a holiday evening? Take it off at once!
JEAN. Then I'll have to ask my lady to step out for a minute, for my black coat's hanging here ... (*Gestures as he goes to the right.*)
JULIE. Are you embarrassed because of me? Changing a coat! Go into your room then and come back! Or you can stay—I'll turn my back.
JEAN. With your permission, my lady! (*Goes to the right; the audience can see his arm when he changes coats.*)

It should be clear from this that Jean remains in the kitchen, where his black coat is hanging (behind the curtain of the right wall). But at the same time Julie's "go into your room" informs us that Jean's room is located to the right of the kitchen, a circumstance of which we have so far been unaware.[2] This piece of information has a preparative aim: very soon Jean and Julie will escape to this room.

By placing the coat in the kitchen rather than in Jean's room, Strindberg is able to visualize Jean's frenetic attempt not to stimulate Julie's sexual appetite. Already at an early point in the play the attention is drawn to Jean's arm. At the end of seq. 3 Julie for the second time invites him to dance. It now no longer concerns a ladies' waltz but a popular schottische; it is obvious that she is lowering herself:

JULIE. /—/ So give me your arm! /—/ (JEAN *offers his arm and conducts* MISS JULIE *out.*)

It is still he who gives her his arm—be it at her command. In seq. 7 Julie has become bolder:

JULIE. /—/ Come! Just out in the park! (*She gives him the arm, and they go out.*)

When he has got a speck of dust in his eye, she "*takes him by the arm, makes him sit down*":

JULIE. /—/ Why, I think you're trembling, you big strong man! (*Feels his upper arm.*) With arms like that!

The touching of his upper arm indicates how strongly Julie is now attracted to it—or to the strength it represents.

In the light of these passages, Julie's teasing "Are you embarrassed because of me? Changing a coat!" seems rather unfair. She wants to indicate that it is he who is prudish, not she who is "crazy", i.e. erotically excited. Perhaps she also wants to provoke him to change coats while she is looking.

Dramaturgically, it is important to note that Jean obviously can hear what Julie and Kristin tell one another, since he is fairly close to them (Josephson, 85). This means that when Jean re-enters the kitchen he knows that Julie knows that he and Kristin have an intimate relation; he can no longer pretend to be altogether independent. But at the same time Strindberg can prevent Jean from joining in their conversation by having him disappear behind the curtain right. By isolating his arm—from the spectator's point of view—the playwright is further able to stress its erotic significance.

Symbolically, Jean's changing of coats amounts to a change of social roles; once he has taken off his livery, he is no longer Julie's humble servant. The example illustrates how even such stage business as the changing of costume may affect a speech situation considerably.[3]

Psychologically, it is evident that Jean's decision to stay, characterizes him in one way or another. But how? One interpretation may read as follows:

> As a servant unfamiliar with the possibility of making a choice, Jean takes Julie's second suggestion to be a command which he has to follow.

But it is also possible to interpret his decision as follows:

> When Julie has declared that she will turn her back on him while he changes coats, Jean sees no reason for leaving the kitchen.

Here we assume both that Jean trusts Julie and that he is still anxious not to stimulate her desire. Instead of the mechanical response of a subaltern, we have a balanced, deliberate, ethically respectable reaction. A more complicated alternative is the following:

> Jean does not trust Julie's promise. When he chooses to stay, thereby risking that she will stealthily glance at him, he gives way to his own desire for an erotic adventure. But it is important to him that *she* takes the initiative. It gives him a comfortable feeling of irresponsibility.

Jean here appears less balanced, morally more dubious but perhaps also more human. Yet even this alternative appears rather simple compared to the one that was eventually dramatized in the successful 1949 production at the Royal Dramatic Theatre in Stockholm; commenting on this passage, director Alf Sjöberg states (letter to Törnqvist, November 6, 1979):

> Strindberg has always had an extremely comical manner of saying (i.e. have his heroes say) "Out!"—*after which they themselves leave the stage.* It is a clown trick, almost on the same level as that of Beckett's clowns as they say: "Let's go"—after which they remain seated until the curtain falls.
>
> Jean's speech (and that is what makes it treacherous) means that *Jean drives Julie out.* (And he does it by means of the implicit code that a gentleman does not take off his coat in the presence of a lady.)
>
> The speech with this code as alibi—*drives her brutally out*—he demonstrates power, shows what a noble, hell of a fellow he is—but he contradicts himself (in Strindberg's tricky manner) *he leaves himself!*
>
> Yet *at the same time* he has made her understand that this brutality and this escape from her—is dictated by a (proposed) *respect* for her.
>
> Julie at once senses the banishment. How does she show that? By immediately

inverting *the meaning of the speech.* She implies, that he wants her to go, because he is *himself embarrassed.*

Julie. Are you embarrassed *because of me?* etc.

At the same time she *lowers herself. "Because of me."* "I am not the high-spirited lady you think—we are on the same level." And then she says what Jean should have understood himself: "if he does not want to embarrass *her,* the possibility of withdrawing always remains." But this possibility he has *not* implied.

The conclusion, then, is: "Or you can stay—I'll turn my back."

Jean has *got her where he wants her.* He can start the undressing, the first step to the intercourse and it is *she who has taken the initiative.*

Jean. "With your permission, my lady."

The speech—or the whole passage—is not an expression of Jean's discomfort. It is part and parcel of his fullblown strategy to let the victim decide her own fall.

The four alternatives, presenting four rather different portraits of the servant, are all possible. We cannot, with any certainty, determine Jean's intentions. It goes without saying that if such a short passage can give rise to such a variety of interpretations, this variety becomes much more encompassing when we deal with the play at large. It is not surprising that Jean's part has been recreated in a number of ways in different stage productions. Psychological analysis implies by necessity that the intentions of the characters are made an object of discussion; yet this is a highly speculative concern since it involves numerous interpretative alternatives.

If the speech situation of our coat-changing example undergoes merely a slight change with regard to character constellation, a more decisive alteration in this respect takes place a little later when Kristin falls asleep in her chair by the stove. It is, we may protest, not very plausible that the cook should fall asleep shortly after she has appeared most affectionate towards her fiancé and even made herself up to celebrate Midsummer Eve with him (Dyfverman, 139). The dramaturgic reason for Kristin's falling asleep in this part of the play is obviously that she has no function there. Strindberg must get rid of her. But why in this manner?

Presumably because in this phase of the seduction we are confronted with a tense intermediate situation. We get the following development:

Seq. 6:	*J*	*Ju*	*K*
	J	*Ju*	K
	J	*Ju*	K (asleep)
Seq. 7:	*J*	*Ju*	
	J	*Ju*	(*P*)
Seq. 8:			*P* / J Ju (= offstage intercourse)

At the end of seq. 6 Jean and Julie are for the first time in a sense alone together.[4] Erotic advances are now possible—within certain limits. For Kristin is still there and she *can* wake up at any moment. A new situation is created when Julie wakes her up and Kristin leaves for her room. Jean and Julie are now all by themselves. We have come one step closer to the intercourse which is finally facilitated by the arrival of the peasants.

However, it is noteworthy that Kristin does not immediately leave the kitchen. She awakens gradually:

JULIE. /—/ Kristin! Are you asleep?
(KRISTIN *mutters in her sleep.*)
JULIE. Kristin!—She certainly can sleep!
KRISTIN (*in her sleep*). The count's boots have been brushed—put on the coffee—right away, right away—ho ho—puh!
JULIE (*takes* KRISTIN *by her nose*). Will you wake up?
JEAN (*sternly*). Don't disturb the one who's sleeping!
JULIE (*sharply*) What!
JEAN. The one who's stood by the stove all day can be tired when night comes. And sleep should be respected ...
JULIE (*changing her tone*). That's a lovely thought, and it does credit to you—thank you! (*Puts out her hand to* JEAN.) Come out and pick some lilacs for me!
(*During the following speeches* KRISTIN *awakens, goes—stupefied with sleep—to the right to lie down.*)

When "a sleeper talks in his sleep", Strindberg says in the Preface to the play (*ASD,* III, 307), we deal with a motivated monologue, i.e. a speech situation which fulfills the demands for plausibility and which therefore is permissible also in illusionistic plays. In our terminology we are here rather confronted with a soliloquy: Kristin is hardly aware of the presence of others.

In several respects the passage corresponds to certain speeches at the end of the play. Thus we find a counterpart of Julie's condescending attitude to Kristin and Jean's defense of her in seq. 17, where the cook scornfully refers to her mistress as "that creature", while Jean again "*sharply*" rebukes her for her lack of respect. The symmetrical arrangement underlines the reversal that has taken place between the two women while at the same time Jean's intermediate social position is brought out.

It is significant that the sleepy Kristin speaks of the chores which have to be done early in the morning. Brushing the boots would seem to be Jean's business; in seq. 7 he wishes to return to his work with the excuse: "The Count wants his boots ready"; and when the play opens he enters carrying the Count's boots. Making coffee is, of course, exclusively Kristin's business.

It is obvious that Strindberg has shaped Kristin's sleepy speech in such a way that it corresponds to Jean's conversation with the Count at the end:

JEAN. /—/ Yes, sir! Right away! /—/
JULIE. /—/ What did he say? /—/
JEAN. He wanted his boots and his coffee in half an hour.

It is now clear that Kristin's speech need not be interpreted as a recapitulation of what must be done early in the morning; alternatively, it can be seen as an answer to the orders habitually given by the Count via the speaking-tube. Her "the count's" is in that case a vocative form and the speech is indeed a monologue. In any case, it prepares for Jean's submissive attitude to the Count at the end; even in her sleep Kristin is filled with a sense of duty toward her superiors.

When Strindberg chooses to have her go to sleep only to be awakened later and to have her leave the room in a state between sleep and awakening, the reason may also well be that in this way Julie's final exit is foreboded:

JULIE (*ecstatically*). I'm already asleep—the whole room is like smoke to me ... and you look like an iron stove ... which resembles a man dressed in black and wearing a high hat—and your eyes are glowing like coals when the fire is going out—and your face is a white spot like white ashes—
/—/
JEAN (*takes the razor and puts it into her hand*). Here's the broom! Go while it's light—out to the barn—and ... (*Whispers in her ear.*)
JULIE (*awake*). Thank you! Now I'm going to my rest!
/—/
(JULIE *goes determinedly out through the door.*)

Note how Julie and Jean here stick to Kristin's sphere of occupation: making up fire, sweeping the floor; even the barn we associate with her rather than with the aristocratic Julie. But while Kristin's sleepy speech is highly prosaic, Julie's is ecstatic: in poetical images she verbalizes her vision, her dream of extinction. And while Kristin goes to bed "*stupefied with sleep*", Julie is fully awake (despite her heavy drinking!) when she "*determinedly*" leaves the room on her way to everlasting rest. In short: the similarity between the two situations underlines on the one hand Julie's descension, on the other the contrast between the cook and the 'countess', between an average person and an exceptional one.

When Jean in seq. 16 disappears into his room, he does so with the altogether acceptable excuse that he must shave; after all, he has just decided to accompany Julie on her journey; he must now tidy himself up. The situation at this point is that Jean knows that Kristin knows that he and Julie have had sexual intercourse with one another. But Jean has denied to Julie that Kristin knows anything about this. When Kristin is now confronted with Julie for the first time after the sexual aberration, there is an obvious risk that his lie will be revealed—the more so since Julie now sees Kristin, being a woman, as a friend and Jean, being a man, as an enemy. When he chooses to leave "the ladies" at this point, our impression is indeed, as Dyfverman (140) notes, that of a cowardly escape. Strindberg's acting direction is expressive: Jean "*steals out*" of the kitchen. He may or may not hear what is being said at this point; there is no reason for him to take part in the conversation. Significantly he returns when Julie begins to recapitulate what he has just said about the attractive life at Lake Como.

Dramaturgically, Jean's exit/entrance is connected with Strindberg's attempt to introduce the razor, the suicidal weapon, as naturally as possible. To have Jean shave in his own room is obviously no solution. To have him shave in the kitchen is unnatural. Instead of this Strindberg has him prepare the shaving in his room and then provide Julie with speeches which arouse his curiosity and motivate his return to the kitchen. Note, by the way, how prominent the razor becomes through Jean's way of handling it:

(JEAN *can be seen in the right wing, sharpening his razor on a strop which he holds with his teeth and his left hand; listens with satisfaction to the conversation and nods in agreement now and then.*)

The sharpening of the razor, the exposed teeth, the satisfied expression—we are not very far from the end where Jean in self-defense incites Julie to suicide. The connection becomes especially poignant when we realize that the sharpening of the razor still occurs as Julie "*collapses on the bench; puts her head between her arms on the table*". It is evident that Julie grows dormant at this point—she has no speeches until more than a page later—and we get a situation which not only points backwards to the one in seq. 6 but also forwards to Julie's death at the end—and Jean's share in it.

As we have already noted, seq. 17 is merely formally a triologue; at closer inspection we can see that, in fact, it consists of three subsequent duologues:

(1) *Ju* *K* J (Julie tries to persuade Kristin to join herself and Jean on their trip to Switzerland)
(2) Ju *K* *J* (Kristin's contempt for Julie, quarrel Kristin–Jean)
(3) *Ju* *K* J (Kristin puts an end to the plans to escape)

Is Julie aware of what Jean and Kristin say in (2)? Do they experience her as a listener? This cannot be determined with any certainty. All we can state is that Kristin's contempt for her mistress appears more brutal but also more straightforward if she believes Julie to be listening. Kristin's nature is in other words in part determined by how we interpret this speech situation.

It may seem as though Strindberg in (2) turns our attention away from the protagonist and concentrates on the secondary figures. However, their accusations against one another are also relevant with regard to their mistress. Just as Julie, Kristin has slept with Jean, without being legally allied to him, the servant indicates. And just as the servants for years have been robbing the Count, so Julie has recently stolen money from him. Their sins are hers. The crimes evoke thoughts of punishment which in turn, on Kristin's part, give way to the hope for a forgiving Jesus. And now Julie becomes again wide awake, for atonement is precisely what she is longing for. For a moment she feels the temptation to "lay the blame on Jesus", as she later puts it. But she cannot share Kristin's faith and finally she chooses the more honorable alternative of taking full responsibility for what she has done.

In two places—both appearing in the final sequence—we come across the fairly rare phenomenon which we have termed 'silent speech'. The first place, just quoted, consists of Jean's whisper as he puts the razor into Julie's hand. The second place is the Count's order to Jean through the speaking-tube. In both cases we deal with speeches unheard by the audience.

What Jean whispers to Julie we can guess. In one way or another he admonishes her to commit suicide, presumably he also tells her how to do it. But why does he say this whisperingly? After all, they are now alone. Three different explanations may be given:

(1) They are indeed alone but via the speaking-tube the Count may hear what is being said, and since Jean is anxious not to be held responsible for Julie's death he prefers to whisper.
(2) Jean wants to send Julie to her death as considerately as possible. He therefore whispers.
(3) It would appear both superfluous and artless to the audience were Jean explicitly to admonish Julie to commit suicide. As for the manner, Julie may certainly need some information (law of plausibility) but not the audience to whom such information would merely seem disturbing.

Of these explanations, (1) does not seem acceptable since Jean, granted that the Count is able to hear what is being said, has already compromised himself when he begins to whisper. The psychological explanation (2) seems of secondary importance. More convincing than these is the dramaturgic explanation (3), which interestingly demonstrates how Strindberg—despite the postulated naturalism of *Miss Julie*—has not created a pure fourth-wall-gone drama.

The second example is somewhat different:

(*The bell rings sharply twice.* MISS JULIE *leaps up;* JEAN *changes his coat.*)
JEAN. The count is home! Imagine if Kristin—(*Goes to the speaking tube; knocks; and listens.*)
JULIE. Now he has been at his desk?
JEAN. This is Jean, sir! (*Listens. Note: the audience cannot hear what the count says.*) Yes, sir! (*Listens.*) Yes, sir! (*Listens.*) Yes, right away. In half an hour.
JULIE (*extremely anxious*). What did he say? Good Lord, what did he say?
JEAN. He wanted his boots and his coffee in half an hour.

It is of course not to be expected that the spectator should hear what the Count says. But what concerns us here is how efficiently Strindberg has utilized this circumstance. By having both Jean and Julie express their worry that the Count has discovered what has taken place and by shaping Jean's answers so that this worry is not put to rest, Strindberg has the recipient experience a tension comparable to Julie's; when she puts her anxious questions, he can easily identify himself with her. Not until Jean answers her does this tension ebb away. The Count has not yet discovered anything. But how long will he remain ignorant? This question dominates the final pages—until it is answered when "*the bell rings sharply twice*". Not in the last instance through Jean's and Julie's earlier anxiety are we prepared for the ringing of the bell and do we know what it signifies. The sound initiates Julie's final exit.

We can now answer the question we initially posed: Why does the Count not appear in person? Does the Strindbergian variant offer any advantages? To this may be said: The return of the Count is highly significant. There is a cruel irony in the fact that it is the father who (unwittingly) puts his daughter to death. Moreover: with this arrangement Jean appears less reckless than he otherwise would; his coolness toward Julie must be seen in relation to his awe of her father.

By keeping the Count invisible Strindberg plays down our feeling that we are dealing with a living human being. Rather than an individual, the Count seems a representative of a system. Via the vertical speaking-tube his presence/absence is vividly visualized in hierarchical terms suggesting the conflict between higher and lower classes. One may even go so far as to say that the Count grows into a mythic figure, an incarnation of the Fate (heredity and environment) which ultimately causes Julie's death, a naturalistic—i.e. immanent and plausible—counterpart of the *deus ex machina* of classical tragedy.[5]

The speech situations in our quotation from seq. 18 could be designed as follows:

(1) *J* *Ju*
(2) *J* (*G*)
(3) *J* *Ju*

Three duologues of which (2) is a variant (silent speech on the part of one character). The first of these situations could, however, be categorized in another way; the two speeches read:

JEAN. The count is home! Imagine if Kristin—
JULIE. Now he has been at his desk?

It is of course possible to see this as a regular duologue between Jean and Julie. But it is also possible to interpret the speeches as two soliloquies: Jean and Julie do not address one another; each of them thinks aloud; the moment they voice their speeches they experience themselves as alone. Two more variants are possible. On one hand we may imagine that Jean directs himself to Julie who, lost in her own thoughts, thinks aloud; on the other that Jean thinks aloud, while Julie anxiously poses her question to him. We thus get a total of four alternatives which may be formalized as follows:

(1) *J* ↔ *Ju*
(2) *J* / *Ju*
(3) *J* →/ *Ju*
(4) *J* /← *Ju*

There are arguments for each alternative; the labelling of the speeches is a matter of interpretation.

Something similar is true of many other speeches in the play. The uncertainty as to which speech situation we are faced with at every single moment contributes to the suggestiveness and multiplicity of Strindberg's dialogue. One more example—Julie's escape monologue—may illustrate the problem of demarcation. The concluding part of this monologue reads:

Of course, you won't be working at the stove yourself—and you'll have to be nicely and neatly dressed when you're to see people—and with your looks—I'm not flattering you—you'll be able to catch a man one fine day! A rich Englishman, you see—that kind of person it's so easy to—(*Slows down.*)—catch ... and then we'll get rich—and build a villa on Lake Como—oh, it rains there a little now and then—but—(*Subsiding.*)—the sun must shine sometimes ... though it looks so dark ... and—then—otherwise we can return home again—and come back—(*Pause.*) ... here—or somewhere else ...

We here deal with the final part of a long, descriptive and analytical speech, with a monologue. But this monologue can, as far as the quoted passage is concerned, be interpreted either as directed to the speaking partner (Kristin) from beginning to end or—according to a more convincing and theatrically more rewarding view—as a monologue turning into a soliloquy. In support of the latter view we may note how Strindberg not only by means of acting directions and pauses indicates how Julie gradually becomes alienated, solipsistic; he does it also by allowing the frequent, intimate 'you' forms (Sw. 'du'), indicating contact, suddenly to cease.[6] In addition, we have the change from persuasive optimism in the first part of the speech to disheartened pessimism in the latter part testifying to a complete congruence between what Julie says and the way she says it. As these examples demonstrate, there is always reason to ask to whom a speech is directed—even when merely two characters are on the stage. In *Miss Julie,* however, Strindberg rarely leaves us in doubt, mostly due to the distinct way in which he arranges the speech situations.

To whom is the speech directed? The question may be posed also from a different point of view. In every drama we normally deal with a communication in two directions: the speeches are meant both for one or more of the onstage characters and for the audience. The ideal situation occurs when the information given in the speeches is natural and appropriate to both these receiving categories. But here a difficult problem arises. On the one hand the audience must partake of the information in a particular way and in a particular order for structural and esthetic reasons, notably the building of suspense. On the other hand these dramaturgic reasons, especially in a realistic/naturalistic drama, must be disguised as much as possible so that the illusion that not *we* but the characters are addressed, is maintained. Notably at the beginning of a play this problem is urgent, since here the discrepancy between the total ignorance of the audience and the partial knowledge of the characters concerning the actual situation is greatest. This is the way *Miss Julie* opens:

JEAN. Tonight Miss Julie's crazy again—absolutely crazy!
KRISTIN. Oh, you're here?
JEAN. I took the Count to the station, and when I came back I passed the barn and went in to dance. And who do I see there but the young lady leading the dance with the forester. But when she catches sight of me, she rushes right up to me and invites me to the ladies' waltz. And since then she's been waltzing so—I've never been in on anything like it. She is crazy!

The two-way communication here functions exceedingly well, mostly because what Jean relates concerns a very recent event of which Kristin is as unaware as the audience. Yet the reference to the Count is clearly inserted not for her sake but for the sake of the recipient; the absence of the Count is one of the important prerequisites for the intimate relation between Jean and Julie and the audience must realize that well in advance. As far as this reference is concerned, Kristin functions merely as a feigned addressee. Yet even this piece of information does not disturb us, since Kristin's preceding question connotes a fairly long absence on Jean's part; his mention of the Count explains why this is so.

But in the next speech Strindberg has not altogether managed to keep the natural tone:

KRISTIN. She always has been, but not quite as bad as the last fortnight since her engagement was broken.

As far as Jean is concerned, the speech could have been better phrased either in this way: "She always has been, but not quite as bad as this last fortnight." Or: "She always has been, but not quite as bad as since the engagement was broken off." The only thing Jean needs to know is how long Julie has been *especially* "crazy". *He* knows when the engagement was broken off. But the audience does not—enough reason to include also this piece of information. It is important that *we* learn not only that the engagement has ceased but also that this has happened recently, since this explains Julie's unstable state of mind at the moment.

When Jean continues to describe the situation—that it was the fiancé, not Julie who broke off the engagement—her instability becomes even more comprehensible. It is, of course, surprising that Kristin, Jean's fiancée, has not heard him tell about this event before. It is again obvious that his description is meant in the first place for the recipient. The last two examples illustrate the tension that easily arises between the need to provide functional information and the need to create a completely natural dialogue. They demonstrate, in short, how difficult it is to create realistic speech situations in drama.

The complexity and roundness of a drama character are partly determined by quantitative factors. How often and how long does he/she appear on the stage? How often and how long does he/she speak? In *Miss Julie* we find the following pattern:

Character	*Stage presence, number of seq.*	*Speaking part, number of seq.*	*Number of speeches*	*Number of lines*
Jean	13	11	258	610
Julie	10	9	225	482
Kristin	10	8	67	125
People	1	2	2	24

Somewhat surprisingly, Jean's share in the play is more extensive than Julie's; it confirms our impression that his part is almost as central as hers.[7] Yet no one would question the fact that she is the protagonist and that the play title is adequate. That we experience the situation in this manner is primarily due to the fact that Julie figures prominently also in the speeches of Jean (and Kristin). When measuring the importance of a character we must, in other words, also take into account how extensively he/she is commented on by the others.[8] The reason Jean scores high with regard to stage presence, speech situations and speeches is that he, dramaturgically, has a double part. He is both partner/antagonist to the central character and informant. It may also seem surprising that Kristin has a speaking part in almost as many sequences as Julie. But here the great difference in speeches/lines indicates that the cook is, after all, a minor figure.

As for the *kind* of speech situations found in *Miss Julie,* we may state, by way of summary, that the play consists of eight duologue sequences (plus other brief sequences) and four triologue sequences which, however, are more or less disguised duologues. Thus Kristin has only one speech in seq. 3. Seq. 6 consists of two duologues (*Ju K, Ju J*) and a combination of a duologue and a soliloquy (*Ju J/K*). In seq. 15 Jean has only one (exit) speech. Seq. 17, finally, consists of three duologues: *Ju K, K J, Ju K.* We may thus safely conclude that *Miss Julie* by and large is constructed as a series of duologues.

Why has Strindberg shown such a preference for this particular type? Why has he not anywhere in the play created a genuine triologue, a true conversation between all the three characters? The answer is not difficult to find. As has often been pointed out, the play is socially very firmly constructed. Each character represents a particular level or class. As an intermediate figure Jean can communicate both upwards with Julie and downwards with Kristin. But Julie can only communicate with the cook when she has lowered herself, and even then she does it, significantly enough, in the form of a monologue, that is, an 'undemocratic' speech situation. Besides the social factor we have the erotic one. Here Julie and Kristin appear as rivals for Jean, a circumstance which hardly paves the way for triologues. In short: the duologic structure is conditioned by the two major themes of the play. Partly for this reason is *Miss Julie* one of Strindberg's best constructed plays.

5. *Den starkare/The Stronger* —a Monodrama

The musical monodrama died out at the beginning of the nineteenth century. Toward the end of the same century another kind of monodrama was born with Strindberg's *The Stronger.*[1] The play dramatizes a random meeting between two actresses in a café. In the course of Mrs. X's monologue—Mlle Y does not utter a single word—it becomes clear both to us and to herself that Mlle Y has been, and probably still is, her husband's mistress.

The Stronger may be classified as a combination of monologue and duodrama.[2] Mlle Y's reactions are extremely important, since they at once motivate and qualify Mrs. X's statements. The fact that we are dealing with a monologue presents certain problems. Whereas in a 'normal' play the exposition is usually handled by minor characters, whose 'objective' information often contrasts ironically with the versions of the main characters, in *The Stronger* Mrs. X has to handle the exposition herself, although she is the protagonist of the play. As a result, we find her constantly alternating between her objective role (that of presenting facts) and her subjective one (that of interpreting these facts).

Impressed by the naturalistic *quart d'heure* plays, Strindberg wrote *The Stronger* for the Scandinavian experimental theatre he was trying to bring to life around this time, and it is likely that he wrote not only the part of Mrs. X but also that of Mlle Y for his own wife, Siri von Essen: for performances in Sweden, Siri could do the speaking part; for performances in the other Scandinavian countries, she could do the silent one. The fact that apart from Siri, his little acting company consisted of a few Danes, may be a major reason why Strindberg chose to write a monodrama. According to another hypothesis (Smedmark, 1970, 7 f.), he wrote the play to demonstrate that the monologue need not be excluded from naturalistic drama. In the Preface to *Miss Julie,* he notes: "Monologue is now condemned by our realists as unnatural but if one provides motives for it, one makes it natural, and then can use it to advantage". By including Mlle Y in the play, Strindberg could make Mrs. X's speech acceptable from a *tranche-de-vie* point of view, even though a closer inspection of it reveals that the speech sometimes comes closer to soliloquy than monologue: occasionally Mrs. X appears to be thinking aloud rather than addressing the rival. It is partly these fluctuations between monologue and soliloquy which make Strindberg's monodrama so vivid and psychologically penetrating.

As the title indicates, the problem of power stands central in the playlet—as in so many of Strindberg's dramas around this time:

CAPTAIN. I feel that in this struggle one of us must go under.
LAURA. Who?
CAPTAIN. The weaker, naturally.
LAURA. And the stronger is right?
CAPTAIN. Always right since he has the power. (*The Father*)

JULIE. What terrible power drew me to you? The weak to the strong? The falling to the rising? (*Miss Julie*)

GUSTAV. /—/ do you know why you two were bound to get the worst of it in this fight? /—/ And why you let yourselves be tricked? Because I'm stronger than you and wiser too. (*Creditors*)

MRS. X. /—/ Maybe when all is said I'm really the stronger right now /—/. (*The Stronger*)

Mr. X. You are an entirely different person from what I am. /—/ I don't know whether you are stronger or weaker. And whether you are more or less of a criminal is none of my business. /—/ But one thing is certain: you are more stupid! (*Pariah*)

Who, then, is the stronger in Strindberg's drama by that title? The question may seem spurious. After all, does Mrs. X not make the matter completely clear in the statement just quoted? And if we are still in doubt, there is in addition Strindberg's letter to his wife—who did the part of Mrs. X at the opening night—in which he explains that Mrs. X is the stronger of the two women because she is the more pliable (*ASB,* VII, 263). As Mrs. X tells Mlle Y in an important statement at the end of the play: "You couldn't learn from others, you couldn't bend—so you broke like a dry reed—but I didn't!"

Mrs. X's statements, coupled with Strindberg's remark to his wife, have clearly shaped the opinions of those writers who have commented on the play. Nearly all of them accept the conclusion that Mrs. X is the stronger. Madsen's analysis (121) reflects this conventional view:

At the beginning of the play it looks as if Mlle Y is the stronger of the two women. With the quiet strength of the person who does not speak and is rendered temporarily superior to Mrs. X by her knowledge of Mr. X's infidelity (a knowledge which Mrs. X has not as yet discovered), she calmly allows Mrs. X to give an exhibition of her foolish ignorance and vulgarity. But at the point where Mrs. X discovers the existence of the affair between her husband and Mlle Y, the tables are turned. Mrs. X now becomes the stronger because she is able to accept this fact and go on living with it.

If what Madsen says is true, it must nonetheless be admitted that Mrs. X's adjustment to the new situation would be psychologically convincing only if Strindberg had demonstrated her complete indifference to her husband's love affairs. But this is not the case. On the contrary, he shows that Mrs. X readily falls victim to jealousy. The alternatives left to us, then, are either that Strindberg has drawn an incoherent figure—a view that is hard to reconcile with the international reputation of the playlet—or else that Mrs. X does not adjust as well to the new situation as she seems to do and as the critics have assumed; in other words: that she is not as strong as she pretends to be, and that, conversely, Mlle Y is stronger than Mrs. X wants to admit.

More doubt on Mrs. X's claim to strength is cast by another circumstance. Commenting on the play in the Danish paper *Politiken* on January 24, 1889—that is, shortly after it was written and sixteen days before it was produced—Strindberg remarked that "the heroine does not say a word" (Ollén, 171). The playwright could hardly have identified the heroine with the weaker character. In several productions of the play Mlle Y has also appeared to be the stronger woman to the critics. A Finnish actress, who had herself played the part of Mrs. X, once declared that in her opinion Strindberg considered Mlle Y the victorious one in the play (Ollén, 174). Similarly, Paul (1976, 286) explicitly states that Mlle Y is the stronger of the two.[3] It should also be noticed how hesitant several commentators are with regard to this matter. Thus Lamm (1940, 276) only grudgingly accepts the view that Mrs. X is the stronger. And Gierow (1967, 132) describes Mlle Y as "la rivale vaincue, qui garde une attitude invincible". Apparently Strindberg has created a delicate balance. When producing the play, the director can attribute the greater strength to either of the women, or he can demonstrate a transference of strength from one character to the other, as Madsen suggests and as we have earlier witnessed in *The First Warning.* But what does 'strength' really amount to? 'Strong'—with regard to what? In order to answer these questions we must turn to the play itself.

From Mrs. X's monologue we learn that she and Mlle Y are both actresses. But while Mrs. X is engaged at the Grand Theatre, is married and has three children, Mlle Y is unmarried and is no longer employed at the house in question. Mrs. X's husband, Bob, is an influential person—also with regard to the hiring of actors and actresses. He has earlier had a love affair with Mlle Y. For some reason, not made clear, he then turned to Mrs. X. Several years after their marriage—we may suppose—Mlle Y left the company, presumably at the instigation of Mrs. X. In an attempt to console herself, Mlle Y then became engaged. As though her engagement had once more made her attractive in Bob's eyes, his old interest in Mlle Y flared up:

> Then the two of you really got so friendly that it looked as if you dared to show your real feelings when you felt secure /—/. And I remember at the christening when you were godmother I made him kiss you—he did, but you got upset /—/.

The christening undoubtedly was that of little Eskil, named after Mlle Y's father. Eventually Mlle Y's engagement was broken off. This must have happened less than a year before the start of the scenic action, since we learn that she had stayed with her fiancé's family the preceding Christmas. Why did this relationship go to pieces? Mrs. X indicates a reason when she says:

You know what, Amelia! I think you would have been better off if you had kept him! Remember I was the first one who told you to forgive him!

In other words: the fiancé has been unfaithful to Mlle Y; when she learns this, she drops him. Strindberg's reason for including the statement in the play is clear enough. It depicts Mlle Y as a morally rigorous person and it prepares for Mrs. X's contrasting reaction later on, when she learns that her husband has been unfaithful to her. As Mrs. X puts it toward the end: "I suppose you expected me to go my own way—as you did, and which you regret now—but you see I'm not going to leave him!" Dramaturgically, Mrs. X's statement makes sense, but does it psychologically? How are we to combine it with the indication that the old love between Bob and Mlle Y revived as soon as the latter got engaged? Could it be that the true reason is the opposite one: that the fiancé has discovered that Mlle Y has been unfaithful to him with Bob? And that Mrs. X's explanation merely reflects what Bob, anxious to cover up his liaison with Mlle Y, has told her? Mrs. X actually comes to see the broken-off engagement in this light as soon as she discovers that Mlle Y is her husband's mistress:

Why did you break your engagement? Why did you never come to our house after that? Why don't you want to come to us this evening? /—/ Quiet! You don't need to say anything—now I understand everything! That was why! That was why! Yes! Everything falls into place now!

It is apparently while Mrs. X is on tour in Norway that the relationship between Bob and Mlle Y turns into an intimate one. Again Mrs. X is kept in ignorance of the true state of things by her husband:

And then I know he's faithful to me, you see—yes, I do know! He told me so himself . . . What are you grinning about? . . . that when I was on that tour in Norway that nasty Frederique tried to seduce him—can you imagine? /—/ It's a good thing Bob told me himself so I didn't have to hear it from others.

The French name undoubtedly serves to relate Frederique to the true seducer Mlle Y, named Amelie.

Bob's infatuation with Mlle Y is revealed also by the fact that he virtually turns his wife into another Mlle Y; in Mrs. X's words:

That's why I had to embroider tulips, which I hate, on his slippers—because you like tulips: that's why /—/ we had to live on Lake Mälare in the summer because you couldn't stand the sea; that's why my son was to be christened Eskil, because that was your father's name; that's why I had to wear your colors, read your authors, eat your favorite dishes, drink your drinks—your chocolate, for example.

Mrs. X here depicts herself as a slave of her husband and an imitator of his mistress—a rather degrading and certainly weak position. And yet, shortly after this, she declares herself stronger than Mlle Y. From "others" and from life she has learned to adjust, to compromise, "to bend—and rise again" as Strindberg puts it in his letter to Siri von Essen.

Mrs. X's whole line of reasoning rests on the assumption that she is in the process of getting her husband back. "To judge by certain signs, I think you've already lost him", she tells her rival. What these signs are, however, remains a mystery. Nothing of what Mrs. X says and does suggests that she is correct in her assumption. Her hatred of Mlle Y—she symbolically shoots her—indicates, rather, that Bob is still Mlle Y's lover. So does the fact that Mrs. X continues to imitate her rival, drinking the drink Mlle Y used to relish (but, be it noted, relishes no more; she has turned from chocolate to beer, a stronger, more masculine drink), and presenting her husband with the flowers Mlle Y likes, because Bob "has to have tulips on everything". Her description of Bob points in the same direction:

(*puts a hand in each slipper*). Do you see what small feet Bob has? See? And you should see how elegantly he walks! You've never seen him in slippers! (MLLE Y *laughs aloud.*)

The choice of a Christmas present is significant to a Swede ('slippers' = Sw. 'tofflor'; Sw. 'toffelhjälte' = 'henpecked man'). Mrs. X's way of ridiculing her husband—she derogatorily refers to him as "a fine little man"—suggests that he is indeed henpecked. However, I have earlier indicated that Mrs. X is actually her husband's obedient servant. This seeming contradiction can be resolved if we regard Mrs. X's ridicule as an attempt to attribute a strength to herself which she does not possess. When she puts her hands in the slippers and walks them across the table, she certainly expresses merely her desire to rule her husband.

The slippers also have other connotations. Imitating the husband at home, Mrs. X quotes him:

And then there's a draft on the floor, and his feet get cold: "Ugh, how cold it is! Those damned idiots who can't keep the fire going!" (*She rubs the sole of one slipper against the top of the other.* MLLE Y *laughs uproariously.*)

Here we get a glimpse of the frozen relations between husband and wife. To Mlle Y the description is as comical as was Mrs. X's earlier assumption that she, Mlle Y, would never have seen Bob in slippers. When Bob is together with his mistress there is no need for slippers; he can then keep his feet warm in other ways.

From beginning to end Mrs. X demonstrates a weak person's need to assert herself against a stronger one. Her first words are literally: "How do you do, little Amelie! You look as lonely on Christmas Eve as a poor bachelor." The patronizing tone is obvious; she later tells Mlle Y explicitly: "you are the little one" (Sw. 'den lille', note the masculine form!). Christmas Eve is, of course, the family holiday *par excellence,* and Mrs. X is not slow in reminding the unmarried Mlle Y how happy she was the previous Christmas and how miserable her present existence is compared to that of Mrs. X. Her display of the Christmas presents she has just bought for her family is, consciously or unconsciously, designed to hurt Mlle Y. But the rival can listen calmly and with an ironic smile to Mrs. X's boasting, since she knows that Bob belongs to her. When Mrs. X discovers the true state of things, all the pent-up hatred against Mlle Y bursts forth. She now describes Mlle Y as a worm ("your soul stole into mine"), a snake ("with your dark eyes you fascinated me"), a giant crab ("ready to seize me in your claws"). Here Strindberg touches on one of his favorite notions of the time: the idea of hypnosis or suggestion, and the theory that a stronger brain can exercise an influence over a weaker one (H. Lindström, 1952). Finally Mrs. X explodes: "I hate you! Oh how I hate you!"

What follows demonstrates her desperate attempt to restore her shattered illusions of her own strength. She offers the rather Jesuitical argument that it does not matter if she imitates Mlle Y as long as she gains her purpose: the love of Bob. Her triumphant exit line is: "Thank you for teaching my husband to make love. Now I'm going home to make love to him." But, as we have noted, there is no evidence at all that Bob will be receptive to Mrs. X's love-making. The departing speech should therefore, I think, be regarded merely as a desperate attempt to make the rival believe what Mrs. X can hardly make herself believe: that she will get her husband back and thus prove herself to be the stronger of the two.

Similarly, we may ask ourselves whether some of Mrs. X's statements about Mlle Y are not more meaningful when applied to Mrs. X herself. Consider, for example, her initial anecdote about the deserted bride in Paris:

> /—/ the bride was sitting reading a humor magazine while the bridegroom was playing billiards with the witnesses. Huh, I thought, with a start like that how will it go and how will it end! He played billiards on his wedding night!

Mrs. X sees a parallel between the deserted bride and Mlle Y, abandoned—as she believes—by her unfaithful fiancé. The parallel holds good at this point in the play when we are not yet aware of the real situation. Later, it is more meaningful to regard the anecdote as an ironic illustration of Mrs. X's own situation. For has not Bob—playing the bridegroom's part—deserted his wife, not for any of the wedding witnesses, it is true, but for a person performing a similar duty: the godmother of his son. At the end of the play we may well ask ourselves with regard to Mrs. X's marriage: "with a start like that how will it go and how will it end"?

Again, when Mrs. X tells Mlle Y: "I know you're unhappy, unhappy like someone who has been hurt, and nasty because you're hurt!"—does her description not fit herself much better than it does the rival? After all, it is Mrs. X who has just been seriously wounded and who shows definite signs of viciousness.

Our analysis has revealed that the play title is far more ambiguous than first appears. Of the two women, Mlle Y is intellectually clearly the stronger—no critic has denied it. Morally, she at least does not appear weaker than Mrs. X, if by 'strength' we mean firm moral principles. This need not mean that Mlle Y is impeccable, although it is interesting to note that her name, Amelie, means precisely 'the impeccable one'. In the erotic triangle, finally, her position, as far as we can judge is again stronger than Mrs. X's.[4]

Yet, it must be admitted that there is something to be said for Mrs. X's claim, as a general principle, that the person who can adjust easily to new situations is stronger, better equipped for the struggle of life than the one who cannot. In this sense, and in this sense alone, Valency (282) is right when he says that "the weaker [meaning Mrs. X] is the stronger of the two". It is also noteworthy that while Mrs. X is decidedly feminine, Mlle Y has certain masculine characteristics turning her into what Strindberg called a half-woman: it is significant that she is drinking beer, not chocolate (or coffee). It might be argued that just as Mrs. X imitates Mlle Y, so Mlle Y imitates the male sex.

The balanced conflict in *The Stronger*—the cause of which may undoubtedly partly be traced back to biographical circumstances (Törnqvist, 1970, 305 ff.)[5]—is not unique in Strindberg's *oeuvre*. As initially indicated, it has a counterpart in *Pariah,* in *Creditors* and even in *Miss Julie,* where Julie is morally the stronger character—"she cannot live without honor", Strindberg says in the Preface—while Jean is the stronger in the struggle for life. And just as Strindberg's sympathies are clearly divided between Jean and Julie, favoring the former in the Preface and the latter in the play (Törnqvist, 1976, 102 f.), so his—and our—sympathies are clearly divided between the two women in *The Stronger.* The conflict between the sense of honor and the urge to live at all costs—a conflict we all recognize—is vividly brought out in the play. There is some virtue, or at least some attraction, in each alternative;[6] hence the delicate balance between the characters representing these contrasting dispositions.

6. *Till Damaskus I* / *To Damascus I*—a Drama of Half-Reality

The technique in *To Damscus I*[1] is rather like the one adopted with regard to that familiar black-and-white picture which can be seen either as a white urn framed by blackness or as two black faces in profile staring at each other. One spectator sees the white urn, another the two faces. Once we discover both the urn and the faces, we can agree that the picture can be viewed in two different ways. Our double vision has, you might say, resulted in a truer, richer understanding of the picture.

When Strindberg, in the first hotel room scene, has the Stranger discover how the flowers on the wallpaper form a pattern resembling the face of the Doctor, he employs essentially the same kind of double-vision technique. And this is but a very obvious example of a fundamental technique underlying the whole drama. By constantly alternating our vision, by constantly forcing the double vision upon us, Strindberg makes us partake of the Stranger's own uncertainty as to what reality actually is.

The plot of *To Damascus I* is very simple; in Brandell's (1974*a*, 251 f.) words:

> The Stranger meets the Lady and abducts her from her first husband. They marry, and economic need drives them to seek refuge with her family in the country, where they find a mixed reception. The Mother coaxes the Lady to read the Stranger's latest book. The Stranger leaves her and later finds himself in an asylum. After the moral crisis that he undergoes there, he retraces his steps—part of the time accompanied by the Lady—and discovers that he has treated people unjustly. When he returns to his point of departure, he finds a money order that had been awaiting him all the time at the post office. The play ends with a bit of moralistic wisdom: "It was my own stupidity, or my wickedness . . . I did not want to be life's dupe, and therefore that is exactly what I did become!"

For all its novelty, the play is quite traditionally divided not only into scenes but also into (five) acts. Although the scene division is much more important than the act division—since the scene progression is related to the fundamental compositional device: the mirror technique—Strindberg chose to number the acts rather than the scenes, hereby (intentionally?) obscuring the originality of his composition.

While the three-act structure of *The Father* is easy to defend,[2] the five-act structure of *To Damascus I* appears somewhat haphazard.[3] It certainly seems surprising that Strindberg has not made the act division conform with the mirror scheme. Yet, if we place the first kitchen scene at the beginning of Act III instead of at the end of Act II as Strindberg has it, we get a symmetrical arrangement harmonizing with the symmetrical scene progression. There is, it would seem, only one likely reason why Strindberg chose to begin Act III with the first rose chamber scene. At the beginning of this scene the Lady acquaints herself with the contents of the Stranger's latest book; this constitutes a major sin on her part, since she has promised the Stranger not to do so, a fact which he immediately recognizes by leaving her. The Lady's act, we shall see, is comparable to Eve's eating of the apple, and just as the biblical Fall constitutes a new stage—indeed a peripety—in the history of man, so the Lady's new-gained knowledge motivates a new act in Strindberg's play.

It is easier to see why the first two scenes together form Act I. This act is a kind of prelude to the wandering beginning with Act II. Scene 1 states the situation in which the Stranger and, to some extent, the Lady find themselves; Scene 2 describes the liberation of the Lady from her "werewolf"; only after this is she free to follow the Stranger. The division between Act III and IV seems motivated by the fact that the Stranger at the end of the former, instigated by the Mother, sets out on his penitentiary pilgrimage. Act V, finally, consisting of Scenes 16 and 17, clearly corresponds to Act I and thus emphasizes the symmetry of the act division.

While the act division may seem rather superfluous, the highly symmetrical arrangement of the scenes in quite another way reflects the theme of the play; moreover, it gives it a firm, even rigid, outward structure, as appears from the following scheme:

17, 1 Street corner
16 Doctor's home 2 Doctor's home
15 Hotel room 3 Hotel room
14 Sea 4 Sea
13 Road 5 Road
12 Ravine 6 Ravine
11 Kitchen 7 Kitchen
10 Rose chamber 8 Rose chamber
9 Asylum

In an interesting letter to the fellow-writer Gustaf af Geijerstam (17.3.1898) Strindberg has himself indicated the significance of the scene progression:

The art lies in the composition, which symbolizes the repetition that Kierkegaard speaks of. The action unrolls forward as it leads up to the asylum; there it hits the 'point' and then moves backward, kicking against the pricks, through the pilgrimage, the relearning, the ruminations, and then it starts anew in the same place at which the game ends and where it began.

As G. Lindström (1964, 18) has pointed out, we here find a direct allusion to the conversion of St. Paul. On his way "to Damascus" Saul according to The Acts 26: 14, was surrounded by bright sunlight and heard a voice speaking to him, saying: "Saul, Saul, why persecutest thou me? It is hard for thee to kick against the pricks". In these words Strindberg apparently saw a compositional possibility. Morally, the mirror composition underlines the (Old Testament) idea that man must reap as he has sown; in the words of the Mother: "My son: you have left Jerusalem and you are on the way to Damascus. Go there. The same way you came here. And plant a cross at each station, but stop at the seventh. You don't have fourteen, as He had."

If we assume that the scene in which these words are uttered (Sc. 11) represents the first station, then each of the remaining scenes may be classified as one of the predicted stations of the cross. These seven stations of penance may be combined with the seven hells which the Stranger refers to in Scene 1; but more relevant are the following words from Deuteronomy 28:25, quoted by the Confessor: "thou shalt go out one way against them [i.e. thine enemies], and flee seven ways before them". In Scene 1 we witness how the Stranger goes out against his enemies in traditional fairy-tale fashion. "Battling dragons, liberating princesses, slaying werewolves—that's more like living", he triumphantly exclaims. In the following seven scenes preceding Scene 9 we witness how he flees his enemies, one after the other. If we ask ourselves why Strindberg has settled for 17 scenes in the play, a possible answer is to be found in the following formula: 1+7 (from Deuteronomy) ×2 (mirror technique) +1 (asylum scene/peripety) =17.

According to Sprinchorn (1964, 272) also the figure nine has significance:

Since the sufferings of the hero remind him of the torments of hell, the scenes are arranged to suggest a descent into the inferno, the seventeen scenes forming an inverted cone with the nine scenes of the descent suggesting, though not corresponding to, the nine circles of Dante's Inferno.

It seems, in view of this, hardly a coincidence that the work by Strindberg most intimately connected with *To Damascus I* is entitled *Inferno*; that the Stranger in Scene 1 speaks of "the seventh hell"; and that he, after his stay in the asylum, tells the Mother that he has returned "from hell". Since the Stranger's torments gradually grow worse, it is quite appropriate to see his journey as a descent into hell, the asylum corresponding to the pit.

In the scheme outlining the scene progression three principles underlying the composition have been indicated: (1) the circle, related—as we shall see—to the concept of time, (2) the (normal and inverted) cone, related to the descent-into-hell idea as well as to the ascendance–penance idea (Damascus, Golgotha), (3) the mirror, related to the idea of repetition according to the *lex talionis*.

In *The Father* Strindberg still adheres to plot in the traditional sense, that is a cause-and-effect pattern based largely on interhuman relations. As in *Oedipus Rex* and *Ghosts*—though not to the same extent—*prescenic* events play an important determining role in the scenic action; the information concerning these events has a certain complexity (it deals with both positive and negative experiences); it is fairly spread out over the play; and the provided data can to some extent be chronologically arranged. Within the *scenic* action the causal structure is very compact; one event follows almost by necessity upon another; the Captain and Laura are not unlike two chess players: the move of one is followed by the counter-move of the other. It is also noteworthy that the plot of each of these three plays revolves around some crime(s), factual or suspected; as it happens adultery is at stake in all of them.

The structure of *To Damascus I* is quite different. Here the information about prescenic circumstances is too sparse to allow any elaborate causal and/or temporal pattern. We learn something about the Stranger's childhood and relations to others (notably his family) in Scene 1, but the information is largely additive and patterned, it would seem, on the kind of plaintive parallelisms we find in the Bible—not surprisingly, since the experiences of the Stranger are meant to conform to the misfortunes related in the quotation from Deuteronomy 28: 15–67 in Scene 9.

Within the scenic action, similarly, the causal pattern is much vaguer than in *The Father*. In the latter rational reasons are, for example, usually given for the entrances and exits of the characters; in *To Damascus I* such reasons are often lacking. Instead of a central, palpable crime, forming a focus for the action, we deal with something much vaguer: the evil of mankind, original sin. While the Captain (the male) is pitted against Laura (the female), the Stranger is seen as essentially akin to his fellow-men, as a representative of man. As a result of this, conflict does not play the same role in *To Damascus I* as in *The Father*. This is especially true of the part succeeding the asylum scene, where the Stranger is out to seek reconciliation. Strindberg was here presented with a technical problem: how could he make this part dramatic? If the Stranger were already to be presented in Scene 10 as a fullfledged convert, the suspense of the latter part of the play would be destroyed and the inner meaning of the Stranger's *via dolorosa*—that of gradually paying off one's debts, receiving insight in return—would be lost. Instead Strindberg chose to let the Stranger show a certain distrust of the Powers even after the asylum scene: in this way the tension between the conflicting parties could to some extent be retained. The dispute is, in fact, never completely resolved; even at the end the

Stranger remains somewhat skeptical; he is prepared to pass through the church but not to stay.

The fact that the Stranger, unlike the Captain, has an invisible, omnipotent antagonist has very definite consequences for the plot. While we are given frequent opportunities to look into Laura's machinations, so that we know what she is up to before the Captain is aware of it (dramatic irony), we are virtually in the same situation as the Stranger, wondering, like him, what the following step by the Invisible will be. Our possibility to identify ourselves with the Stranger is, as a result of this, much greater, and *To Damascus I* is clearly a much more subjectivist drama than *The Father*.

Let us summarize. The plot of *To Damascus I* is less tight and the causal pattern much vaguer than that of *The Father*. The reasons for this, we have found, are primarily the following: (1) as a representative of man—rather than of the male sex—the protagonist is not fundamentally different from his fellows; (2) ethically, the play does not deal with a palpable crime but with evil as such; (3) the antagonist is not visible but invisible.

No single characteristic of *To Damascus I* has attracted more attention among scholars than the relationship between the Stranger and the other characters. This is not surprising, for here we deal with one of the most striking consequences of Strindberg's subjectivism. Yet the critics who have commented on this important aspect of the play have usually done so *en passant* and/or with special regard to the biographical background.

With regard to *dramatis personae* in general we can distinguish between the following types: (1) Those who have an exclusively *objective* existence, that is, an existence as autonomous, flesh-and-blood creatures. (2) Those who have an exclusively *subjective* existence, that is, an existence only in the mind of (one of) the characters, usually the protagonist; according to this alternative, the characters are not what they seem to be; they represent something; they are incarnations of thoughts, emotions, drives within the character to whom they 'belong'; we deal here with a convention within the modern theatre comparable to earlier conventions such as the implausibilities—even in realistic drama—concerning time (the time that passes is not the time that seems to pass) or dialogue (the dialogue representing everyday conversation is rather different from everyday conversation). (3) Those who have an *objective–subjective* existence, that is, an existence as partly realistic, partly symbolic creatures.

With respect to *To Damascus I* no critic has, to my knowledge, claimed the first alternative; several non-Swedish critics (Dahlström, Jolivet, Børge, Szondi) have claimed that the second alternative applies; whereas Swedish scholars (Lamm, Brandell, Ollén) lean toward the third alternative.

Let us begin by examining the subjectivist standpoint (alt. 2). It is theoretically quite valid, of course, and it is also easy to see its attraction: if it can be

proved to be true, then *To Damascus I* signifies indeed a radical break with the drama preceding it. Characteristic of the defenders of the subjectivist standpoint is that they make much of those characters who especially lend themselves to this view—notably the Beggar—but make little or no comment on the others; and the hypothesis, it would seem, stands and falls with the question whether *all* the subordinate characters can be regarded as *"Ausstrahlungen des Ichs"*—to use Dahlström's expression—or only some of them.

It is in this context important to take note of the Stranger's stage presence. A division of the drama based on stage presence (a sequence scheme) reveals that of the 48 sequences of the play, the Stranger is present in 25, that is a little more than 50%. It is obvious that it is rather difficult for a spectator to imagine that a character incarnates a drive within the protagonist if the latter is not even present on the stage.[4] If we are to grasp this, the author must make it clear that the two are in some sense related, and in a rather special sense at that. Let us examine the various characters from this point of view.

The figure who bears the closest resemblance to the Stranger is the Beggar. Already before he enters, we are informed of his half-reality:

THE STRANGER. /—/ In my loneliness I meet someone. I don't know whether it's myself or someone else. All I know is that in the midst of my loneliness I'm not alone. The air thickens, congeals, certain presences begin to take shape, invisible but tangible, and possessing a life of their own.

This statement is of tremendous importance, since it tells us not only how we are to consider the Beggar but also the other subordinate characters and, indeed, the whole ensuing action. It indicates, very clearly, that the key to an understanding of the drama is to be found in what we have earlier termed the double vision of the objective–subjective reality (alt. 3).

The Stranger's hesitation as to the objective or subjective reality of the shapes he is confronted with in his loneliness is visually acted out in the sequence with the Beggar:

THE STRANGER. /—/ Are you real? Let me touch you. (*He feels* THE BEGGAR'S *arm.*) Yes, you are.

Also by his appearance the Beggar is a border-line case, an incarnation of half-reality: "*Very strange-looking*". The fact that he is a most unusual kind of beggar, excelling in Latin maxims, a result of his "university education", further stresses the strange, subjective aspect of the man—especially since the traits fit the Stranger.

The primary reason why the Beggar, more than any of the other characters, has been regarded as the Stranger's double is that the two also in appearance are exceedingly similar. This is made clear in the sequence in which the Café Proprietor mistakes the one for the other, because the description furnished by the police fits both of them. Before this we already have learnt that the two have an unusual outward characteristic in common: a scar on the forehead; the Stranger has received it from "a brother", the Beggar from "a close relative". Both men drink too much—the Beggar is a little worse—and they even stick to the same kind of alcohol:

THE STRANGER. /—/ I just hope this is all part of my hangover. Too much Moselle.
THE BEGGAR. Waiter!—A bottle of Moselle.

Very obvious—and certainly adding to the mood of half-reality that Strindberg seeks to create—are the verbal echoes linking the two. Thus the Stranger repeats—or "chews" as he puts it—the Beggar's "Virtus post nummos". The word is carefully chosen; it suggests that the Stranger is chewing (1) the cud, (2) cigar butts (the Stranger has just been figuratively referring to the seeking of cigar butts), and (3) Latin maxims. The Beggar is literally chewing cigar butts thrown away by others and thus, as it were, chewing the cud; he is also, as we have noted, constantly using the words of others—the maxims of the Romans—as his own. What Strindberg wants to indicate is, clearly, that the one activity is as much a sign of poverty, of dependence, as the other. It is therefore highly ironical when the Beggar characterizes himself as "an independent man", and even more ironical when the Stranger, who is echoing an 'echo' (the Beggar), has the same pretensions.

The two are also alike in their experience of life:

THE STRANGER. /—/ I've often sensed that two different spirits were in control of my destiny. The one gives me everything I ask for while the other stands beside him and wipes filth on it, so that when the gift is handed to me, I don't even want to touch it. It's really true, I've had all I wished for in life—but I've found it all worthless.

THE BEGGAR. /—/ You see before you a man who has succeeded in everything he's tried his hand at, for the very good reason that he hasn't ever done anything. I should call myself Polycrates—Polycrates of the golden ring. Do you know, I've had everything I've wanted from life. But I never really wanted anything, and, bored by my easy success, I threw away the ring. Now that I'm getting on in years, I regret my action and spend my time looking for it in the gutters.

The Stranger spends his time waiting for luck, the Beggar spends his searching for it; since we are usually alternatively active and passive, it might be said that together they illustrate two fundamental attitudes of man with regard to the future; a third attitude, we shall see, is connected with the corpse in Scene 1. Both the Stranger and the Beggar, we notice, describe their lives in fairy-tale terms (the tale of the Sleeping Beauty, the story of Polycrates) and their 'autobiographies', though not identical, have a definite kinship: they both relate how blessedness is replaced by misery. Behind the two tales we divine a third: the story of the Fall. Strindberg draws attention to the connection in the following lines:

THE STRANGER. /—/ whenever the golden fruit fell into my hands, it turned out to be poisoned or rotten inside.

This seems like a contamination of the story of the Fall and—with regard to the repetition of the disappointment—the story of Tantalus.

While Tantalus and Adam and Eve were punished because they offended "the Powers"—to use Strindberg's favorite expression—Polycrates was reduced to misery *although* he did his best not to offend the gods—in this sense he resembles Job to whom the Stranger once compares himself; it was precisely because he did not wish to stir up the jealousy of the gods that Polycrates threw away his greatest treasure, the golden ring. Both in the Greek myth and in Strindberg's play the ring obviously represents fortune, luck, happiness, a state of blessedness. The Stranger and the Beggar give, as it were, two versions of the same story: while the former blames some outward force (a spirit), the latter blames himself (Stockenström, 313); again we are faced with a case of double vision.

Very characteristic of Strindberg's tendency to tie dialogue elements to visual action, thereby tightening his play structure, is the fact that the Polycrates episode is later dramatized:

THE STRANGER. /—/ I tell you, someone's fighting against me.
THE LADY. Well, you challenged him!
THE STRANGER. I wanted a fair fight with clean weapons—not with unpaid bills and empty pockets. But if that's the way it's going to be, here's my last cent. Old Nix the water sprite is welcome to it—if he exists. (*He throws a coin into the stream.*)

The Beggar has earlier compared himself to Polycrates; now we see the Stranger performing the act of Polycrates. When the two meet again (Sc. 13), the Beggar says:

Talking about flaps reminds me: a little bird once told me about Polycrates and his ring, and how he got all the good things in the world but he didn't know what to do with them. So he prophesied in the east and in the west about the empty universe he had helped to create out of the universal void. Now I wouldn't insist it was you, except I'm so dead certain I'd take my dying oath on it.

In other words: the story we have earlier heard the Beggar tell the Stranger, he now claims to have heard from the Stranger. The roles of the two appear interchangeable.

Also the poverty of the Beggar is shared by the Stranger. At an early point he tells the Lady of his "poverty, beggary and dishonor"; later he informs her that he has money "now and then, but not very often". In Scene 3 he dislikes the idea that he and the Lady turn up like "beggars" at the home of her parents. In Scene 5 he admits that they actually look like beggars, and a sign informs them that vagrancy is forbidden in the district. In the kitchen of the parents (Sc. 7) the Stranger feels like a beggar:

THE MOTHER. /—/ Go and eat your supper.
THE STRANGER (*indicating the table for the poor*). At that table?
THE MOTHER. A very poor joke, but it might come true.

Similarly, in Scene I we hear the Café Proprietor shout to the Beggar: "You'll get a free trip to the poorhouse if you don't clear out of here—quick!" Later, the poorhouse can be seen through the rear windows of the rose chamber. It appears from this that the Stranger grows more and more like the Beggar. After the asylum scene he is actually begging—not for money or bread, to be sure, but for forgiveness from the ones he has trespassed against.

A beggar can be defined as a person who has no worldly possessions—a desirable situation according to the Sermon on the Mount—and who lives from the grace of others; by begging he recognizes his dependence on his fellows. It is obvious that this mentality sharply contrasts with that of the Stranger in the first part of the play, where he still boasts of his own importance and independence and where he spites both his fellows and the Invisible. But it is equally obvious that this mentality agrees fairly well with the one the Stranger embraces in the second part.

The Beggar is the Stranger's complementary figure; when the Stranger moves in one direction, the Beggar moves in the opposite one; their relationship is comparable to the struggle between conflicting impulses that takes place within man; now one impulse comes to the fore, suppressing the counter-impulse, now the situation is reversed. It is, in view of this, not surprising that the Beggar does not appear to be a very coherent figure.

But the Beggar not only represents an aspect of the Stranger's self; he has also an objective existence; he is, as the Stranger puts it, "someone else". Yet, even as an autonomous figure he takes on a mystical note, for we cannot help being influenced by the Stranger's view that if the characters he comes across exist outside his mind, then they must be Messengers sent out by the Invisible to punish, warn or instruct him, the Stranger. The fascination and dramatic effectiveness of the Beggar—like that of the other subordinate characters to a varying degree—rests precisely in the fact that he has *both* psychological and metaphysical significance, that he is half-real.

Somewhat surprisingly, also the corpse that is carried in by the Pallbearers in Scene I is the Stranger's double. In the beginning it is made clear that the Stranger has left wife and children; that he is contemplating suicide; and that he has not been able to "take anything really seriously"; we later learn that he drinks too much. About the dead man we hear that he "let others provide for his wife and children". The dead man resembles the Stranger in all but one thing: that of being dead. But since the Stranger has already indicated that he contemplates suicide, there is a close link between them also in this respect. As a matter of fact, the Stranger at this point may be seen as a living dead. The whole funeral scene, once the parallels are established, takes on a subjective character. It visualizes not only the Stranger's death instinct and his lack of vitality, it is also the logical continuation of his initial thoughts of suicide in the sense that it dramatizes the question: How will I be judged after my death?

Thus we see how Strindberg at a very early point in the play dramatizes three fundamental human attitudes: (1) the passive waiting for luck (the Stranger), (2) the active searching for luck (the Beggar)—both expressions of the life instinct, and (3) the death instinct (suicide), that is, complete disbelief in the possibility of finding happiness in life (the corpse). If the life instinct proves victorious, it is partly because the Stranger, with his strong sense of pride, cannot accept a completely negative obituary; the verdict on the dead man actually prepares for the cursing of the Stranger in the asylum scene, and just as the curse does not crush the Stranger but on the contrary convinces him that he must live on to pay off his debts, so the obituary makes it clear to him that he must not depart from life with such a poor record.

Scene 2 introduces two new male characters: the Doctor and Caesar. Both can easily be related to the Stranger. The relationship between the Doctor and the Stranger is rich in facets: they have been childhood friends; yet, as a child the Doctor has been punished for a crime committed by the Stranger; as a result of this, the Doctor has for a long time hated the Stranger; the Doctor admires the Stranger as a writer and claims that he has "learned a lot" from him; he has a portrait of him in his study; the Doctor claims that he has given the Lady "a life of freedom in contrast to the virtual imprisonment she had known before"—but this is precisely what the Stranger claims when he liberates the Lady from the Doctor, "the werewolf"; like the Stranger, the Doctor in the early part of the play is financially badly off and tired of life; finally, the Stranger's changing attitude to the Powers is paralleled by that of the Doctor.

The last point needs further comment. In the case of the Doctor the struggle with the Invisible, as Stockenström (318) has noted, is illustrated by his concern with the woodpile. In the middle of his yard there is "*a large, high woodpile shaped like an Oriental cupola*". We learn that although "lightning has knocked it down twice", the Doctor not only lets it remain but builds it higher—an obvious symbol of how he dares spite the Powers. In the early part of the play the Stranger demonstrates precisely the same attitude; in Scene 4, where his hubris culminates, he bares his chest, glances spitefully upwards and exclaims: "Strike me with your lightning—if you dare! Scare me with your thunder—if you can!" Yet shortly before the Stranger visits him, the Doctor seems to have changed his attitude:

THE SISTER. You say you haven't bowed down before anything, but you crawl on your belly for a chimera you call fate.
THE DOCTOR. Experience has taught me not to waste time and energy struggling against the inevitable.

In Scene 16 this new attitude has affected the woodpile; says the Doctor to the Stranger: "You challenged fate and you lost. /—/ I did too, but as you can see, I've cut the woodpile down in size. I want the thunder to stay out of my house, and I no longer play with lightning."

The relationship between the Stranger and the Doctor may be seen in metaphysical terms as a story of crime and punishment. For his childhood crime against the Doctor the Stranger is punished by being confronted with him and with Caesar, the Doctor's mad 'servant'; for his crime of stealing the Doctor's wife he is punished by being haunted by "the werewolf" to the point of imagining that the Doctor marries his former wife; for his crime of spiting the Powers he is punished—like the Doctor—by being struck with misery; for his crime of doubting Their goodness, he is 'punished' by *not* reaping (from the Doctor who forgives him) as he has sown. On the metaphysical level, the Doctor functions as another agent of the Powers; he is one of the Erinyes eventually turning into the Eumenides.

At the same time we can't help feeling that also the Doctor, up to a point, is a double of the Stranger; in Scene 16 the Doctor significantly knows why the Stranger has returned to see him without the Stranger's actually telling him. Yet the difference between the Doctor and the former doubles (the Beggar, the corpse) should not be overlooked. While the subjective nature of the Beggar is enforced by the fact that he and the Stranger are isolated together on the stage—the natural way of visualizing the mind's talking to itself—and while the corpse sequence may well be interpreted as a hallucination on the part of the Stranger, the Doctor twice appears alone with his Sister, whom the Stranger never meets. As a result of this, the Doctor's objective existence appears far stronger than those of the other two doubles.

As a boy the Stranger was nicknamed Caesar, and "in memory of" him the Doctor calls the madman staying in his house Caesar. The nickname alludes to a special form of insanity: Caesarmadness or megalomania (Brandell, 1974*a*, 254). While the Doctor spites the Powers with his woodpile, Caesar "wanders about the garden, putting nature to rights", irritated by the lack of plan and purpose there. But this is of course precisely the Stranger's attitude. "I want to take it all [that is, the whole universe] in my hands and knead it into something more nearly perfect, more enduring, more beautiful", he exclaims in his Promethean monologue by the sea. This outburst is significantly followed by the Lady's admonition: "don't compare yourself to the Creator. You remind me of Caesar back home". Strangely costumed like the Beggar, Caesar too may be seen as a double of the Stranger; just as the Beggar incarnates the Stranger's fear of physical misery, so Caesar incarnates his fear of mental collapse; both are grotesque versions of tendencies within the Stranger himself; or, if we adopt the objective point of view, harbingers of the fate that may befall him if he does not look out, and in this sense agents of the Invisible.

A problem is presented by the Doctor's sister, the only character in the play who is never brought into contact with the Stranger. Yet her mentality is not unlike that of the protagonist such as it appears in the early part of the play; hatred and escapism characterize both of them.

The Old Man, appearing in Scene 7, has a long life of suffering behind him, and like the Stranger he longs for death. On the other hand, unlike the Stranger he has given up hunting others and has learnt to accept the adversities of life as a necessary punishment, as a penance. But this attitude merely presages that of the Stranger in the latter part of the play; here every adversity is greeted with joy, since it means the crossing out of an entry in the Great Book of Debts.

The Mother is fundamentally akin to the Stranger. Her subjective nature appears from the following lines:

THE STRANGER. /—/ How can you think such thoughts?
THE MOTHER. They are yours.

Later she states: "I don't know if it's myself or someone else who is punishing me"—a double-vision idea completely in agreement with the Stranger's uncertainty of the nature of reality. Like the Stranger the Mother is "mean" and revengeful; like him she suffers from intense guilt feelings. But instead of trying to rid herself of her bad conscience by putting the blame on others (as the Stranger does in the beginning), she practices self-punishment: "I make use of religion in the same way I'de make use of a hair shirt and a stone floor." But this, after all, completely corresponds to the Stranger's behavior in the latter part of the play. Deeply related to him, the Mother has unusual qualifications to function as an "agent of Providence" for the Stranger. It is significant that even before he meets them, the Stranger sees both the Old Man and the Mother in a vison; in this way Strindberg could indicate that they are *Ausstrahlungen des Ichs* or—if we are inclined to believe in the supernatural—agents of God.

With the Confessor we arrive at an attitude toward the Powers diametrically opposed to the Stranger's initial one but in agreement with his later one[5]—as Strindberg indicates through costume and stage position: dressed in a "*Dominican habit*" the Confessor places himself "*behind* THE STRANGER" who is seated, while reading to him from "Dies irae, dies illa"; in Scene 12 the Stranger appears dressed in a friar-like habit: "*a brown 'Kaisermantel' /—/ with hood*".

If the Confessor, who curses the Stranger in the words of Deuteronomy voices the severe law of the Old Testament, the Abbess who exercises charity incarnates the Christian gospel of love.

One character remains to be considered: the Lady. Unlike the others she accompanies the Stranger throughout the play and appears in no less than 33 sequences, that is in 8 more than the Stranger himself. Both the Stranger and the Lady express the opinion that she is an agent of Fate. As Beatrice helped Dante on his way through Inferno and Purgatorio,[6] so the Lady helps the Stranger through his spiritual inferno, away from the funeral music in the beginning to the "new songs" she promises him in the church at the end. Her guiding role is not in the last instance indicated in the scene endings: at the end of Scene 1 the Stranger "*hurries out after* THE LADY"; at the end of Scene 2 she insists on leaving first; at the end of Scene 4 she tells him: "Come"; at the end of Scene 6 she says: "Follow me and you shall see . . ." [that goodness exists];[7] after which the Stranger hurries past the infernal blacksmith and follows the Lady; at the end of the play, outside the church, she again tells him: "Come!"; and he follows her.

The metaphysical aspect is stressed even more in the Lady's stage business: from the first scene to the fifteenth we see her crocheting. The Stranger clarifies the symbolic meaning of this when he says: "You sit there like one of the three Fates, drawing the threads between your fingers . . .". It is, after this, not surprising that, in the asylum scene, the woman resembling the Lady is the only one of the group who does not curse the Stranger; she just keeps crocheting—like a Moira, blind to the weal and woe of man. In Scene 15 the Lady's work is finished; it is white no longer; the Stranger compares it to his own and the Lady's life story, "written in blood and tears and the dust of the road". The Lady, it will be seen from this, has a double function: on the realistic level, she is the Stranger's partner in life, sharer of his fate; on the metaphysical one, she is weaver of his fate and guide to a wiser understanding of life. In this respect she comes quite close to Christ—god *and* man—and she antedates Indra's Daughter in *A Dream Play.*[8]

Yet the Lady, no less than the other characters, can alternatively be seen as a radiation of the Stranger's ego, a product of his imagination, a wish fulfillment. This is strongly suggested when the Stranger early in Scene 1 'creates' her by providing her with age, name and character. Nor should we overlook the hint that the Stranger was intoxicated when the Lady first appeared to him the day before the action begins. Was she a hallucination?

Her first entrance is in line with this:

THE STRANGER. Ah, there you are. I was almost certain you would come.
THE LADY. Then you did call for me. I might have known. I could feel it.

In other words: she comes because he is longing for her. The situation is repeated a little later:

THE LADY. /—/ The light went out on the altar and a cold wind blew across my face just when I heard you call for me.
THE STRANGER. I didn't call. I only longed for you . . .

Revealing, too, for a subjective interpretation of her role, is the Lady's explanation that "there's nothing I can tell him [the Stranger] that he hasn't heard before". And the crocheting is significantly seen not only as an outer but also as an inner fate:

THE STRANGER. It looks like a net of nerves and knots to catch your thoughts. I bet your brain looks like that inside.
THE LADY. If only I had half the thoughts you say I have! But I haven't any at all.

Taken literally, the last sentence assures us of the Lady's subjective nature. But even with a more modest reading it is clear that the Stranger is describing his own, not the Lady's brain.

Let us summarize our impression of the subordinate characters. As we have seen they can all be related to the Stranger (1) as incarnations of drives within him and/or (2) as agents—positive or negative—of the Invisible. And the point is that neither we nor the Stranger can be sure of their true nature. If the subordinate characters seem incoherent and flat, it is precisely because they are included in the play not so much for their own sake as for that of the protagonist; it is his spiritual development they serve to illuminate. To regard them as autonomous or realistic figures is to see merely the veneer.

Rather than speak of different characters we should perhaps speak of different characteristics—in the manner of *Everyman*—or drives. (I disregard for the moment the metaphysical aspect.) If Strindberg had chosen a linear composition, showing how the Stranger on his pilgrimage meets one after the other, the situation would have been relatively simple; each person could then have been provided with precisely those qualities or drives which at that particular moment dominate the protagonist. By choosing a circular composition and making (most of) the characters reappear, Strindberg considerably complicated the situation.

The examination of the relationship between the protagonist and the subordinate characters has already revealed how complex a figure the Stranger is. When Strindberg chose to christen him "the Stranger" or, more correctly, "the Unknown" (Sw. "Den Okände"), he may have done so because he felt that this was an adequate label for a character representing everyman; after the 'discovery' of the unconscious this designation seems even more meaningful.

But *To Damascus I* is not only a psychological drama; it is also, we have noted, a metaphysical one. By relating his protagonist to a number of archetypal figures, Strindberg could indicate that the hero is not just a representative of man here and now—or in 1898—but of man such as he always has been and presumably always will be. The references to the archetypal figures, in other words, serve to give the play a wide scope; it is part of the universalizing technique.

In his introduction to the drama, Sprinchorn (1964, 272) lists a number of these archetypal figures: "If the Stranger is Saul being persecuted by God, he is also Lucifer asserting his pride and Loki stirring up mischief. He is Jacob wrestling with God; he is Cain against whom every man's hand is raised; and he is Jesus who must suffer through the stations of the cross." The list could easily be extended.

As early as in Scene 1 the Stranger compares himself to the devil, and in the following scene the Sister states that "he looks like the devil himself". The Old Man, who himself has a rather godlike apparition, follows suit: "I've never detested a man I never met as much as I detest him. He sees evil everywhere he looks, but there's no man I've heard more evil about than him." Later he remarks: "Well, that was no angel"; and the Mother adds: "At least not an angel of light", an obvious reference to Lucifer, the fallen angel (cf. Genesis 6: 1 ff.). Finally, there is the Doctor's remark to the Stranger: "if there were a hell, you'd be its commandant". The accident which brings the Stranger to the asylum is described as follows: "You were seen in the mountains above the ravine, with a cross you had torn down from a calvary, and you were using it to challenge someone you imagined you could see in the clouds. You had a fever, and you fell over the cliff." This compares rather well with God's plunging of the rebellious Lucifer from heaven to hell. An explicit reference to this event—as well as to the Stranger's 'fall'—is the Mother's: "You beautiful morning star—why have you fallen so far from heaven?" In the asylum there is fittingly, "*a painting of Michael slaying the Evil One*". In Scene 1 the Stranger had expressed his joy at "battling dragons"; now he has discovered that he is himself the dragon: when he looks at Michael he feels ashamed. When the Stranger is said to "belong to the children of the Evil One", the reference is rather sophisticated. Strindberg has noted (*OD*, July 10, 1897) that *To Damascus I* was first called *Robert le Diable* after the hero of a French medieval folktale. A product of the devil's coition with a duchess, Robert commits all kinds of terrible crimes. Suddenly he realizes his own depravity, goes on a pilgrimage to Rome, is forgiven for his sins and ends his life as a hermit. It is obvious that this tale, as Lindström (1964*a,* 10f.) has pointed out and Stockenström (290f.) at length has demonstrated, has provided Strindberg with a basic outline for his play.

Somewhat akin to the Lucifer episode is the one describing Jacob's wrestling with God (cf. Genesis 32:25). Strindberg alludes to this when he makes the Stranger suffer from a pain in his thigh and again when he has him state that he would not be afraid to climb Mount Sinai and face God Almighty Himself (cf. Genesis 32:30). Jacob—like Prometheus—serves as an example to the Stranger that "man can wrestle with God, and not without success".

More integrated in the total play are the many references to the story of the Fall. The (apple) tree of knowledge is discreetly brought in here and there, for example in the reference to the golden fruit which turns out to be rotten inside (Sc. 1); in the Stranger's statement about his family: "From that kind of tree, this kind of fruit!" (Sc. 1); in the scenery of Scene 5, where the road is "*lined with fruit trees*", contrasting with the crosses of the calvaries, just as the sinner (Adam) is traditionally contrasted with the redeemer (Christ); in the Mother's question (Sc. 7) whether she should give the Stranger and the Lady cider.

Early in Scene 1 we witness a kind of mock creation. Just as God created Eve out of Adam's rib, so the Stranger 'creates' his Eve—her real name is Ingeborg—out of his imagination:

THE STRANGER. I gave her a name of my own choosing in order to make her mine. I intend to re-create her according to my tastes and desires—.
THE MOTHER. In your image! (*She smiles.*) I've heard how the black magicians up in the hills carve a figure of the one they want to bewitch, and baptize it with the name of the person they want to destroy. That's how you're planning to use your self-made Eve to destroy her whole sex.
THE STRANGER. (*stares astonished at* THE MOTHER). Well I'll be damned!

The Mother's interpretation is truly infernal; if the Stranger compares to Adam and the Lady to Eve, then the Mother compares to the serpent, an allusion missed in the translation of the last speech.[9] When the Mother tells the Lady to read the Stranger's latest book, which the Lady has promised not to read, she fulfills precisely the function of the serpent which tempted Eve. In Scene 8 the Stranger significantly compares the Mother to a "crushed snake". Yet Strindberg would hardly have inserted the Mother's suspicion if it did not contain a fundamental, if partial, truth. As an archetypal figure Eve fulfills four major roles; she is the first (1) woman, (2) virgin, (3) mother and (4) sinner. The Stranger 'creates' his Eve because he needs all four (cf. Børge, 82): the woman as a life companion and love partner, the innocent woman (Beatrice) as an ideal, the mother as a consoler, the sinner as a scapegoat delivering him from an excessive burden of guilt.

As Eve before the Fall the Lady is innocent; this is why the Mother can say about her, in Scene 7, that she has "no misgivings and no conscience". After her 'fall', in Scene 8, the situation is changed. "After reading your terrible book", the Lady tells the Stranger, "I feel as if I'd eaten of the tree of knowledge. My eyes have been opened, and I know the difference between good and evil. Now I see what an evil man you really are, and I know why you wanted to call me Eve. But if the first mother brought sin to the earth, another mother brought redemption. If sin came with the first, atonement came with the second!" In Scene 14 the Stranger logically remarks: "We've been driven out of the Garden of Eden. All we can do is pick our way over the stones and thorns." And just as Adam and Eve tried to hide themselves after the Fall, so the Stranger and the Lady decide to hide themselves in the mountains "where [they] can be alone with [their] misery".

The mother bringing redemption, the Virgin Mary, seems alluded to by the Stranger in Scene 1 when he says that he believes that the Lady has been sent to save him. In the first hotel room scene we are again reminded of the connection the Lady–Mary:

THE STRANGER. (*with an overnight bag in his hand*). You mean this is the only room available?
THE WAITER. That's right.
THE STRANGER. But I can't stay in this one.
THE LADY. There isn't any other. And every hotel in town is filled.

This is Strindberg's version of "because there was no room for them in the inn" (Luke 2:7); we are not surprised to learn that there is a Christmas rose in the hotel room.

In the early part of the play the Stranger nourishes the atheist's inclination to turn himself into a superman replacing God. This is, partly, the significance of his 'creating' Eve in his own image. In Scene 4 this tendency is made explicit in the following words: "My head reaches as high as the heavens and I look out over the whole universe, which is all me, and I feel all the strength and power of the creator in me, for he and I are one." This is subjectivism stretched to its logical extreme. Again when, in Scene 8, the Stranger's book is compared to the tree of knowledge, the implication is that the creator of the book is comparable to the creator of the tree, that the Stranger and God are one. And indeed there is this resemblance—highly relevant in this subjectivist play—that the Stranger feels as omnipotent in his fictitious world as God does in his real one. This alone explains why the major conflict in the drama is the conflict between the Stranger and the Invisible—Den Okände and Den Osynlige—suggestive labels indicating a connection between man and god.

Also with regard to scenery Strindberg adopts his method of double vision: what we see possesses both an outer and inner reality. With few exceptions—notably the asylum scene, where Strindberg allows his 'chorus' to be covered with gauze to indicate their subjective nature—there is nothing in the play that completely breaks with illusionism. There are, to be sure, elements which from a strict slice-of-life point of view may seem odd—the Doctor's turtle, the proximity of the blacksmith shop and the mill in the ravine scenes, the dominance of red in the first rose chamber scene—but unthinkable in real life they are not.

In the first scene we see a post office, a church, a café and a street corner. All very real. And at the same time very symbolic. For at the end of the play, when this scenery returns, it is clear that the café represents a secular (decadent) existence, the church a religious one, while the post office functions as a kind of supernatural instance delivering both letters of demand (punishment) and reward (blessing). It is significant that the Stranger at the beginning spends his time at the café and shuns the church (where the Lady spends much of her time), while at the end he ignores the café and follows the Lady into the church. It is a symbolic exchange of localities somewhat in the spirit of the medieval exchange of one *mansion* for another. The scenery of Scene 1, we might say, visualizes the essence of the Stranger's inner development, the essential subject of the play.

Of great interest are the brown-clad Mourners and Pallbearers, one of whom is carrying a flag decorated with the insignia of the carpenters' guild and a brown crape. Although both the stage directions and the Stranger state that these people are dressed in brown, they themselves claim that they are dressed in black—as indeed we would expect them to be. Here Strindberg, perhaps for the first time in the history of drama, makes his audience doubt their own senses. By forcing us to see reality with the eyes of the Stranger and at the same time realize that this reality is absurd, contrary to all expectation, Strindberg upsets our conventional evaluation and includes us, as it were, in the action. It is a truly subjectivist device stressing a basic theme in the play: nothing is what it seems to be.

But why has Strindberg, of all colors, selected brown? Presumably because this color has significance in the religious context. We easily associate brown with monks, and the brown-black controversy could in fact be seen in monastic terms: the Carmelites were first dressed in brown, later in black.[10] In the second rose room scene the furniture is "*covered with brown sheets*" as a sign of the Stranger's penance, and in Scene 12 we see him "*dressed in a brown 'Kaisermantel' with pelerine and hood*", that is, very similar to a monk.[11] A monk-like existence is, in fact, already suggested in Scene 2, where the Doctor's house is rather like a "Buddhist monastery".

While the hotel room scenes contain almost no comments on the scenery, the scenes by the sea provide telling information. In the first (Sc. 4) we read:

A cabin on the brow of a hill at the seashore. Outside are a table and some chairs. THE STRANGER *and* THE LADY, *dressed in light-colored clothes, appear younger-looking than in the previous scene.*

In the second (Sc. 14) we read:

The same landscape as before, but now it is winter. The sea is blue-black. Clouds like giant heads tower up on the horizon. In the distance are the three white, unrigged masts of a foundered ship, resembling three white crosses. The table and the bench are still there, but the chairs are gone.

While the first scene is marked by summer, sun, open sea—youthful optimism and pride—the second is characterized by winter, cold, darkening clouds resembling heavenly giants—the Powers grown mighty in the eyes of the Stranger—and under them the three crosses of Golgotha, indicating the Stranger's feeling that he is, as he says, driven out of the Garden of Eden and suffering from the burden of the cross he has to carry. That Strindberg in the latter scene has settled for a winter landscape has to do with the color symbolism of the play, white representing penance. The significant changes in the scenery thus illustrate significant changes within the Stranger; the two scenes depict two radically different inner climates.

No scenery relates more closely to the play title than that of the road scenes, for the road, as Strindberg himself remarks in his ms. notes for the play, allegorizes the Stranger's pilgrimage. Again, the contrast between the two road scenes is marked by a change of season illustrating an inner change: while the trees in Scene 5 are still green and full of fruit, in Scene 13 they must be bare, 'dead' since it is late autumn.

More stylized than the rest are the ravine scenes with their marked contrast between height and depth, black (the blacksmith shop) and white (the mill).[12] The Stranger makes the following comment on the scenery: "Why is the shop black and the mill white? Because one's covered with soot and the other with flour [=objective view], but all the same, when I saw the blacksmith standing in the red glow of his fire directly opposite that white miller girl, I couldn't help thinking of an old poem ..." [= subjective view]. Again a case of double vision. The old poem is presumably *Divina Commedia,* the blacksmith shop corresponding to the Inferno and the white mill to the sunlit Mount of Purgatory.

The black-and-white pattern returns in the following scenes. Thus the walls of the kitchen are whitewashed while "*the beamed ceiling is black with soot*"; and the Mother is "*dressed in black and white*", a costume which links her with the Abbess, who appears in the "*black-and-white habit of the Augustinians*".

In Scene 11, playing at night, the kitchen has become a veritable "witches' kitchen":

It is dark, but the moon throws on the floor shifting shadows of the window lattices as storm clouds draw by.

Under the crucifix in the corner to the right, where THE OLD MAN *used to sit, a horn, a gun, and a hunting bag are hanging on the wall. A stuffed bird of prey stands on the table. The windows are open and the curtains are fluttering, and the rags and cloths, the aprons and towels that hang on a line in front of the stove are flapping in the wind. One can hear the soughing of the wind, the roar of a distant waterfall, and now and then the sound of pounding on the wooden floor.*

The Stranger's anguish has here found its visual and aural expression. Although there is nothing in the scene that cannot be explained rationally, the light and the sounds give a touch of nightmare to it. And the Stranger shows by his reactions that he is prone to interpret supernaturally what he sees and hears. Thus when facing the bird of prey, he stops "*petrified*" and exclaims: "Jesus Christ!" A little later he complains: "Ohh! He's here, here in this room—and he's tearing my heart from my chest. Ohh!" We are reminded of Prometheus tormented by the eagle.

Located on either side of the asylum scene, the two rose chamber scenes strongly contrast with each other. In the first we find the following description:

A simply furnished but cozy room in the forester's lodge. The walls have been calcimined with a rose-red solution. The curtains are thin, rose-red muslin. Flowers are standing in the rather small lattice windows. To the right, a desk and a bookcase. To the left, a sofa, with rose-red drapes above it arranged to form a baldachin. Chairs and tables in Old German style.

A door in the rear. Outside, a landscape and the poorhouse, a dark, dismal building, its black windows curtainless. The sun is shining brightly.

It is striking how Strindberg here contrasts the cozy interior with the horrifying exterior—notably by limiting himself to two colors: rose-red against black.

What does the rose-red color stand for? To answer this question we must relate it to the rose symbolism pervading the play. Traditionally, the rose of course represents such things as the (passing) beauty of woman or love. And since there is a vague suggestion that the rose chamber primarily belongs to the Lady such an interpretation is quite possible; but it is hardly telling. Much more interesting is the rather special kind of rose symbolism we find in the play. In Scene I we see the Lady appearing with a Christmas rose (*Helleborus niger*) in her bosom.[13] The Stranger points out that "it stands for evil and slander, as a symbol. As a medicine it was formerly used to cure madness". Thus the Christmas rose has to him both a negative, destructive quality (relating it to the mandragora) and a positive, healing one. When the Lady offers the Stranger the rose, she is performing an ambiguous action, later enlarged upon when, on the one hand, the Mother's slander causes the Lady to betray the Stranger and when, on the other, the Lady eventually manages to heal him from his sickness unto death.

It is significant, I think, that the chapel favored by the Lady is furnished with a rose window and dedicated to Saint Elizabeth (of Thüringen), famous for her charity and usually depicted with roses; compare the Abbess' remark that charity is to be found in a rose-red room. At the Doctor's house there is "*a rambler rosebush*", and in his garden there are (withering) Christmas roses, planted by Caesar; here the connection between the *Helleborus* and madness is evident not only because the planter is a lunatic but also because these flowers do not belong in the garden at this season; they are 'abnormal'. In the hotel room, we have already noted, the withering Christmas rose is found again.

It is also meaningful, in this religious drama, to think of the thorns that go with the rose; significantly, Christ's wreath of thorns appears twice in the ms. notes for the play, and the following passage from *Inferno* indicates that the name of the Austrian village where Strindberg spent some time in the early 1890's together with the Uhl family has helped him to see his own life and that of the Stranger as a *via dolorosa*: "Farewell white house in Dornach, the field of thorns and of roses!" In Scene 6 the Stranger remarks that his clothes have been ripped and torn after "hiking through thorn bushes". 'The rose chamber', Strindberg himself points out in *Inferno,* was what the old torture chamber in Stockholm was called. To make it clear that the scenery of the rose chamber is directly related to the Stranger, Strindberg has the Mother read from his latest book with *"red covers".* It should be noticed in this context that the 'torture' the Stranger suffers in the asylum takes place in "a bed with steel rails, painted red". When the Stranger, in Scene 15, declares that his and the Lady's life has been one of "tears and blood" and that the Lady's hand-work, symbolizing this life, should therefore properly be "rose-red", he again draws attention to the aspect of suffering.

As we have seen, the rose-red color and, indirectly, the rose chamber carry connotations of love, charity, suffering, torture, madness. This may seem paradoxical but is not necessarily so if we accept the idea—as Strindberg obviously did—that there is charity in suffering.

It might be claimed that the emphasis on the rose-red color in the first rose chamber scene primarily serves to bring out the contrast to the second one where it has almost disappeared:

The curtains have been removed. The windows gape like black holes into the darkness outside. The furniture is covered with brown sheets and pushed together in the center of the room. The flowers are gone. A large black stove is lit. THE MOTHER *stands ironing white curtains by the light of a single lamp.*

It will be seen from this description that the poorhouse, earlier figuring in the background, has as it were moved into the rose room. The coziness is gone; the black stove, recalling the blacksmith shop, suggests that the Stranger is still living in hell; the monkish brown and the pure white combined with the Mother's significant action suggest penance.

In the asylum scene—the only one lacking a pendant—the mirror effect is created in another manner. At one table we find the Stranger "*dressed in a white hospital gown*"; at another all his 'victims' are seated:

All are dressed in white but over their white gowns they are wearing gauze costumes in various colors. Their faces are waxen and deathly white. Their whole appearance and all their gestures are ghostlike.

In other words: on the objective level we are faced with a crowd of inmates dressed in hospital costume; on the subjective one with a man and the ghosts that haunt his mind. The gauze costumes parallel the brown dresses of the Pallbearers and Mourners in Scene 1: again we are confronted with the protagonist's way of experiencing reality; says the Abbess: "If they appear strange to you, it may be because you still have the fever—or because of something else." Again Strindberg provides the audience with a case of double vision, of half-reality; the true reason is left open, handed over to us.

The vacillation between outer and inner reality also characterizes the dialogue with its constant transpositions from an everyday realistic level to an existential, mystical one. An excellent example we find already at the very beginning:

THE STRANGER. Ah, there you are. I was almost certain you would come.
THE LADY. Then you did call for me. I might have known. I could feel it.

Isolated from what follows, the Stranger's speech appears completely realistic, even banal. But the impression quickly changes, for in the following speech (by the Lady) a mystical note is struck. Now it is clear that the two have not agreed to meet on this street corner; the Stranger has not even called for the Lady; she has only felt it that way. Telepathy clearly plays a part here. However, we are still inclined to regard the Lady as a realistic figure and to rationalize: the two know each other very well, perhaps, and this would then explain their intuitive contact with one another. But soon we learn that they have just become acquainted. New surprise. Step by step we are pushed away from a realistic toward a symbolic interpretation.

The Lady asks: "But why are you standing here on the street corner?" The Stranger answers: "I don't know. Have to stand somewhere while I'm waiting." Later we get the commonplace explanation: "Actually I'm waiting for the post-office to open. There's a letter waiting for me." But it is very characteristic of Strindberg's dialogue technique that the question is not answered the way we expect the first time; we do not expect a man appearing in a realistic environment—for the decor of Scene 1 is at least superficially realistic—to answer an everyday question—"Waiting for what?"—posed by a realistically costumed lady in the following way: "For forty years I've been waiting for something. Luck, I believe it's called. Or at least the end of bad luck." This answer signifies a transposition of the whole situation to another, existential level. Yet we cannot free ourselves from what we see with our eyes: that the man stands waiting on a street corner. The impressions of what we see and what we hear are fused and the result is a feeling that the man has indeed been waiting on this street corner for forty years. But this is, of course, from a realistic point of view impossible. To solve the contradiction, we become inclined to see the street corner not as an ordinary street corner but as a point where the ways of life part, where a (moral) decision has to be taken. This agrees very well with our earlier observation of how Strindberg dramatizes the conflicting drives within the Stranger. Here is a modern Hercules at the cross-roads, waiting "for something", like the Officer in *A Dream Play* and like

Vladimir and Estragon in *Waiting for Godot.*[14] When the Stranger later gives his commonplace explanation it is actually, at closer inspection, a concretization of his earlier reply, for he is really expecting the letter at the post office to be a letter of luck.

When does the action of *To Damascus I* take place? The question is not easy to answer, for we never get any definite information as to how long it is supposed to last. On the other hand we get surprisingly accurate information as to when it begins. In Scene 1 the Stranger tells the Lady: "From here on you shall be thirty-four, and consequently born in 1864"; from which we can conclude that the scene takes place in 1898, that is, the year the play was written and published. Undoubtedly Strindberg inserted this implied date to indicate the autobiographical nature of the drama.[15] But this kind of exactness is exceptional and the rule, both concerning time and place, is that the author is non-committal, vague. However, there are a number of hints and by combining these we can arrive at a likely time schedule.

Thus, in Scene 2 the Doctor remarks that the fruit in the orchard should be picked and that the woodpile should go into the woodshed "come autumn"—from which we must conclude that it is late summer. Since the visit at the Doctor's house occurs one day after the meeting on the street corner—cf. the Stranger's remark: "Why did you kiss me yesterday?"—it follows that the play begins in late summer. The time lapse between Scenes 2 and 4 is uncertain and the decor—hotel room, sea, road—gives us little idea of the distance between the different places. All we can say is that there is nothing that contradicts the view that it is still late summer in these scenes. In Scene 5 there are "*fruit trees*" to be seen and it is explicitly said that "it will soon be fall". There are strong suggestions that Scenes 5–13—road, ravine, kitchen, rose chamber, asylum, rose chamber, kitchen, ravine, road—take place in the same neighborhood with only short distances between the various places. The time lapse between these scenes is usually uncertain; however, we learn that the Stranger spends exactly three months in the asylum, and it is obvious that Scene 11 follows almost immediately upon Scene 10. If we assume, as we rightly may, that it is late summer in all the scenes preceding Scene 9 and add the three months the Stranger spends in the asylum, we logically arrive at late fall in Scene 10. Neither here nor in the following scene do we receive any sure indications of the season—although color and mood in these interior scenes are certainly autumnal. In Scenes 12 and 13 it is explicitly said: "*now it is autumn*". Scene 14 announces: "*now it is winter*". In Scene 15 there is "spring in the air". The time lapse between Scenes 15 and 17 is again uncertain, but since the decor of Scenes 16 and 17 is almost or completely unchanged, we must assume that it is, again, late summer. We thus arrive at the following schedule:

Scene	*Time*	*Place*
1–8	late summer	street corner – Doctor's home – hotel room – sea – road – ravine – kitchen – rose chamber
9	fall	asylum
10–13	late fall	rose chamber – kitchen – ravine – road
14	winter	sea
15	early spring	hotel room
16–17	late summer	Doctor's home – street corner

The action thus proceeds from summer to summer, and the seasonal cycle helps to enforce the circular composition of the play. The various seasons naturally have their symbolic connotations: we deal, as we have seen, largely with inner climates.

Our one-year schedule is based on the assumption that all the scenes belong to the present and that the play describes a real pilgrimage beginning and ending on the street corner. From quite a different point of view it might, however, be argued that only the framing scenes (1 and 17) belong to the present, while all the intermediate scenes belong to the past, that is, that they are dramatizations of what the Stranger has earlier experienced and what he is now recalling. If we apply this time concept, then Scenes 2–16 have already occurred when the action begins. It should be noted in this context that Scenes 1 and 17 are the only pair of scenes in the play which do not reveal any change at all in the decor; besides, the decor is here more realistic than in the other scenes. Moreover, in Scene 1 we find this:

THE STRANGER (*sits down and writes in the sand with his cane*).
THE LADY (*returns*). /—/ You *still* sitting here? (my italics)

Scene 17 opens as follows:

Same as in the first act. THE STRANGER *is sitting on the bench under the tree, writing in the sand.*
THE LADY (*entering*). What are you doing?
THE STRANGER. Writing in the sand. *Still at it.* (my italics)

It should be noticed that it is in Scene 1, after she has been away only for a short while, that the Lady suggests—through the word "still"—that a fairly long time has passed, whereas in Scene 17 her initial speech suggests rather the opposite. The Stranger's "still at it", echoing her earlier question, may well suggest that a fairly long time has passed, but what is here of primary importance is that it gives the right sense of continuous action. With regard to the time Strindberg has, it would seem, found a formula for mingling the past and the present, of dramatizing *la durée*; also here the double vision applies.

To Damascus I has often been hailed as a mile-stone in the history of drama—usually for two reasons. On one hand Strindberg has here employed a loose, 'plotless' structure. On the other he has reduced all the characters surrounding the protagonist to *Ausstrahlungen des Ichs,* so that we can here speak of the first *Ich*-drama. Yet both the *Stationen* technique and the *Ich* structure can be traced back to medieval drama, and Ibsen comes at least quite close to both devices in *Peer Gynt.* I do not, of course, deny that there are elements of novelty in the way Strindberg handles these techniques, but a better claim to genuine novelty we find, I believe, in the way Strindberg, by applying his double-vision method to practically all play elements, manages to make an audience *experience*—not just rationally learn—that life is a "terrible half-reality"—Strindberg's own characterization of *To Damascus I* (letter March 17, 1898)—a dream-like mystery, a battle with shadows.

The three techniques are naturally interrelated and the common denominator is to be found in the subjectivism of the play. Presumably for the first time in the history of drama we are confronted with a play in which an inner reality is *consistently* dramatized (Rinman, 93) or better: in which the border between outer and inner reality is blotted out so that we can indeed, with Strindberg, speak of a drama of "half-reality". A good case can certainly be made for the statement that modern drama begins in 1898 with the first part of *To Damascus*.

7. The Plot of *Erik XIV*

In Strindberg's historical plays we are faced with a situation differing from the one in the contemporary or lyrical dramas: the content is to a great extent verifiable. It is naturally of interest to see in what respect the reality created in the plays differs from historical reality—not because it informs us of the value of the dramas but because it indirectly says something about their themes and structure. For it seems reasonable to assume that a writer of historical dramas never departs from historical reality unless he has strong reasons to do so, whether of a dramaturgic, psychological or ideological kind. In other words: the observation that the playwright is 'unhistorical', in itself trite, leads to the intriguing question why this is so.[1]

Since the value of *Erik XIV,* then, has little to do with Strindberg's accuracy with regard to historical reality—those who claim this are guilty of a historical fallacy—but much to do with its quality as drama, it seems more relevant to study the play on its own conditions as a product meant to function efficiently on the stage. As such it has been appreciated by foreign audiences, lacking knowledge of the historical background (Ollén, 288 ff.).

As an independent play it has often been produced with great success. This alone disproves Lamm's view (1926, 147) that the play is intelligible only in relation to *Gustav Vasa,* the second part of the so-called Vasa trilogy. Naturally, the two dramas have much in common. But nobody would seriously argue that *Erik XIV* should only be produced as a sequel to *Gustav Vasa,* the logical consequence of Lamm's argument.[2] With Johnson (1963, 126) we could rather claim that *Erik XIV* "is both a companion play for *Gustav Vasa* and an independent play".

As an independent play *Erik XIV* will be examined here from one—neglected—point of view. The question which will concern us is: How is the plot constructed? By 'plot' is meant here the action of the drama in the order of presentation found in the play, by 'story' is meant the same events in chronological order. Plot and story thus include the same elements, structured in different ways. By 'fable', finally, I mean the most essential parts of the story in abstract form, i.e. without any relation to a specific time and place and to specific characters. Plot, story and fable are three different ways of retelling the action of a play.[3]

By examining, within the plot, the relation between main plot and subplots and between the subplots amongst themselves, it is possible to throw light on the fairly complex structure of the play:

Act Sc.	Seq.	*line in SS* XXXI	*On stage*																
I	A	281/2																	
	1	281/7	K	Ma															
	2	286/1	K		G	(E)													
	3	290/5	K			E	c^+												
	4	290/17	K			E		N											
	5	292/18	K			E		N	KS										
	6	293/12	K			E		N											
	7	294/1	K			E				J									
	8	295/11	K			E													
	9	297/9	K			E	c^+												
	10	297/14	K			E													
	11	297/25	K			E					SS	NS	ES						
	12	300/7	K			E					SS								
	13	300/18	K			E													
	14	301/4	K			E	c^+												
	15	301/10	K			E													
	16	301/16				E								NG					
	17	303/17				E													
	18	303/21			G	E													
	19	307/12			G	E	c^+												
	20	307/18			G	E													
	21	309/17			G	E	c^+												
	22	311/4–11			G	E													
II	B	312/2																	
	23	312/5			G										Gm				
	24	315/29			G										Gm	A	M		
	25	317/7			G						SS				Gm	A	M		
	26	321/27			G										Gm	A	M		
	27	322/28		Ma	G										Gm	A	M		
	28	325/1			G	E									Gm	A	M		
	29	330/25			G	E									Gm	A	M	MK	
	30	333/16			G	E									Gm	A	M		
	31	334/21			G										Gm	A	M		
	32	334/23			G										Gm	A	M		P
	33	335/15–27			G										Gm	A	M		

Act	Sc.	Seq.	Page/ line in SS XXXI	On stage																					
III	1	C	336/2																						
		34	336/6		G								NG												
		35	338/1											P	g										
		36	339/15		G									P	g										
		37	340/5							SS	NS	ES		P	g	L	S	g1							
		38	342/19						J	SS	NS	ES							g2						
		39	343/1							SS	NS	ES	NG	P	g	L	S	g1		g3					
		40	344/14		G								NG	P	g										
	2	D	345/16																						
		41	345/20		G	E															g4	Å			
		42	347/15	K	G	E															g4				
		43	347/29	K	G	E															g4		Gu	Si	
		44	348/26	K	G	E	c+														g4		Gu	Si	
		45	348/28	K	G	E															g4		Gu	Si	
		46	349/3	K	G																g4		Gu	Si	
		47	350/21	K	G		c														g4		Gu	Si	
		48	350/22	K			c+														g4		Gu	Si	
		49	350/27	K				KS													g4		Gu	Si	
		50	353/3	K				KS													g4		Gu	Si	lm
		51	353/10	K				KS													g4				
		52	353/19	K				KS													g4				lm+
		53	353/22	K				KS													g4				
		54	355/1			E															g4				
		55	355/4		G	E															g4				
		56	357/22		G	E	c														g4				
		57	359/10		G	E															g4				
		58	359/18		G	E							NG								g4				
		59	361/7		G	E							NG	P							g4				
		60	361/11		G	E								P							g4				
		61	362/13		G	E															g4				
		62	364/29		G																g4				
		63	365/1		G																g4				
		64	365/3, 368/5		G	E															g4				

Act	Sc.	Seq.	line in SS XXXI	On stage										
IV	1	E	369/2											
		65	369/3								MK			
		66	369/7								MK P			
		67	372/14	K							MK P			
		68	372/17								MK P			
		69	373/4	K							MK			
		70	374/17	K		E					MK			
	2	F	376/1											
		71	376/1				J					C		
		72	376/6				J					C		
	3	G	379/11											
		73	379/12	K		E								
		74	380/26	K		E		NG						
		75	381/5	K		E		NG	Gm	A M	MK		g5	
		76	382/10	K		E		NG+	Gm	A M	MK		g5	
		77	382/13			E								
		78	382/19		G	E								
		79	385/5		G	E		NG						
		80	385/28		G	E		NG		A M	MK		g5	
		81	386/20		G	E		NG		A M	MK		g5	
		82	387/3		G	E				A M	MK		g5 g6	
		83	391/17		G	E		NG		A M	MK		g5 g6	
		84	393/5							A M	MK		g5 g6 l+	
		85	395/18						Gm	A M	MK		g5 g6	
		86	396/6							A M	MK		g5 g6	
		87	396/12							A M	MK P		g5 g6	
		88	397/1						Gm	A M	MK P		g5 g6	
		89	397/14					NG	Gm	A M	MK P		g5 g6	
		90	397/23–399/22				J	NG	Gm	A M	MK P	C	g5 g6	g7 g8

Abbreviations

K = Karin Månsdotter, the king's mistress, later his queen
Ma = Max, ensign
G = Göran Persson, the king's friend, later procurator
E = Erik XIV
c = A courtier
N = Nigel Goldsmith
KS = Katarina Stenbock, widow of King Gustav I Vasa
J = Duke John, Erik's half-brother
SS = Count Svante Sture
NS = Lord Nils Sture
ES = Lord Erik Sture
NG = Nils Gyllenstjerna, marshal to the king
Gm = Göran's mother
A = Agda
M = Maria, Agda's daughter
MK = Måns Knekt, a soldier, Karin's father
P = Peder Welamson, Göran's nephew
g = A guard at the bridge
L = Lord Lejonhuvud
S = Lord Stenbock
g1 = Group 1 (suite of the Stures)
g2 = Group 2 (John's guardians)
g3 = Group 3 (Erik's soldiers)
g4 = Group 4 (members of the estates)
Å = Duke Magnus (of Åbo), Erik's half-brother
Gu = Prince Gustav
Si = Princess Sigrid
lm = A ladies' maid
C = Duke Charles, Erik's half-brother
g5 = Group 5 (people)
g6 = Group 6 (people)
l = A lackey
g7 = Group 7 (John's suite)
g8 = Group 8 (Charles' suite)

+ designates exit not indicated by Strindberg.

While the sequence scheme numbers 34 different *dramatis personae,* including group designations, only 20 are found in Strindberg's list of characters.

The bare facts presented in the scheme provide us with a firm basis for an analysis of the plot, since we are much concerned with the question when and in what order the various events take place. Only in this way can we get an idea of the dynamic structure of the play.

Before turning to the actual analysis of the plot, a few comments on the problems related to the sequence scheme may be appropriate. On the whole Strindberg has in this drama been quite accurate in indicating entrances and exits. The exits which have not been marked, concern (in accordance with

French practice) servants in seven cases out of eight; it has been taken for granted here that the servants leave as soon as they have fulfilled their task.

The eighth exit, not indicated by Strindberg, appears in seq. 76, which ends with the exit of the people. Since Erik in seq. 75 has ordered Gyllenstjerna to drive the people out, we must conclude that Gyllenstjerna leaves together with the crowd. Erik is now left alone; in seq. 77 he voices the single soliloquy of the play. Alternatively, we may imagine that Gyllenstjerna remains on the stage until seq. 78; in that case there is of course no question of any soliloquy. A director must make a choice here; how he chooses obviously says something about his view of Erik and his relationship to Gyllenstjerna.

One example of the relatively rare sequence type (3)—cf. p. 15—can be found in the play: seq. 62–63. In both sequences Göran is alone on the stage—if we disregard the members of the four estates who are merely background accessories. The curtain between the sequences indicates that a certain amount of time has passed, the time Erik needs to get down to the cellar, witness the killing of the Stures and return to Göran.

The division into sequences is not always unproblematic. Seq. 1–2 and seq. 24 illustrate this. The play opens with a tense situation. While Karin and Max talk to one another on the terrace of the royal palace, Erik is perched in a window (off-stage), spying on them. Behind the bushes Göran is regarding them. This constellation has not been indicated in the scheme, since this would have been in conflict with our definition of the term 'sequence'; neither Erik nor Göran are seen or heard by the audience. In seq. 2, however, Erik has several speeches; the audience is now aware of his presence and a form of communication with the visible characters, Karin and Göran, takes place. We now deal with a character who is at once (acoustically) present and (visually) absent. The sequence is unique in the play; it is a border case—as has been indicated by putting Erik within brackets.

We find a similar situation in seq. 24, playing in Göran's home. In the large room we see a fireplace and a dining room table to the right (the mother's work place) and a desk to the left (Göran's work place). Even after Agda and Maria have entered, the room remains undivided. But when there is a knock on the door, Göran "*puts a partition screen*" before the dining women. During the rest of the act the room remains divided. To the left Göran receives a number of male visitors, to the right the women continue their meal. We are thus confronted with two simultaneous activities. The division of the room means that the women can listen to what the men say; the audience and Göran are aware of this, his visitors usually not. The grouping here, it will be seen, is a variant of the spy grouping in seq. 1–2. The difference is that in seq. 24 all the characters can be seen by the audience. In a sense there is a change of place; it is, however, not radical enough to motivate a sequence division.

Erik XIV has so often been regarded as a penetrating character study that people tend to forget that we are dealing here with a psychological portrait *in a drama.* It is true that the action of the play is determined to a great extent by the psyche of the title figure,[4] but at the same time we cannot disregard the fact that the head of a state has a position of power which in itself is dramatic—quite apart from how he is as an individual. The central conflict of the play—the rivalry between Erik and John—is not so much determined by Erik's psychic constitution as by his (quite normal) desire to increase his power and John's opposite desire to deprive him of this power—to increase his own. In this central sense *Erik XIV* does not differ from the bulk of plays about royalty—by Strindberg or others. A closer look at the text shows that it is above all a number of political events which carry the action forward.

The essential points in the struggle for power between Erik and John are the following:

7 Erik promises John that he may marry Catherine of Poland.
19 Erik gives order to seize John, "dead or alive".
21 John has secretly married Catherine.
28 Supported by the Finns, John has rebelled against Erik.
34 John has been condemned to death by the four estates but been pardoned by Erik.
38 John is brought to prison.
66 Erik has released John from prison.
72 John promises Charles half the kingdom, provided Charles supports him in his struggle against Erik.
88 John has arrested Erik.
90 John is proclaimed king.

In this list, the figures left represent sequences. Present tense stands for dramatized (scenic) activities, perfect tense for reported (off-stage) activities. The distinction is important, since it forms a sound basis for any discussion about why the author has chosen to visualize certain activities and not others, which advantages and disadvantages the choice signifies, etc. It is easy to see why Strindberg has preferred the report type in seq. 21, 28, 34 and 66; here the place of action plays a decisive role. But it is not as easy to see why he has preferred this type also in seq. 88; the arrest of Erik could easily have been shown. Conversely, seq. 72—the conversation between John and Charles—clearly deviates from the pattern set in the rest of the play. Strindberg realized that the audience must be prepared well in advance for the end of the play: the dethronement of Erik. We must somehow get to know that John is supported by Charles and that the threat against Erik is therefore aggravated. At the same time Erik must himself be unaware of these circumstances. Strindberg's problem, in this situation, was that he lacked a character who could receive a message of the impending menace without letting Erik in on it. The best he could do was to dramatize the bond between John and Charles. It is an enforced solution determined by the one-sided point of view which Strindberg has chosen; we will shortly return to this.

The list of the elements forming the main plot provides us with the framework around which the play is built. With this list as a starting-point we can see how Strindberg enriches the action in various ways. To become fully comprehensible, the list needs, however, to be complemented with a number of causal explanations. Thus seq. 19 dramatizes Erik's fear that John will deprive him of power—already here is the end anticipated—while seq. 21 reveals ("secretly") that John is aware of the fact that Erik is chasing him. Seq. 28 tells us that John has violated the Arboga articles, according to which the dukes had promised to obey the king. This is the reason why he is condemned to death by the four estates. Erik's pardoning him has to do with his unwillingness to have a half-brother executed; possibly he also regards it as a tactical move; fear of revenge is a third possibility. The capital punishment is thus transformed into imprisonment (seq. 38). All these sequences can be explained within the frame of the main plot. A different case is found in seq. 7 and 66.

In order to motivate Erik's thoughtless promise to John in seq. 7, Strindberg in the beginning of the play introduces a secondary plot: Erik's courting of Queen Elizabeth of England. Erik is convinced that Elizabeth will accept him, and he already regards himself as king of six countries. It is in this strong position that he generously gives John permission to marry, thereby increasing John's sphere of power eastwards. Presumably he considers it a way of pacifying the ambitious half-brother, a diplomatic move. This equilibrium is upset by Elizabeth's refusal (seq. 11). John suddenly appears as the mightier of the two. Having failed to increase his own hegemony, Erik now strives to diminish that of John.

When Erik releases John from imprisonment (seq. 66)—John's freedom is a necessary condition for his dethronement of Erik at the end—it is the consequence of the development within another secondary plot: Erik's relationship to the Sture family. This family has sided with John. In punishment of this, Erik has several of them killed. But when the surviving members of the family show indulgence to Erik's children whom they have taken hostage, Erik is filled with pangs of conscience. To expiate for his crime he lets John out of the prison.

Both the promise to John and the decision to release him are examples of how Erik's activities are determined more by his own sensitivity and impulsive temperament than by the careful calculation one expects from a head of state.

As we have seen, the two secondary plots (the Elizabeth plot and the Sture plot) are organically related to the main plot (the conflict Erik–John). Within the main plot we may also observe a slight complication:

58 John has escaped from the prison (rumour).
64 John has not escaped from the prison (denial of rumour).

The reason why this complication has been included is, as far as I can see, that the false rumour upsets Erik and thereby helps motivate his brutality against the Stures. (It is obvious that Strindberg has taken pains to mitigate his responsibility for the killing of the Stures.) If this interpretation is correct, it is difficult to understand why Erik later dares to let John out of the prison. His feelings of guilt are apparently now far stronger than his fear.

While John is imprisoned, his followers, the Stures, become Erik's chief antagonists. The role of the Stures, in other words, is partly a vicarious one. Within the Sture plot we may distinguish the following decisive moments:

11 The Stures bring Erik news of Elizabeth's refusal.
38 They pay homage to John on his way to prison.
39 They are arrested by Erik's soldiers.
55 They have been judged innocent by the estates.
64 Some of them have been executed at Erik's command.
66 Erik has asked the relatives of the dead Stures for forgiveness and declared the executed men innocent.
78 The executed Stures have been judged guilty by the estates.

We here have two opposite developments. Erik first considers the Stures guilty, then innocent. The estates come to the opposite conclusion. When the estates first declare the Stures innocent, it is because they lack reliable evidence; when such evidence is presented a sentence of guilt is pronounced. Erik's declaration that the Stures are innocent has nothing to do with their crime; it is exclusively conditioned by his own action (the killing of the Stures) put in relation to that of the surviving Stures (the sparing of Erik's children). As Erik states in seq. 73: "the enemy was nobler than I".

So far I have described the action of the play as though Erik alone were representing the interests of one of the clashing parties. This is of course a simplification of the matter. The king has a very strong and active person at his side: Göran Persson. It is obvious that Göran plays a very central part in the drama. It is now our task to examine his function in the plot. Let us begin by scrutinizing his role in the political sphere:

1 Göran is out of grace with Erik.
18 Erik is reconciled with Göran. Göran suggests that Erik marry Catherine of Poland.
20 Göran is appointed procurator by Erik.
39 Göran has the Stures arrested.
41 Göran has penned the indictment of the Stures.
60 Göran orders Peder Welamson to murder the Stures.
78 Göran has read the indictment against the Stures to the estates. The estates have pronounced the Stures guilty.
88 Göran (and Erik) have been arrested by John.

Why Göran is out of grace when the play opens we never get to know. This situation enables Strindberg to illustrate on the one hand Erik's proneness to moods and his dependence on Göran (cf. seq. 18), on the other Göran's loyalty to Erik: even when he is out of grace, he is faithful to his king.

Göran's suggestion that Erik marry Catherine (after Elizabeth has refused him) is tantamount to: increase your power eastwards if you can't do it westwards. It is this proposal which causes Erik to ask for the arrestation of John; he has just promised him Catherine. A decisive step is taken when Göran, at his own demand, is made procurator. As he himself implies in seq. 20, this office gives him power to act independently. As procurator Göran keeps an eye on the king's adversaries. Especially vis-à-vis the Stures he is very active. It is he who sees to it that they are caught in the act. It is he who composes the indictment against them. It is he who insists on their execution (seq. 55, 57), who decides on the killing of the Stures (seq. 60)—Erik's order in seq. 64 is merely a reiteration of this decision—and who finally justifies the murder by having the estates sanction it. His attitude to the Sture family is completely consistent and markedly contrasts with Erik's vacillating opinion.

When the estates in the first instance refrain from condemning the Stures, it is because Erik has lost Göran's indictment and is himself unable to present any incriminating arguments. The arrangement may seem rather haphazard but it agrees with the aimlessness and self-assurance which characterize Erik. It also throws light on the relationship between the king and his procurator; it is not the only time that Göran must untangle Erik's skein.

The relation between Erik and Göran is based on mutual dependence. A man of strong and sudden emotions, Erik is not fit to rule the country. He needs a cool practical politician at his side. Göran fulfills this function. As "base-born" Göran cannot ascend the throne. His desire for power can best be satisfied through the weak king. As Göran himself puts it in a revealing passage:

> I don't rely on anyone but myself! I wasn't born to wear a crown, but to rule; since I can rule only through my king, he is my sun. (seq. 23)

The friendship between Erik and Göran is not hierarchical. Both have a great desire to rule. That they do not clash is due to the fact that they socially and psychologically complement one another according to the formula: high station (Erik) + capability (Göran) = powerful ruler.

The political conflict in the play we may formulate thus: ruler (Erik + Göran) *vs* lords (John + Charles + the Sture family/nobility). In Shakespearean fashion, Strindberg could have made us partake of both parties in even proportions. But with few exceptions—the Sture's paying homage to John (a pantomime!) and John's scheming with Charles—most sequences are devoted only to the royal party, while a few show the parties in open conflict. We thus learn very little directly about what 'the enemy' is doing; most of it is merely reported to us by 'messengers'.

Parties in conflict usually do not show much understanding for each other's actions. If the audience partakes of the views of both parties, the impression of objectivity is of course much stronger than if it is allowed to share only one point of view. In this respect *Erik XIV*—like many other Strindberg plays (cf. for example the conflict Laura–Adolf in *The Father*)—must be considered a subjective drama.

That Erik's point of view dominates, appears among other things from the fact that we hear much about the crimes of his adversaries and little about his own. An example: Erik's broken promise to John concerning his marriage to Catherine initiates the fraternal struggle. But neither Erik nor John are manifestly upset about this breach of promise. Instead we hear much about John's and the Stures' violation of the Arboga articles, which is a mere consequence of the king's crime. In this way Erik's guilt is played down.

Although the antagonist, then, is allowed to speak very little for himself, Strindberg could of course have provided John, Charles and the Stures with strong arguments in the few sequences in which they could present them. This he has not done. On the contrary, the leading figure, John, strikes us as being a dishonest and ambitious person. Erik's negative view of him is confirmed. As far as John is concerned we are not inclined to regard Erik as suffering from misanthropy and persecution mania. How can the Stures prefer John to Erik? The explanation must be sought in their need to rule by division. The picture of the Stures is much more favorable than that of John but they have the ambition and the violation of the Arboga articles in common.

The only adversary who comes off fairly well is Duke Charles. At the beginning he vacillates between Erik and John. When he finally sides with the latter, he does it for two reasons: (1) he believes that John will be willing to "share the throne with him"—apparently he too is ambitious—and (2) he prefers John's religious nature to Erik's irreligious one. In fact, John's religiousness is to Charles a guarantee that he will fulfill his promise. When this proves a wrong conclusion, Charles immediately opposes John. At the end of the play the Strindbergian idea of retribution is brought out with strong irony. The conflict between the brothers is not only a reiteration of the fraternal struggles of the Folkungs—there are several allusions to this in the play; it is also a reiteration of the conflict we have witnessed throughout the drama. The only difference is that John has replaced Erik as king, while Charles has replaced John as rebellious duke. He who *has* the power will always be opposed by him who *wants* it. The impression of constant recurrence, of dialectic process, is stressed also by the fact that Charles has earlier revealed his animosity towards the nobility. Charles' controversy with John at the end means, as Sjöstedt points out (109 f.), that Erik's democratic policy stands a new chance. We might even imagine that Charles eventually liberates Erik and that they join their forces against King John. He who is unfamiliar with the historical reality may at any rate interpret the end in this spirit. But also without such imaginative additions the end gives us the feeling that we deal with a *perpetuum mobile,* that—as the final words read—"the struggles of life never end".

Related to the political main plot is also Erik's marshal Nils Gyllenstjerna. He is, however, rather passive—as appears from his actions:

16 Gyllenstjerna informs Erik that Elizabeth is in love with the Earl of Leicester. Erik tries to bribe him to murder Leicester but Gyllenstjerna refuses.
34 Gyllenstjerna considers both John and the Stures punishable. He considers himself law-abiding.
39 He points out to the Stures that they have violated the Arboga articles.
58 He has not opposed the decision to declare the Stures guilty.
74 He announces that the people wish to see Queen Karin.
79 He announces that the queen dowager and the lords will not be present at the wedding meal. Erik asks him to let in the riffraff. Gyllenstjerna lays down his marshal's staff at Erik's feet.
83 He informs Erik that the dukes have bribed the guards of the palace and declares his loyalty to King Erik.
89 He proclaims the arrival of the king, John III.

As appears from this list, Gyllenstjerna functions partly as servant/messenger. In nearly all his functions he could be replaced by someone else, for example Nils Sture (seq. 16), Göran (seq. 34, 39), a courtier (seq. 74, 79, 83, 89). But not without problems. It should be noted that Gyllenstjerna takes a position of his own in the political struggle, a position which makes him more suited to perform the above-mentioned activities than the characters just referred to. Erik calls him "Back and Forth", a nickname which indicates his position between the fighting parties. As "a friend of the Vasas" (seq. 34) and "as a kinsman of the Stures" (seq. 39) this intermediate position is, as it were, natural to him. Gyllenstjerna is very loyal to Erik but he is also "one of the lords of the realm" (seq. 34) and as such he is certainly opposed to the king's attempt to increase his own power at the expense of the nobility. This controversy can already be glimpsed in seq. 16 and it returns more powerfully when Gyllenstjerna does not oppose the decision of the estates to declare the Stures innocent although they consider them guilty. But at this point his cowardliness, his inclination to support the stronger one is decisive. This tendency becomes highly ironical in seq. 83 compared to seq. 89; here Gyllenstjerna truly lives up to his nickname "Back and Forth".[5]

The intermediate position and the inclination to avoid taking a stand Gyllenstjerna shares with the people. In this respect he represents the average man, and it is therefore not surprising that Erik and Göran tend to see him as a representative of man in general (seq. 81), a view which seems corroborated also by Gyllenstjerna's inability to live up to his own principles.

If the main plot, then, is political and concerns nationwide interests, several of the subordinate plots deal with private situations. Sometimes the two spheres combine, as in the Karin plot. Erik and Göran function as chief figures in both spheres; in this way a foundation is laid for the intimate connection of the two worlds.

In *Master Olof* Strindberg already shows an inclination to describe his political figures also at home, a method which he had adopted from Shakespeare. In *Erik XIV* he emphasizes this aspect.

Thus Karin Månsdotter is given much attention although her importance for the plot is not very striking:

1 Karin has abandoned Max. Max 'courts' her in vain. Yet Karin is still in love with him.
49 Karin learns that Max has been assassinated.
53 Together with the dowager queen and the children she has by Erik Karin escapes to Hörningsholm, the home of the Stures.
70 Rejected by her father, Måns Knekt, Karin returns to Erik.
73 Karin has just become queen.
88 Karin lets herself be arrested together with Erik (and Göran).

The pattern is fairly simple. First Karin's tender feeling for Max are demonstrated. This is necessary to explain why she later abandons Erik when she learns that Max has been murdered. Strindberg makes use of the classical misunderstanding to make Karin's escape altogether plausible: Karin is convinced that Max has been killed at Erik's request; a few speeches by the king, revealing his jealousy (seq. 8), motivate this conviction of hers.

It is difficult to make her escape from Erik rhyme with her return to him. Since she does not yet know that Erik is innocent of Max' death, her return means that she is prepared to marry the man she believes to be the murderer of her former fiancé. Such an attitude is indeed possible (cf. Hamlet's mother) but it does not agree very well with our over-all picture of Karin. Erik's part in the killing of the Stures and his (possible) insanity after this event would hardly seem attractive to her. Strindberg disguises these matters as much as possible and lays the stress on circumstances which better motivate a return: the brutality of her father, her feeling of being abandoned, her longing to stop being a concubine and have her children legalized.

As soon as she is made queen, Karin becomes at least indirectly a political figure: her son by Erik, Gustav, is now successor to the throne, a development which the dukes and the nobility do not welcome; it is significant that their dethroning of Erik takes place shortly after the wedding; in seq. 73 there is, in other words, an obvious connection between the Karin subplot and the main plot. Another point of intersection we find in seq. 53: the idea that his children have fallen into the hands of the Stures is a major force behind Erik's decision to kill the imprisoned members of the family.

It is interesting to note how Strindberg utilizes the triangular relationship in the play. The object of Erik's tender feelings is named Karin Månsdotter. But, as we have seen, Karin is also loved by ensign Max. We thus get:

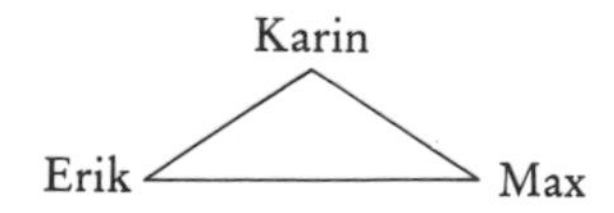

The relevant moments of action in the Max subplot are the following:

1 Karin, now Erik's mistress, has earlier had a relationship with Max. She is still attached to Max but considers herself bound to stay with Erik who needs her.
27 Göran tries to persuade Max to leave Karin alone but Max refuses.
29 Måns Knekt asks Erik for permission to marry his daughter Karin off to Max but the king refuses.
32 Göran requests Peder Welamson to assassinate Max.
35 Max has been assassinated.
49 Karin learns that Max has been assassinated. She holds Erik responsible for this deed.
78 Erik has not had anything to do with the assassination of Max.

As we have seen earlier, the Max subplot is connected with the main plot in seq. 49, since the announcement of Max' fate leads to Karin's escape—which in turn has political repercussions. The dramaturgic problem Strindberg was faced with here can be outlined as follows: Karin and the children must in one way or another abandon Erik for the enemy. In this way the Stures are able to show the magnanimity towards Erik's children—*nota bene* toward the potential successor to the throne—which releases Erik's noble return gesture (the declaration of innocence and the liberation of John), a gesture which in turn leads to his own defeat and John's victory.

Karin's escape is accounted for in several ways. The most powerful reason is that she cannot stay with him who "has murdered [her] only friend, the noblest heart, the one who was ready to restore [her] good name" (seq. 49). As we have seen, it is Göran, not Erik, who gets Max out of the way. He himself presents the reason when he tells Max:

> I don't want your feelings to disturb a human being who is precious to all of us and to our country. Lady Karin can become queen, if you don't upset her with your feelings. (seq. 27)

Göran has a twofold reason to fear that Max will thwart his plans for turning Karin into a queen. On the one hand Max has already in seq. 1 expressed the wish that the king should die; an attempt at revenge on his part cannot be excluded. On the other hand it is obvious that Karin is still in love with Max; a continued liaison between them could result in her abandoning Erik. Göran realizes that the king needs her. He himself needs the king. In the last instance Göran's actions against Max are thus governed by selfish motifs.

It should in this context be pointed out that legally nothing prevents Erik from marrying Karin. Karin is not engaged to Max. Måns Knekt explicitly says: "I don't know that my Karin is betrothed" (seq. 29). Later he points out that Karin and Max "were sort of bethrothed ... well, well, there wasn't anything really between them, as they say" (seq. 75). From this we may conclude that Karin and Max have at most been secretly engaged and that their relationship in any case is not legally defined.[6]

If Karin is legally attached neither to Max nor to Erik, it is on the other hand evident that she has earlier had a Platonic relationship with the former, whereas she now has a sexual one with the latter. Against this background Göran's departing words to Max appear highly ironical:

GÖRAN. /—/ Farewell to you, for eternity!
MAX. With what power do you dare to sentence me?
GÖRAN. With that of justice, and the law, which condemns the man who tempts a betrothed woman! (seq. 27)

As we have seen, Karin is legally betrothed to no one, ethically rather to Max. If anyone, it is Erik who has made himself guilty of tempting a betrothed woman. Göran thus reveals himself as a law-perverter in a double sense.

Even if the need to create a strong reason for Karin's escape is the primary cause for including the Max subplot, it is obvious that Strindberg has tried to disguise this by integrating this subplot in various ways. Thus Max' courting of Karin (seq. 1) corresponds to Erik's proposal to Elizabeth; in both cases the men are refused because the women prefer their lovers. Beside the earlier triangle we now have a new one:

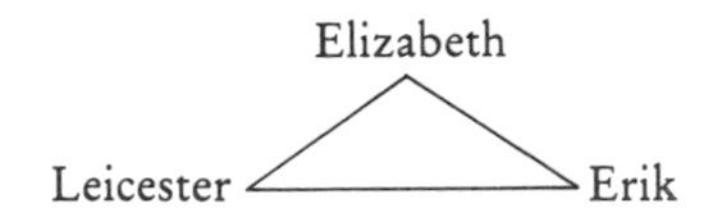

Erik here takes Max' position. It is significant that Erik refers to Elizabeth as a "street whore" who has "a lover" (seq. 18); Karin is generally referred to as "concubine"—Erik also once calls her "street whore" (seq. 56)—and Max calls Erik her "lover" (seq. 1). Erik's diatribe against Elizabeth and Leicester is, in other words, an adequate description of his own relation to Karin. It illustrates his inclination to see only the mote in his brother's eye. The connection between the rivals Max and Erik is further strengthened by the fact that Strindberg has the latter witness the former's courting of Karin at a time when his own proposal to Elizabeth is of current interest. Ironical it is that Max, as a guard, has to protect the man who has caused Karin to abandon him. Finally, the two triangular situations throw a revealing light on Erik's demand that Karin be faithful to him although he himself proposes to another woman.

More *en passant* another triangle can be glimpsed within the frame of the main plot:

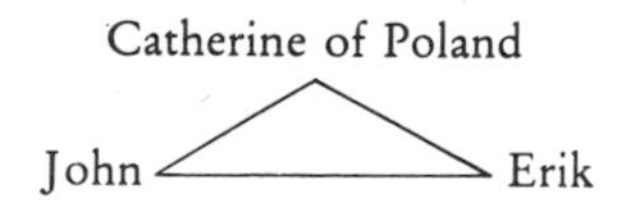

As in the case of Elizabeth, Erik is again defeated.

Our observation that Erik's love for Karin is primarily sexual must, however, be modified. Such it is in the eyes of the people, who regard Karin as his concubine. As a matter of fact, Erik's adoration of her is Platonic, too, as Karin notes in seq. 1. There is, in other words, a strong affinity between him and Max.

More obscure than Erik's love-affair is Göran's:

ERIK. Agda, I suppose?
GÖRAN. No, it's ... someone else.
ERIK. Is she beautiful?
GÖRAN. No, to the world she's ugly, but at a certain moment I saw "the original", as Plato calls it. You know, the revelation of the perfect, the timeless behind the mask of her face, and since then ... hm ... I love her.
ERIK. Strange! When you said the word "love"—and you hesitated to say it—you became really handsome, transformed ...
GÖRAN. Am I so terribly ugly, then?
ERIK. Damnably ugly. Haven't you ever seen yourself in a mirror?
GÖRAN. I avoid mirrors!—But can you imagine anything as crazy as this: she thinks I'm handsome! (*Laughs.*)
ERIK. Does she always think so?
GÖRAN. No, not always. Only ... when I'm not mean.
/—/
ERIK. Do you intend to get married soon?
GÖRAN. Perhaps. (seq. 18)

MOTHER. Göran, your good intentions outstrip your abilities too often ... That's how it was last time, when you helped the deserted Agda and her child.
/—/
GÖRAN. /—/ An unfortunate woman asked for help, and she got it. That's all there is to it.
MOTHER. But they're saying she's your mistress.
GÖRAN. I can imagine, but that, unfortunately, hurts only her.
MOTHER. Are you sure?
GÖRAN. Sure? Hm!
MOTHER. Besides, Agda could begin thinking you had intentions, and then you'd be blamed for having supported her. (seq. 23)

ERIK (*laughs*). I don't know, but I like you better since Cupid caught you, and I trust you more than before. Mayn't I see "the Original" sometime?
GÖRAN. I ask you, valued friend, not to joke about what must be sacred to every man of honor ...
ERIK. You're a beast, Göran!
GÖRAN. I was, but I'm not any more. But this I know: if *she* deserted me, then ... the old Göran would come back! (seq. 28)

GYLLENSTJERNA (*presses an object into* GÖRAN PERSSON'S *hand*). Someone asked me to give you this object with the message that it has been exchanged for another's!
(GÖRAN *stares at the ring he has just received, throws it over his shoulder out the window. Then he takes a miniature from next to his heart and tramps it under his feet.*)
ERIK (*who has observed everything, laughs*). That was the original! A street whore, that one, too! (*Laughs.*)
GÖRAN. Now comes Göran as the devil! (seq. 58)

GÖRAN. Don't imagine I had anything immoral to do with Jacob Israel's Agda, for it is not true. That I took care of her was only one of those whims of ... hm! ... generosity that we all get on rare occasions. (seq. 82)

The first question we must pose is: Who is the woman Göran loves? Lamm (1926, 156) assumes that it is Agda, but Johnson (1963, 126) speaks of "an unidentified woman" and Vogelweith (177) disputes Lamm's assumption when he writes: "On aurait cru qu'il s'agissait d'Agda, l'une des prostituées qui travaillait à la taverne du Pigeon Bleu. Mais il n'en est rien." In support of his point he quotes the passage from seq. 18 just cited.

The advantage of this latter view is that it seems supported not only by the text but also by the manuscript notes, where on the one hand we read that "Agda believes that Göran is in love with her"—which seems to imply that this is not the case; and where on the other the object of Göran's tender feelings is given anonymous designations:

Göran has lost his love.
His beloved has abandoned him.
Göran gets to know that his beloved has sold herself.

Of Agda we know that she and her child have been cared for by Göran and that they now dwell in his house. We may therefore assume that the Platonic love for "the original" has brought out what is good in Göran; this is demonstrated in his generosity toward Agda. Yet this interpretation is not very satisfactory since it integrates neither Agda nor "the original" in the play.

Is it then necessary to see the love relationship in this way? The manuscript jottings are certainly no binding proof. It is not difficult to find examples of how Strindberg has changed his mind while working on a drama, and it is thus quite possible that "the original" of the play is not as anonymous as that of the notes, that Lamm in short is quite right in his assumption that Agda is Göran's sweetheart. What is decisive is whether such an interpretation is reasonable and meaningful in the context of the play. Let us see.

If Göran is in love with Agda, we get of course a very simple explanation of why he has asked her to come and stay at his house. It should in this context be noted that Göran rejects all ideas that he has done this out of magnanimity. Strindberg is indeed very little prone to revealing Göran's feelings for Agda but in seq. 23–24 there is at least an indication. When his mother asks Göran to come to the dining table he protests: he has no time to eat. As soon as Agda has entered, he suggests: "If you're hungry, we'll eat." What is the reason for this change other than his interest in Agda?

But does not Göran himself deny that he is in love with Agda? Not at all! From the context it appears that his statement in seq. 18 should not be understood literally but in a figurative, Platonic sense. When he claims that he does not love Agda, it is because the name to him represents only the woman known to the world: the street whore, the mask, the false copy of the pure and good original which the world does not see. It is this latter woman—the original Agda—Göran loves. In the same way he himself appears ugly to the world, while he appears handsome to Agda; like him, she is attracted by "the original".

The relationship Göran–Agda develops negatively. Agda abandons him for "another"; we thus get a new triangle:

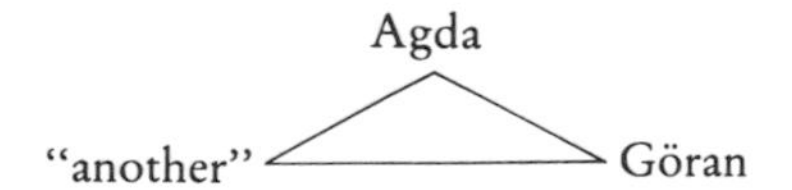

It is in a critical situation that Göran learns about Agda's infidelity. Erik has just failed to convince the estates of the guilt of the Stures. The message that "the original" was merely "a street whore" crushes Göran's faith in the existence of goodness and immediately leads to his evil ("Göran as the devil") decision to kill the Stures. Thus his experience in the private sphere has direct political consequences.[7]

When Göran in seq. 82 again denies that he has "had anything immoral to do" with Agda, his statement can be understood in two ways. On one hand he may be ashamed of the fact that he has been abandoned by a socially inferior woman; although he has never mentioned her name to Erik, he realizes that Erik suspects that it concerns Agda; precisely for this reason he is anxious to tell Erik that this is not the case. Compare the inverted picture Erik presents to Göran of his proposal to Elizabeth: "I've dismissed the Englishwoman!" (seq. 17). But Göran's pronouncement can also be taken as a proof that he is still in love with Agda and wants to protect her against gossip; earlier his mother has warned him to this effect.

Fundamental for an understanding of the Agda subplot is that we see the connection between the relation Göran–Agda and the relation Erik–Karin;[8] that Lamm takes a critical view of the subplot is due to the fact that he has not grasped this connection.[9] Actually, it is not difficult to discover, for Strindberg draws attention to it in a number of corresponding situations. Thus Erik has taken over Karin from Max just as Göran has taken over Agda from Jacob Israel. In both cases the women have substituted a looser relation (cohabitation) for a more respectable one. In Erik's case the postponement of the wedding is caused by Karin's low social status and the king's hope of a politically rewarding marriage. In Göran's case such reasons are lacking. By disguising the fact that his love concerns Agda, Strindberg manages to conceal this difference. This may well be the reason for the secrecy on this point.

Like Erik, Göran cherishes plans to marry. In Erik's case the object is first Elizabeth, then Catherine, finally Karin. Only the last one remains faithful to him. In Göran's case the plans concern only one woman: Agda. The proposal to Elizabeth is made concrete by the crown that has been made at Erik's request. When her refusal is known, he furiously throws it over the balustrade (seq. 11). As we have seen, Göran handles the 'emblems' which he receives from Agda in much the same way, when he learns of her deceit (seq. 58). Elizabeth abandons Erik for Leicester, Agda abandons Göran for "another". Above all: Göran's worship of "the original" has its counterpart in Erik's adoration of Karin. Compare the passage from seq. 18, recently quoted, with the following:

KARIN. /—/ I've flattered myself by believing I could bring out what's best in him, and I've felt his kindly approval has made me a better person. But now—danger is near! For he has the habit of overestimating me. He sees me as his good angel! Wait till he awakens from the dream and discovers how imperfect I am. (seq. 1)

The implication is that "the original" loved by Erik is, in fact, an illusion. The death-blow comes to Erik in seq. 56, when it is clear that Karin has abandoned him and escaped to the Stures (the enemy). Shortly after this, in seq. 58, Göran learns of Agda's deceit. Both women are called "street whore" (seq. 58, 60) by Erik, an allusion to their earlier occupation at the Blue Dove and a rejection of their morals. Göran's and Erik's disillusion concerning their good angels thus occurs more or less simultaneously. With joint forces they now give vent to their aggressions by effectuating the murder of the Stures to whom they both bear a grudge.

We can now see the significance of the Agda subplot in the play. Psychologically, it motivates Göran's way of behavior at an important moment (the killing of the Stures). Moreover, it illustrates his affinity to Erik: however different they may be in other respects, in their view of women they resemble one another. Important, too, is that Strindberg, by demonstrating the parallel between the Karin–Erik relation and the Agda–Göran relation, counteracts the impression that Erik's problems are of a private nature, a risk which otherwise seems imminent when the protagonist, as here, is a mentally unbalanced person. If it can be shown that Göran, despite his contrasting nature, reacts in the same way as Erik when the same fate befalls him, then we obviously deal with a study not in the individual psyche but in that of everyman.

Relatively far from the main plot we find a couple of characters whose function in the play is not immediately evident: Måns Knekt and Göran Persson's mother.

The Måns Knekt subplot has the following significant moments:

29 Måns asks Erik for permission to marry off his daughter Karin to Max but Erik refuses.
69 Måns rejects Karin.
70 Erik explains to Måns that he is going to marry Karin.
75 Måns forgives Karin after Erik has married her and restored her reputation.

Just as Max' primary function is to provide Karin with a reason to abandon Erik, so Måns Knekt's primary function is to make her return to the king. By having Måns reject her, Strindberg so to speak drives her back in the arms of the king. Where else could she go? Meanwhile Erik has come to long so much for Karin that he is now prepared to marry her; he now comes to her rescue. The arrangement is somewhat artificial and Måns is not a very coherent or convincing figure.

In seq. 29 one may still have the impression that in his moral unimpeachability and fearlessness toward the king, Måns functions as a kind of *raisonneur*, but later it appears that his way of acting is exclusively determined by selfish motifs: Måns wants to be rid of the disgrace that has befallen him once his daughter has become the king's mistress. It is difficult to understand why Måns experiences this as a disgrace—rather than an honor. But granted that we accept this, why does Måns want Karin to marry Max rather than Erik? After all, he is later willing to accept the king as his son-in-law. The revelation of Måns' true nature resembles the demasking of Gyllenstjerna, to a certain extent also that of Svante Sture and Duke John. Below a respectable façade, they prove to be "tweedledum and tweedledee" as it says in the manuscript notes.

The function of Göran's mother is, dramaturgically, that of the speaking partner. Vis-à-vis Göran she plays the part of *confidente*; in this way his relationship both to Erik and to Agda can be illuminated. The Mother's influence on the action of the play is negligible. Like Måns Knekt she is a representative of the people but her relation to Göran is the very opposite of that of Måns to his daughter Karin. While Måns only worries about his own reputation, Mother Persson worries about Göran's (and Agda's). When Karin feels deserted by everyone, she visits her father. When Göran feels that his "saga is almost over" (seq. 82), he expresses a longing for his mother. Karin is rejected by her father when she needs him the most. Mother Persson, by contrast, sets out to look for Göran when she feels that he is in danger. With an obvious allusion to the Golgotha situation—it has earlier been indicated that Göran will end on the gallows—she presages the fate of her son:

GÖRAN'S MOTHER (*rushing in*). Good Lord, the king has been taken prisoner! And Göran, my son, my son!

MÅNS. And Karin, my daughter! My daughter!
GÖRAN'S MOTHER. Yes, call her now! She won't go with you . . . (seq. 88)

Paternal egotism is here pitted against maternal love. Even from peripheral characters as these Strindberg manages to extract a thematically significant polarity. In the last instance Mother Persson is, in fact, the character who seems to come closest to Göran's ideal; it is significant that Erik excepts her when he voices his hatred of mankind: "If I could hear what these wretches think, I'd have a cause for hanging all of them . . . except Göran's mother" (seq. 77). These words gain extra weight if they are uttered in the single soliloquy of the play—as we have earlier assumed.

Let us now, on the basis of our examination, schematically indicate the more important character relationships:

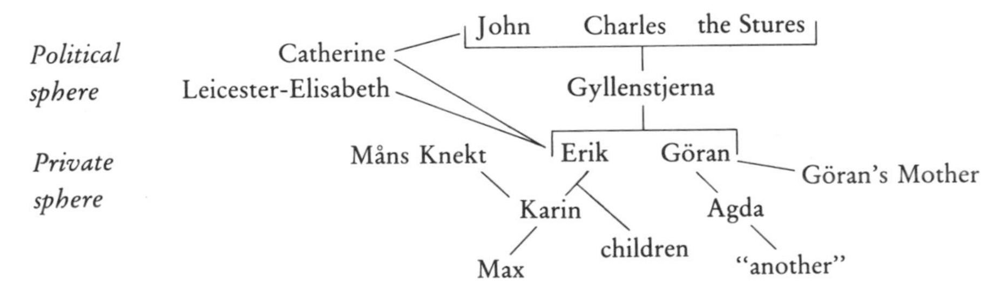

Around Erik and Göran, in the center, we find two spheres of action. Within the political sphere the two appear as a unit (the ruler); within the private sphere they appear as individuals. By synchronizing their private experiences and reactions Strindberg suggests, however, that in spite of all differences they have a close affinity. The unity within the political sphere is, we might say, motivated within the private one.

Ever since the days of Lamm it has been common to regard Göran as the chief plotter and in this sense the protagonist of the play (Lamm, 1926, 156; Ollén, 285; Sjöstedt, 108). It is true, of course, that Göran alone is responsible for the assassination of Max and mainly responsible for the killing of the Stures—two of the decisive elements of the plot. Yet it would be wrong to claim that Strindberg has placed an active procurator next to a passive king. Erik, too, takes a number of decisions and performs a series of actions. The difference is rather that Göran is consistent and does not recoil from using violence, while the far more tender-hearted Erik takes a vacillating attitude and shrinks back from bloodshed. What effectuates the fateful development is precisely that Göran's decisions are often accidentally thwarted by Erik. Somewhat incredibly, Strindberg in fact has Erik take a number of decisions singlehanded to make this tragic development possible. Rather than speak of one protagonist (Erik or Göran) we might speak of a double protagonist. Erik and Göran may even be seen as parts of the same ego.

Opposed to Erik–Göran we find the antagonist John–Charles–the Stures. Gyllenstjerna appears in the scheme in his "Back and Forth" position between the conflicting parties. Within the private sphere we find two parent–child relations (Karin–Måns Knekt and Göran–Mother Persson) contrasting with one another and flanking the central relation Erik–Karin–the children. The two amourous triangles within the private sphere (Erik–Karin–Max and Göran–Agda–"another") have their counterparts in the political sphere (Erik–Elizabeth–Leicester and Erik–Catherine–John).

Lamm has characterized *Erik XIV* as a static drama, despite its many events, a drama without any basic idea or even a strategic pattern—but with ingenious passages and a title character who is one of Strindberg's most masterly creations. The play is static, Lamm argues (1926, 152, 156), because the title figure never changes. Lamm seems to assume that a change within the protagonist is a *sine qua non* in a truly dynamic drama. To my mind the question static or dynamic need not be connected with the characters; rather it concerns the play as a whole. What is decisive, is whether the drama is structured in such a way that at the end *we* arrive at a view different from that at the beginning.

This brings us to the question whether the play has a basic idea or not. Contrary to Lamm I think it has. So does Ollén (285), who formulates it: "the king, the people and its representative Göran Persson struggling against nobility, dukes and other minor royalties who wish to take a position between the king and the people". However, this is hardly a basic *idea*; rather, it is the main plot or conflict. Terminologically more satisfying is Brandell's formulation (1974*b*, 101) when he characterizes the fundamental idea as "the pleading for the rights of the opressed people". But is this view correct?

We hardly get any impression of an oppressed people and the contrast between the people and the lords is not a black-and-white one: Måns Knekt, for example, is not a very likeable person. When Erik is finally confronted with the people (the riffraff at the wedding), his democratic spirit significantly proves to have its limits. One might even ask oneself whether democracy does not primarily have a snob value to Erik— as the manuscript notes suggest. The same question can be posed with regard to Göran, who personally profits from a strong constellation king–people at the expense of the nobility. The effect of all this is that their attitude to the people seems very ambivalent—about as ambivalent as Strindberg's own vacillation between upper and lower classes, two designations which, incidentally, appear in the notes.

As far as I can see, the basic idea—or theme—should not at all be sought within the social or political sphere but within the metaphysical one. As in his other post-Inferno plays, Strindberg is posing here the fundamental question: What is life? The idea that life is a dream, a nightmare, a hell, a prison, an asylum is constantly varied in these plays. In *Erik XIV* Strindberg was, for a change, confronted with a king who by tradition was, or became, insane. That a supposedly insane king must have intrigued a playwright who had sometimes himself had a reason to doubt his mental health, is not surprising; already at the age of twenty Strindberg in fact began to write a five-act tragedy about Erik XIV, whom he considered a Swedish Hamlet (*SS,* L, 75f.). In *The Father* with its mentally disturbed protagnonist, the basic idea may be phrased: Who is really insane, the Captain or the rest (the world)? In *The Ghost Sonata* we learn about the Student's father, who has been taken to the mental asylum, that he "was sound and yet insane", i.e. insane in the eyes of the world, but in fact healthy.

The same idea is at the core of *Erik XIV.* At the beginning the king is constantly referred to as "insane", and as early as in the opening sequence he behaves in a strange way; "a madman" rules the country, we learn. Gradually, however, the difference between Erik and the rest becomes less pronounced. The events are chained to one another in an ironical way and constantly it is demonstrated that the world repays by ingratitude. At the end of the play we are ripe for Erik's question whether it is not the world, rather than he, that is insane (seq. 83). Since this may still seem a defensive statement on Erik's part, it is important that in the final situation, he is supported in his assumption by John: "I think the world has gone mad!". What constitutes the madness is sententiously clarified by the third brother, Charles, in the final words of the play: "the struggles of life never end!". This development from the idea that Erik is insane to the idea that insanity is part and parcel of the world may rightly be considered the carefully structured basic idea of the play.

As for Lamm's complaint about the lack of an artistic plan underlying the drama, we have already seen that it has little justification. It is true that the plot has its weak points; and that historical, political and even psychological probability are occasionally violated. But if we disregard these weaknesses, it is obvious that the drama has a thematically meaningful pattern and a plot which on the whole is carefully and consistently constructed. Of principal interest is Lamm's idea that the title figure in an, according to him, badly constructed play can be "one of Strindberg's most masterly creations for the stage". We may evaluate the play in different ways. But we can hardly, as Lamm does, separate the action from the agent, Erik XIV from *Erik XIV*.

8. The Opening of *Dödsdansen I/ The Dance of Death I*

One of the most admired parts of *The Dance of Death I* is the opening dialogue between Edgar and Alice, seemingly straying from one topic to another but in fact very functionally constructed. A close reading of their conversation may throw light not only on Strindberg's dramatic dialogue but also on dramatic dialogue in general. How are the speeches related to the speeches in the rest of the drama? To acting and stage directions? How are they interpreted by the receivers: Edgar/Alice and the reader/spectator respectively? How ambiguous are they? What are the reasons for topical shifts? In the following I shall try to answer these questions. To give the reader optimal chances of checking the interpretations offered, the opening sequence will be quoted *in extenso*.

For the play as a whole Strindberg gives the following stage directions:

(A) *The interior of a round fortress tower of granite.*

At the rear, a large gateway with French windows, through which can be seen a seashore with battery emplacements, and the sea.

On either side of the entrance, a window with flowers and birds.

To the right of the entrance, an upright piano; further downstage a sewing table and two reclining chairs.

On the left, in the middle of the stage, a writing table with a telegraph apparatus; closer downstage a whatnot with framed portraits. Nearby a chaise longue to lie down on.

A lamp in the ceiling. On the wall, by the piano, two large laurel wreaths, with ribbons attached; they flank the framed portrait of a woman in stage costume.

By the door a hat- and coat-stand with uniform equipment, sabres, etc. Close by a bureau-desk.

To the left of the doorway hangs a mercury barometer.

In addition to these *play* directions we get the following *act* directions:

(B) *It is a mild autumn evening. The French windows stand open and outside by the coastal battery emplacement can be seen an artilleryman on sentry duty; he is dressed in cap and sabre; from time to time his sabre reflects the red light of the setting sun. The sea lies dark and calm.*

As often with Strindberg, the stage directions are not complete. Apart from the gateway rear there are two other doors in the room, one to the right, obviously leading to the kitchen, since the maid, Jenny, enters from here, the other to the left, apparently leading to the hall, since Kurt enters from this direction. From a realistic point of view the gateway is superfluous; Edgar could just as well enter and leave through the door to the left. But symbolically it plays an important part, as we shall see.

The play deals with a man in the shadow of death and a wife impatiently hoping that his death will set her free. The scenery effectively visualizes the situation. It is easy to see that the sea stands for freedom. Yet the sea can also be seen as a (negative) symbol of death; while the cannons turned toward the sea may be regarded as a visualization of Edgar's attempt to protect himself against approaching death. Viewed in this way, it is hardly a coincidence that the battery emplacement is found in the area between land and sea, life and death; the coast corresponds, we might say, to the change from one condition to another: the death-struggle Edgar has to face.[1]

If the exterior seems markedly masculine, the interior is decidedly feminine: the upright piano, the sewing table, the laurel wreaths, the female portrait, the whatnot, the flowers and the birds—all these things we tend to relate to Alice. The only masculine piece of property is Edgar's uniform equipment which, however, belongs as much to the exterior.

Aging (autumn evening, sunset) and death (dark and calm sea): the exterior primarily relates to Edgar. The connection is strengthened by the fact that the Sentry is so closely linked with him: Edgar too is soon to put on a cap and sabre. He himself indicates the relationship when he says: "Sir Bluebeard and the maiden in the tower—and outside the sentry paces back and forth with drawn sabre, keeping watch over the fair maiden." Compare this speech with Alice's statement that she has "spent a lifetime in this tower, this prison, guarded by a man I have always hated". The Sentry obviously represents Edgar, or rather, a certain aspect of him.

The jealousy of an aging husband toward his younger wife can be divined in Edgar's speech. He does not trust Alice; that is why he has to watch over her. In this context it is interesting to note that *she* never leaves the tower, while *he* repeatedly does so. Alice dreams of a reversed situation; in a speech echoing the one just quoted she bursts out: "Oh! The fortress gates shall open and the sentry with drawn sabre will no longer be guarding me, but him."

Yet Alice's hope is not fulfilled. Even at the close of the play the Sentry can be seen outside the tower. Alice is doomed to remain with her husband after Kurt has left her.

From a realistic point of view the guard concerns not Alice but the sea; it is from there that an enemy may come. But also in this case the Sentry is linked with the sick and aging Edgar, guarding himself against death. The Captain's power to resist death and survive the stroke is, we might claim, visualized in the Sentry at the end of the play.

The initial stage directions are succeeded by the first acting directions and speeches of the play:

(1) THE CAPTAIN *is seated in the armchair by the sewing table, fingering an extinguished cigar. He is dressed in a worn fatigue uniform and riding boots with spurs. He looks tired and bored.*

ALICE *sits in the armchair on the right, doing nothing. Looks tired and expectant.*

C. Won't you play something for me?
A. (*indifferent but not snappish*). What shall I play?
C. Whatever you want.
A. But you don't like my repertory.
C. And you don't like mine.

The play opens in a mood of apathy, not so much because Edgar and Alice are especially bored at this moment but because their married life is characterized by tedium. The opening is primarily ritual; in this respect it corresponds to the end of the play with its resigned "erase, and keep going". We feel that we are in a sense back where we started, although the situation at the end is not identical with that in the beginning.

The opening situation is remarkably static. The sea lies "*dark and calm*". Edgar and Alice are seated in their armchairs, immobile apart from his fingering his cigar. The picture presented to us before a single word has been uttered is that of two people buried alive, the tower functioning as a dome-shaped sepulchre. Strindberg does not explicitly state that the play opens with a moment of silence but the acting directions certainly suggest this. Already at this point a director can choose between a more realistic (no/short silence) and a more expressionistic/absurdistic manner of acting (long silence). The longer the silence, the more desperate Edgar's opening speech will appear—an attempt to break an unbearable stillness.

Edgar's activity indicates his extinguished passion for his wife as well as his impotence, brought about by old age and illness—compare his compensatory need to keep "*his sabre between his knees*" during the conversation between Kurt and Alice in Act II. This need is in fact visualized also in the exterior: while the fingering of the *extinguished* cigar indicates the aging man's attempt at self-stimulation, the cannons and the sabre, in the *red* sunlight, visualize the desired male potency.

Even the Captain's uniform testifies to the fact that Edgar is worn out, tired to death. His fatigue uniform, the military everyday costume, markedly contrasts with the splendid uniform by the (rear?) door, indicating the gap between the masculine façade Edgar shows to the world and the far less impressive person we meet at home, the gap between his imaginary and his true self.

Alice, who is ten years younger and still healthy, does not need to regard her life as finished; her boredom concerns the husband rather than life—as her "*expectant*" expression clarifies. What does she wait for? Edgar's death? Kurt's arrival? A new and better life? Presumably all of these things. We touch here on a fundamental problem in the play: the question whether life would have turned out differently for Edgar and Alice, had they chosen another partner.[2] Both of them react ambivalently to this question; their vacillation seems extremely recognizable.

The last speech of this segment may appear puzzling. On the surface it has to do with Edgar's musical taste, his predilection for marches etc. With regard to Alice—she has been an actress—we may also think of the world of the theatre; in that case Edgar's dislike of her repertory illustrates his later documented skepticism about her as an actress. But the words "repertory" and "play" can also be given a wider meaning: in the last instance they indicate the role-playing to which Edgar and Alice as human beings devote themselves —and their limited repertory in this respect.

From the very beginning, then, the dialogue is multilevelled: on the surface realistic, dealing with two individuals, underneath universally significant. The different shades of meaning that can be extracted from the dialogue are a result of Strindberg's suggestively vague manner of expressing himself. We need only substitute, let us say, 'play a piece of music' for "play something" to realize how easily the suggestiveness could be spoilt.

The conversation now takes a new turn:

(2) A. (*evasively*). Do you want the doors to be left open?
C. If you so wish!
A. Let them stay open then! ... (*Pause.*)

The open doors function as a stimulus to which Alice can react. Instead of having her *say* that it begins to get cool, Strindberg has her imply this. Dramaturgically, her question prepares for the imminent storm. Does Alice feel cold? Or is it out of concern for her sickly husband that she poses the question? The acting direction "*evasively*" indicates that the primary reason is that Alice wants to change the topic of conversation. She does not want to play the kind of music Edgar likes and she herself (therefore?) dislikes. But she does not want to refuse point-blank. She solves the dilemma by posing a pacifying question. Does Edgar interpret the question as a friendly gesture which he will chivalrously return? Or does he feel that Alice is hinting at his frailness? And does his insistence that she decide mean something like: an old, hardened soldier like me is not afraid of cold, but if you feel cold you are welcome to shut the doors? After which Alice makes it plain to him that she does not mind the cold either. Attempt at reconciliation or struggle for power—it is not easy to determine what is here at stake.

But since Alice, as we have seen, experiences the tower as a prison it is legitimate to see a deeper significance in her question. Ultimately, it is an appeal to Edgar for another type of married life. Edgar represents a policy of closed doors: separation from the surrounding world. Alice regards herself as a victim of this attitude. She wishes to end the isolation and establish contact with others. Edgar understands her problem but is unable to take any initiative; he lets her choose for herself. And naturally she chooses freedom.

The transition from this segment to the next is indicated by a pause in the middle of Alice's speech. Again we have a conspicuous change of topic:

(3) [A.] Why aren't you smoking?
C. Strong tobacco doesn't agree with me any more.
A. (*almost kindly*). Smoke something milder, then—since you say smoking is your only joy.
C. Joy! What is that?
A. Don't ask me. I am as ignorant as you! . . .

We here get the first hint that Edgar is no longer as healthy as he has been. The extinguished cigar suddenly gains a new significance. Has he deliberately let it go out, having been warned by the doctor against smoking? Does he feel anything around his heart? The segment points forward to the following passage:

A. Soon I have forgotten how to laugh . . .
C. (*lighting his cigar*). You must never forget that . . . life is boring enough, as it is!

If we omit segm. 3, this passage loses much of its significance; the smoking becomes irrelevant. As it is, it dramatizes the *carpe diem* mentality which characterizes Edgar at this point—while at the same time it contributes to motivate the impending stroke.

Is Alice's kindness genuine? Or is her generosity feigned, determined by her desire to promote the death of her husband? After all, she knows that smoking is bad for him.

The segment ends with an essential piece of information: both Edgar and Alice experience life as joyless. How did we suddenly arrive here? A less skillful playwright would probably have dealt with the whole of Alice's speech and let Edgar either confirm or deny the correctness of her statement. Strindberg, by contrast, has Edgar react only to the word "joy", which from his mouth becomes more pregnant than from Alice's. Note how important it is that she uses precisely the expression "your only joy" instead of, for example, 'your only pleasure'; "joy" has an elevated value lacking in 'pleasure'. Alice implies that there are different joys in life; Edgar questions the existence of joy as such.

A short pause (. . .) in the middle of Alice's speech is followed by a change of topic:

(4) [A.] Don't you want your whiskey now?
C. Not just yet.

The transition seems associative. Alice is thinking of another source of joy for Edgar: liquor. Does she want to get him into a gayer mood after his somber comment on the joylessness of life? Or does she, on the contrary, try another way of killing him, having failed with regard to smoking? Edgar is still on his guard. Whiskey is not good for weak hearts. Very soon he will forget about that—and pave the way for a stroke.

Edgar's problem is that he does not wish to reveal his true condition to his wife, and hardly to himself. Still pretending to be a man of men, he is ashamed of all symptoms of frailness. He is not willing to admit that whiskey is too strong for him. But he does postpone the drinking, and hastens to change the topic:

(5) [C.] What are we having for dinner?
A. How should I know? Ask Kristin.
C. Isn't it time for mackerel soon? It's autumn, isn't it?
A. Yes, it's autumn.
C. Outside and inside. But irrespective of the cold that comes with autumn—outside and inside—a grilled mackerel with a slice of lemon and a glass of white Burgundy is not to be disdained.
A. How eloquent!
C. Have we any Burgundy left in the wine cellar?
A. I didn't know that we had had a wine cellar for the last five years . . .
C. You never know what's what.

Not only does Edgar like to smoke a good cigar and to drink whiskey; he is also a gourmet. The picture of a materialist is successively built up.

Alice's reaction to Edgar's introductory question reveals that she leaves the housekeeping to the servants: Kristin and Jenny. When both resign, we realize how difficult the situation becomes for Alice. Their departure is not only painful in the sense that Alice must herself now perform a number of domestic duties which she considers below her standing; it also means an increasing isolation for husband and wife, a lack of safety-valve when the pressure between them becomes too strong. It is of course no coincidence that their isolation reaches a culmen shortly before Kurt's arrival; in this way their need of him becomes exceedingly urgent. The mention of Kristin forms the first link in this chain.

The choice of dish—before the existence of deepfreeze food—enables us to establish season and place. We are on the Swedish west coast, where mackerel is caught (H. Lindström, 1976, 64), not in the Stockholm archipelago, as several commentators believe. Already in the initial stage direction the reader has learned that it is autumn; the spectator does not learn of it until now. Edgar's trivial reference to the season gains a deeper meaning through Alice's echoing it. From a concrete level we are transposed to a figurative one, while at the same time a precise meaning is replaced by a vague one. Traditionally we associate autumn with withering, aging and death, and it is reasonable to assume that Alice alludes to all these conditions, all of them painful to Edgar. Her seemingly innocent philosophizing is yet another reminder of what awaits him. Edgar develops the figurative meaning but significantly lays the stress elsewhere when he states that the couple in the autumn of their life suffer from insensibility. He also returns very quickly to his culinary fantasies. The thought of wine, the need to get drunk, naturally leads to the idea of the wine cellar, the most striking example of Edgar's epicurean nature. Alice's crushing remark that they have not had a wine cellar for five years indicates economic deterioration. Edgar protests, it is true, but it is obvious that she is to be believed on this matter. There is no reason for her to lie about a situation which he knows as well as she does. Edgar's case is different. It is quite in line with his nature not to be willing to admit that for a moment he has been dreaming of the good old days. His capital mistake throws light on a fundamental trait in him: the discrepancy between fantasy and reality.

Contrary to what Edgar claims, it is Alice who is well informed. It is significant that he does not go further into the question about the wine cellar but prefers to change the topic:

(6) [C.] However, we *must* purvey for our silver wedding ...
A. Are you really going to celebrate that?
C. But of course!
A. It would be more natural to hide our misery—our twenty-five years of misery ...
C. Dear Alice, miserable it has been, but we have also had our moments of joy! And one must make use of the short time, for after that comes the end!
A. The end? I wish it were!
C. It *is* the end! Just so much as can be carted out in a wheelbarrow and put on the garden plot.
A. And so much fuss for a garden plot!
C. Yes, that's how it is; it is not of my doing.
A. So much fuss! (*Pause.*)

Note how Edgar here expresses himself as though he would have to purvey (a military term!) for the wine cellar which does not exist. In that respect the initial speech bridges the two segments. The reference to the silver wedding is important. Strindberg signficantly chooses to describe, not only a marriage in which the partners fight one another but a marriage in an utterly critical situation. On one hand Edgar's health has now become so precarious that the marriage may be dissolved at any time through his death. On the other hand it is soon time for a silver wedding. Funeral or 'wedding', that is the question.

Yet Edgar and Alice do not merely hate but also love one another. It is precisely their love-hatred which explains why they have been able to cope so long with a marriage which neither holds nor bursts. On a symbolic level, their love-hatred may be seen as an intensified image of human relations in general, as an illustration of the thesis that out of self-preservation people are doomed to torment each other and that (co)existence therefore means suffering. Edgar and Alice are to be pitied primarily because they are human beings.

Alice wants to forget about the silver wedding; she wants to conceal their life-long misery. Her way of expressing herself agrees with Edgar's view. He too wants to conceal their misery—but in quite a different manner: by denying its existence. Just as he is able to conjure up a wine cellar which does not exist, so he is able to conjure away the misery of their married life. As an officer he is anxious to show a respectable façade, a social *persona*. Hence his desire to celebrate the silver wedding. Perhaps he also sees it as an opportunity of re-establishing contacts with the environment and putting an end to their isolation; his contempt for the surrounding world seems more compensatory than real.

Dramaturgically, the segment anticipates the end of the play, where Alice agrees to celebrate the silver wedding. Her changed attitude is a result of her experience with Kurt, which strengthens Edgar's position and weakens her own. Instead of leaving the aging husband, she herself is abandoned—by a younger man. Edgar now appears to her as faithful, dependable and, despite all his shortcomings, respectable, a friend in need. Also for her, the silver wedding has become emotionally justified.

The somewhat awkward expression "the short time" points in two directions. In the first place it refers to the short time Edgar still has left; it is this time which should be embellished. Secondly, it may be seen as a reference to life; the moral would then be: be happy as long as you live.

The question whether there is a life beyond this one is of universal interest and may be raised at any time; it does not beome a *dramatic* question until it is raised by someone to whom it is urgent. Edgar's faith in annihilation presumably makes him especially anxious to go on living as long as he can. But this means that he has to refrain from all the extravagances which make life worth living. Edgar thus finds himself caught in a hopeless dilemma.

The reason we share his faith in annihilation at this moment is, however, primarily that it effectively contrasts with the faith in a life hereafter which he later embraces. 'When the Devil grows old, he becomes religious', we say. Edgar's development follows the same pattern. The stroke shocks him; with death within sight he is no longer able to cherish the idea that shortly he will be reduced to a pile of dung.

Alice's view on this matter seems as somber as could be. She believes in eternal suffering, at least as far as she herself is concerned—as though the pain of life would not be punishment enough. And she does not seem to change her mind. One gets the impression that Strindberg has focussed so much on Edgar's view of life that Alice's main task is to provide him with speeches to which he can react.

When Edgar mentions the garden plot for the first time, the implication is that in death man is reduced to something as contemptible as dung. The elliptic "just so much" (Sw. "bara så mycket") stands for 'just so much of man remains'. What is meant is: 'just so little'. In Alice's subsequent speech the expression "så mycket" returns but now as an adjunct of "fuss"; "much" now stands for 'great amount'. "So much fuss!" becomes a comment both on life in general and the married life of Edgar and Alice in particular.

Edgar's juxtaposition of man ("dung") and "garden plot" is concrete and naturalistic, while Alice's combination of "fuss" and "garden plot" is drastically metaphoric. (The figurative "fuss" contaminates, as it were, the garden plot so that this too can be understood figuratively.) That man is reduced to dung (Edgar's speech) is sad enough; that this happens after a painful life (Alice's speech) is even sadder. While Edgar's garden plot is still relatively neutral, Alice's is reduced to something extremely petty, through the expression "so much fuss". The very way in which Edgar expresses himself at this point indicates that he accepts the idea of annihilation more easily than Alice.

When Edgar, in the following speech, declares that "it [the garden plot] is not of my doing", he implies that the Creator does not know how to care for his garden (the world) and that he, Edgar, could have managed much better.[3] Edgar's faith in his own strength knows no limits; his hubris is of Promethean size.

As we have seen, the word "garden plot" undergoes a tremendous semantical expansion through merely three speeches; as usual Strindberg has the power to bring us very swiftly from a concrete to a metaphoric level.

After a pause, which facilitates the transition, we move from the speculations on life and death to more trivial cares:

(7) [A.] Has the mail come?
C. Yes.
A. Was the butcher's bill there?
C. Yes.
A. How much was it?
C. (*takes a sheet of paper from his pocket, puts on his spectacles but soon takes them off again*). You read what it says! I can't see any more ...
A. What's the matter with your eyes?
C. Don't know.
A. Old age.
C. Nonsense! I!
A. Yes, not I!
C. H'm.
A. (*looks at the bill*). Will you be able to pay this?
C. Yes, but not now!
A. Later, in other words! In a year when you have retired on a small pension and it is too late! Later, when the illness comes back ...
C. Illness? I have never been ill, only a bit indisposed once. And I have twenty years yet to go!
A. The doctor had a different opinion.
C. The doctor!
A. Yes, who else could have a trustworthy opinion of your illness?

C. I have no illness, and have never had one. Nor shall I ever have one. I shall drop dead like an old soldier!

The transition from segm. 6 to 7 is difficult to account for. Alice has no obvious reason to change the topic. And it seems surprising that she has not earlier in the day asked for the post.

The chief function of the bill is apparently that of turning the conversation to the distressing economic situation; once we are familiar with this situation, we can see that Edgar's boast to Kurt that "money has been rolling in" is a contribution to the picture of Edgar as a dreamer. By having Edgar not only mention but actually present the bill, Strindberg can inform us of his impaired eyesight, a sign of his aging. And by having Alice express her surprise, the playwright in addition clarifies that the deterioration is of a very recent date. A flaw it is, however, when Edgar declares that he can pay the bill, although he has never learned how large it is.

When the conversation turns to the topic of aging the speeches become short, duel-like. The sense of rivalry comes to the fore. Alice is swift to start the attack. Edgar parries with a haughty "Nonsense! I!". We then get Alice's interesting reaction "Yes, not I!"—a sign of her hypersensitiveness in this matter. After all, Edgar has never blamed her for being old. But his emphatic "I!" (i.e. 'not I') implies to her a blame which she must refute.

Note, by the way, how Alice also in the speech concerning the pension continues to remind Edgar of his age—while at the same time informing us indirectly that he is 64 (provided he retire at 65) and she 54. The idea that Edgar could postpone payment of the bill a whole year seems absurd; Alice exaggerates out of a desire to tease her husband. Nor is it easy to see what the illness has to do with the paying of the bill; possibly Alice is here thinking aloud: the debt had better be paid as soon as possible—while Edgar is still alive.

But Edgar does not want to recognize that he is ill; he prefers to talk about indisposition, although a doctor has obviously been consulted. From Alice's remark we understand that the doctor regards the illness as rather serious, and it is natural to see Edgar's moderation with regard to tobacco and alcohol as a result of the doctor's advice. Edgar's dismissal of the doctor's advice is another example of his faith in his "own strength", another sign of his hubris.

Once introduced the doctor can be further utilized:

(8) A. Speaking of the doctor! You know that he is giving a party this evening.
C. (*agitated*). Well, what of it! We are not invited because we are not on intimate terms with him and his wife, and we are not intimate with them because we don't want to, because I despise both of them. They are riff-raff!
A. You say that of everybody!
C. Because everybody is riff-raff!
A. Except you!

C. Yes, for in all conditions of life I have behaved decently. That's why I am no riff-raff! (*Pause.*)

Edgar's reaction at this point is interesting. His domination over Alice is subtly reflected in the revealing change from "we" to "I". What Edgar has to say about the doctor and his wife may seem reasonable enough. But if it is true that he and Alice are so disinterested, why is Edgar so agitated at the fact that they have not been invited to the party? There is a discrepancy between the Captain's explanation and the manner in which it is delivered. The result is that we distrust what he says. It is even possible to see his variant as an inversion of the true situation, as a plagiarism of the doctor's thoughts about him and Alice: "I despise both of them".

Another interpretation is also quite possible. Socially, the doctor ranks high. Edgar, who is sensitive to outer status, is hurt that he has not been invited—although he dislikes the doctor as a person or perhaps rather as someone he is presently dependent on; Edgar very much fears to be indebted to anyone.

However, the contemptuous characterization of the doctor and his wife immediately becomes invalid when Edgar declares that everybody except himself is riff-raff. The conclusion must be that he cannot be on intimate terms with anyone, and this is precisely the purpose of his misanthropic, conceited statement. Edgar cannot accept the idea that he is rejected by others. So he reshapes reality to suit his needs. The isolation is easier to accept if it is experienced as self-inflicted.

The pause after Edgar's statement about his own excellence indicates that Alice is silent—without agreeing. She just does not wish to protest against such fundamental illusions. Instead she suggests:

(9a) A. Would you like to play cards?
C. All right!
A. (*takes a deck of cards from the drawer of the sewing table and begins to shuffle*).

(10a) [A.] Imagine, the doctor is allowed to have the garrison band for his private party!
C. (*angrily*). That's because he fawns on the colonel in town! Fawns, mind you!—If I could only do that!

(9b) A. (*dealing*).

(10b) [A.] Gerda and I were friends once, but she cheated me ...
C. They are all false! ...

(9c) [C.] What's your trumps over there?
A. Put on your spectacles!
C. They're no help! ... Well, well!
A. Spades are trumps.
C. (*displeased*). Spades? ...
A. (*playing a card*).

(10c) [A.] Maybe so, but as far as the wives of the new officers are concerned we are dropped in any case.

(9d) C. (*plays a card and takes a trick*).

(10d) [C.] What does it matter? We never give parties anyhow, so nobody will notice anything. I can stand being alone ... I always was.
A. So can I. But the children! The children grow up without company.
C. Let them find it for themselves in town! ...

(9e) [C.] That's my trick! Have you another trump?
A. I have one left! This trick is mine.
C. Six and eight makes fifteen ...
A. Fourteen, fourteen!
C. Six and eight gives me fourteen ... I think I have forgotten how to count too! And two makes sixteen ...

(11a) [C.] (*yawning*).

(9f) [C.] It's your turn to deal.

(11b) A. You're tired!

(9g) C. (*dealing*).

(11c) [C.] Not at all!

In segm. 10 the problems with the environment are dealt with. Via the music from the doctor's house, which Alice seems to hear already at this point, Edgar informs us that the doctor has secured certain benefits by flattering the colonel. Friendship with superiors Edgar regards as a sign of ingratiation. His view is of course determined by the fact that he himself is at cross purposes with the colonel: he has never been promoted to major. This does not necessarily mean that Edgar's view is incorrect; true or not—we cannot tell—it expresses a disillusioned view of man: this is the way people behave.

It is in this context interesting to note that the doctor later, when Kurt approaches him, appears to be "very friendly" and immediately prepared to come to Edgar's sick-bed. Here as elsewhere Strindberg puts Edgar's negative view of his fellows to shame to indicate his egocentric inability to see them as they are.[4] Eventually Edgar's faith in his own strength is replaced by the realization that we all, as Kurt puts it, need indulgence. At the end of the play Edgar in fact arrives at the conception of life embraced by Kurt.[5]

Does Alice share her husband's negative view of mankind? The expression "maybe so" *can* be interpreted in this way. But it may also be seen as a pacifying gesture which does not say very much about Alice's own view of the matter. Unlike Edgar, she wants to keep in touch with the environment—for the sake of the children, she *says*; perhaps mostly for her own sake.

Their attitude to others can be evaluated in different ways. Edgar's may be considered consistent and upright, the misanthropist's preference of loneliness above false company. But it can also be seen as stubborn or even cowardly: the Captain does not dare to associate with others since his infatuation with himself is then always put to shame; and as for the consistency, we may ask ourselves how his unwillingness to run parties rhymes with his wish to celebrate the silver wedding.

Similarly, Alice's attitude can be viewed as vacillating and compromising or else as human and indulgent. How we interpret it to a great extent depends on what significance we ascribe to the expression "maybe so". It is in this context important to note that she does not, like Edgar, consider herself an exceptional person; there is a fundamental difference between the statement 'everybody is riff-raff' and the statement 'everybody is riff-raff—except me'. *If* Alice includes herself among imperfect mankind, there is no need for her not to mix with others. Alice, we may conclude, holds a somewhat vague position between Edgar's view (isolation, misanthropy) and that of Kurt (contact, indulgence).

We may now ask ourselves what the function of segm. 9 is. On a trivial, yet essential level the game of cards means a form of stage business, of importance both to the actors (need for activity) and the audience (need for variation). The reason Strindberg settles for a game of cards may have to do with the fact that this is an activity which connotes a lack of activity in a deeper sense. That the game is above all a pastime, a way of passing the time when one is bored, appears not the least from the fact that it is introduced when other pastimes (smoking, drinking, eating) have proved unsuitable. The game of cards is a substitute. Edgar's "allright" is hardly enthusiastic. In this sense the card-game emphasizes the matrimonial tedium.[6]

It may seem as though the game establishes a kind of contact between the partners: they play *with* one another—just as they talk *to* each other. In this respect the game contrasts with the "*solitaire*" which Edgar devotes himself to at the beginning of Act IV, after Alice has left him for Kurt.

A more penetrating interpretation, I think, is to regard the game of cards as a sign of the lack of contact between Alice and Edgar. It is with a feeling of resignation—after all attempts to establish contact in any deeper sense have failed—that they grab for the cards. The conversation accompanying the playing is rather impersonal and can therefore have a neutralizing effect. An even more obvious interpretation in a Strindberg play is to regard the game as a symbol of the struggle for power: after all, the two play *against* one another—just as they contradict each other more than they agree with each other. The game is in other words the counterpart of the verbal duel at the beginning of the play. Its figurative significance is underlined by Alice's statement that she has always played with open cards, as well as by Edgar's comment on Kurt shortly before he appears: "I won't give him a peek at my cards". The game of cards is here, clearly, a metaphor of the struggle for power between two people.

With such an interpretation it is of significance to note who wins the game.

Edgar is displeased when he learns that spades are trumps and one gets the impression that he loses the first game, but who is later the winner remains unclear. Compare this to the struggle for power that is fought between Edgar and Alice throughout the play. Here again Edgar looses the first 'game', when it appears that his health is precarious and when Alice succeeds in stealing Kurt from him. She now has the trumps in her hand. But in the next 'game' Alice loses, when Kurt leaves her. At the end it is clear that nobody has won and nobody has lost, that the game so to speak will continue until one of them will prove too "tired" for it.

The game of cards, we can now see, is a symbol of (married) life, as appears from Alice's words about playing with open cards, i.e. living an honest life; while cheating at the game corresponds to treacherous or hypocritical behavior. Seen in this symbolic perspective Edgar's displeasure with spades may be regarded as an allusion to the power the black color has over him, the triumph of death. Very shortly his life is characterized by his struggle against death; in this 'game' Alice has death on her side, as a card of trumps; Edgar's death means victory for Alice.

A special problem is Edgar's miscalculation. What does it mean? Is it merely another reminder of his senility, an indication of the fatigue he still tries to conceal but soon will be forced to admit? Is it a hint that he is a cheat, someone who wants to get more than he deserves (cf. his hubris)? The passage does not reveal its full significance until it is combined with the following one from Act IV (K = Kurt):

C. What meaning is there to all this medley [life]?
K. In my better moments I have believed its meaning to be that we were not to know the meaning and yet be submissive . . .
C. Be submissive! Without a fixed point outside myself I can't be submissive.
K. Quite correct. But you, as a mathematician, ought to be able to find that unknown point, when you have several given ones . . .
C. I have searched for it, and—I haven't found it.
K. Then you have made some miscalculation, start all over again!
C. I will.

When Edgar counts in his own favor at the game of cards, it corresponds to his inclination to make absurd demands on life and his fellows. When he later counts correctly, to his own disadvantage, it corresponds to the repentance he undergoes at the end of the play, when he lowers his demands and learns to accept the rules of life in the conviction that they are meaningful. In a way the whole play in this figurative sense demonstrates how Edgar learns to count; this lesson is laconically anticipated in the counting of the cards.

The music from the doctor's house which verbally—perhaps also acoustically (for Alice)—has already been introduced, now functions as an outside stimulus motivating a change of topic:

(12) A. (*listening outwards*). You can hear the music all the way here! (*Pause.*)

This exceedingly short segment has two functions. First, the idea of music is kept alive in the imagination of the audience; it will return more extensively in segm. 17. Second, it introduces Kurt in the conversation via the associative chain 'music (stimulus) – the doctor's party – guests':

(13) [A.] Do you think Kurt is invited?
C. He arrived this morning, so he should have had time to unpack his tails, although he hasn't had time to call on us!
A. Quarantine master? Is there to be a quarantine station here?
C. Yes! ...
A. He is, after all, my cousin, and I once had the same name as him ...
C. That was certainly no honor ...
A. Now listen ... (*Sharply.*) You leave my family alone if you wish me to leave yours alone!
C. Now, now! Are we going to start that all over again!

So far the exposition has been a rather inconspicuous part of the dialogue; now it becomes more obvious. The difference is due to the fact that at the beginning Edgar and Alice talk either about themselves or about people they are presently in touch with, however imperfectly. Kurt, by contrast, is a person they have earlier known quite well but whom they have not seen for years: a traditional expository figure. It is rather natural that they recapitulate various matters previous to the expected visit.

But how do they do it? Let us consider Edgar's first speech and the problem the playwright was faced with here. The audience must get to know in a short time that Kurt has just arrived on the island; for this explains why Edgar is soon to inform him about the local situation. But at the same time Edgar and Alice must be aware of Kurt's arrival and any information about it would disturb our sense of plausibility. Strindberg tries to solve the difficulty by having Edgar present this piece of information in the form of a sarcasm: although Kurt has spent a whole day on the island, he has not had sense enough to visit his relatives yet. By choosing for this temperamental reaction Strindberg not only tells us that Kurt has just arrived; he also indicates that Edgar makes certain claims on him, and that Kurt hardly pines to see his relatives—for reasons which will be clarified later. Yet the speech is not altogether natural; Strindberg does not completely manage to obliterate the impression that the information is meant more for the audience than for Alice.

Kurt's occupation slips in rather naturally. That he is a quarantine master is of course no accident. As such he will be a subordinate to the doctor, that is, he will have a tricky intermediate position between him and the relatives. But the occupation is also of symbolic significance. Kurt's task is to see to it that the internees are freed from their contagion so that they do not represent any danger to their environment when they return to a normal life. This is applicable to Edgar and Alice. Isolated from the surrounding world they figuratively find themselves in quarantine, contaminated by self-sufficiency and misanthropy. Kurt's visit signifies a purification. As we have already noted, Edgar is converted to Kurt's faith in the meaning of life despite everything, and in the need to accept and forgive. The basis for a contact with the surrounding world has been laid. Also with regard to Alice we may speak of an inner change. The quarantine master has cured them.

Alice's remark that Kurt is her cousin indicates, the way it is phrased, her need to ally herself with him; the reference to her maiden name testifies to her contempt for the name she now carries, i.e. for her marriage. The implication is: 'once I had a respectable name'. No wonder that Edgar reacts with his "that was certainly no honor". The indirect accusation against Edgar is thus met by an indirect accusation against Kurt: "honor" points forward to Kurt's lack of honor in the next segment. Similarly the designation "cousin" suggests a link with the cousin of the von Krafft family who "committed a crime" so that "the family name was disgraced". Parallels like these support Edgar's conviction that "the life is the same for everyone". In this way the playwright pounds home the idea that Edgar's and Alice's situation is paradigmatic.

At the end of the segment Edgar notes that they have "again" entered the area of family quarrel. None of them wants, however, to continue this meaningless discussion. We get a pacifying change of topic:

(14) A. Is the quarantine master a physician?
C. No, he is merely a sort of civilian administrator or book-keeper, and Kurt never really got anywhere!
A. He was a weakling . . .
C. Who has cost me a good deal of money . . . And when he abandoned his wife and children, he became a dishonorable man!
A. Not quite so severe, Edgar!
C. Yes, he was! . . . What has he been doing in America since then? Well, I can't say I long for him! But it was an agreeable boy and I liked to argue with him!
A. Because he would always yield to you . . .
C. (*haughtily*). Yielding or not, he was at any rate someone you could talk to . . . Here on this island there is not a single person, who knows what I am talking about . . . it's a collection of idiots . . .

The presentation of Kurt continues but it should be noted that the exposition is partly misleading: it is not Kurt who has left his family but, as we later learn, the family which has left him, in connection with Edgar's suspect interests in his wife. The false exposition contributes to the characterization of Edgar: again he stands out as a man who tries to liberate himself from his pangs of conscience by reshaping the past. His own crime is projected onto someone else. Kurt, who really deserves the designation "agreeable boy", functions as scapegoat. However, this procedure has the effect that in segm.

14 we are momentarily inclined to take sides against Kurt, since at this point we accept Edgar's version. It is part of the basic conception of the play that we initially tend to identify ourselves with Edgar only to discover later that he is far less likeable than we had assumed. But as soon as we have discovered this, Edgar is ready to be converted. In this way he never actually appears to be an altogether dislikable person.

Why, then, does Alice not protest against Edgar's history-writing? The reason is not that she is in good faith—as we are. She obviously finds it senseless to confront Edgar with the truth. If Kurt is "a weakling" in her eyes, it is because he has let himself be manipulated by Edgar.

When the Captain shows a tendency to repeat the old complaint about the world, Alice interrupts him and switches the subject back to Kurt:

(15) A. It's strange that Kurt should arrive here just at the time of our silver wedding ... whether we celebrate it or not ...
C. Why is that so strange? ... Oh yes, it was he who brought us together, or married you off, as it was said!
A. Well, didn't he?
C. Yes, he did! ... It was one of those ideas of his ... it's up to you to judge that!
A. A frivolous idea ...
C. For which *we* have had to suffer, not *he*!
A. Yes, just imagine, if I had remained in the theatre! All of my women friends are now stars.

We here have a new case of false exposition. The truth is that Edgar has asked Kurt to act as marriage agent but Kurt, considering Alice an unsuitable wife for Edgar, has refused. Again the Captain reverses the situation, and for the same reason. The idea that he himself is responsible for his (sad) fate is too hard; by laying the blame on someone else, he appears in his own eyes as the offended one. Yet the role of a martyr does not agree very well with that of a man of men which he also wants to play. It is therefore significant that Edgar uses the expression "married you off" instead of the less flattering, but more truthful, 'married me off'; it is the wife's unoriginality, not his own, that he wishes to emphasize.

The addition "as it was said" makes Kurt's role somewhat unclear. It may be more gossip than reality. But Alice does not oppose the idea. She too seems in need of a scapegoat.

Edgar's speculations about the conjugal misery causes Alice to think of what the alternative for her as unmarried woman—or married to someone else—would have been like. Spelled out, the final speech of the segment means: 'I could have been a star if I hadn't married you.' This is a variation of the scapegoat pattern; it does not concern personal guilt projected onto someone else; it concerns personal success thwarted by someone else.

Faced with this indirect attack, the Captain has every reason to shift the topic of conversation—especially since he undoubtedly knows Alice's dreams of success by heart and finds it difficult to cope with what strikingly resembles his own megalomanic fantasies. We thus get a new segment:

(16) C. (*rising*). Well, well, well . . . Now I'll have my glass of grog! (*Goes to the cabinet and mixes himself a grog, which he drinks standing.*) We ought to have a rail here to put one's foot on, so that one could imagine oneself in Copenhagen, at the American Bar.
A. We'll have one made, just to remind us of Copenhagen. After all, we had our best moments there!
C. (*drinking heavily*). Yes! Do you remember Nimb's *navarin aux pommes*! Wow!
A. No, but I remember the concerts at the Tivoli!
C. You have such a superior taste!
A. That ought to please you, having a wife with good taste!
C. It does . . .
A. Sometimes, when you feel the need to boast about her . . .

Edgar is now ripe for the whiskey alluded to already in segm. 4. The boredom has become too much for him. Note how his drinking is dramatized. Instead of having him remain in his chair, dreaming of the American Bar, Strindberg moves him to the cabinet, which now due to his position ("*drinks standing*") and comment ("a rail") visualizes the bar of the Copenhagen pub. The connection is further strengthened by the acting direction "*drinking heavily*": such tests of virility we associate with bars; as Edgar later points out: "I want to drink immeasurably, or not at all! A guy should be able to stand up to a tumbler!" (Naturally, the violent drinking has been included also to motivate the imminent stroke.) By visualizing Edgar's dream in this way, the passage not only becomes dramatically effective: Edgar appears far more obsessed by his dream than would have been the case, had it merely been verbalized. The little 'dream' section also becomes a concrete example of Edgar's power to reshape reality.

But why *American* Bar? The name should be combined with the following speeches:

C. /—/ Have you ever been to Copenhagen?
K. (*smiling*). No, I've mostly been in America . . .

Here Kurt with his worldly experience is contrasted with the provincial Edgar who has never been further abroad than Copenhagen and who now, adopting his usual method of inversion, wants to give Kurt the impression that Copenhagen equals the world. His visits to the American Bar in this context seem significant. Pitted against Kurt who has really been to America we find Edgar who has merely dreamt of being there. Opposed to the man of the world, experienced in life, we have the insular man, isolated, prejudiced.

If Copenhagen represents the little world, it also signifies the short moments of happiness the couple have had in the past. Yet even then it has hardly been a *shared* happiness. He has enjoyed the food at Nimb, she the music next door.

A sharp remark from Alice, the significance of which is that he makes use of her more refined taste for his own purposes instead of simply appreciating it, causes the Captain to change the subject:

(17) C. (*drinking*). They must be dancing over at the doctor's . . . I can hear the three-four time of the brass tubas—boom—boom—boom!
A. I can hear the strains of the *Alcazar Waltz*, from beginning to end. Well— it wasn't yesterday I was waltzing . . .
C. Would you still manage that?
A. Still?
C. Yes? You're out of the dance, aren't you, you as well as me?
A. I am ten years younger than you, remember!
C. Then we are both the same age, since the lady should be ten years younger!
A. Shame on you! You're an old man; but I am in my best years!
C. Oh yes, of course, you can be very charming—to others, when you put yourself to it.

The music at the doctor's now functions as a stimulus for Edgar; as a military person he especially notes the tubas and the rhythm. Alice, by contrast, being more musical, listens to the melody, which she can also identify. The title is significant. 'Alcazar' is in Spain the name for castles which are not only, or even primarily, built for the purpose of defense; the word comes from Arabic *Al-kasr*, meaning 'the castle'. Is it not precisely such a castle (marriage, life) Edgar and Alice dream of—instead of the prison cave they have landed in? A light, growing castle, to speak with the author of *A Dream Play*.

Alice's remark that she has not waltzed for a long time is a disguised reproach against the husband. The blow is immediately met by a counterblow: Alice is too old to dance. The expression "out of the dance" stresses the symbolic aspect of the dancing, and we may in this context note how the mobility at the doctor's contrasts with the immobility inside the fortress tower. It is life as opposed to death.

Edgar is impressed by the music. To the tunes of 'The Entry of the Boyars' he is soon to try a few dance steps in a vain attempt to demonstrate his preserved vigor. It now appears that he is the one who does not manage. Once the stroke hits him the dance, meant to be a manifestation of strength (of life), becomes a *danse macabre*, a dance of death.[7] Edgar is finally punished for his hubris and his unwillingness to face the truth. As in Holbein's engravings, we deal with a human being dancing with Death without really knowing it. In this new situation the expression 'out of the dance' becomes synonymous with 'being dead'. The meaning of the expression, in other words, changes from a stress on the life component (the dance) to an emphasis of the death aspect (out of the dance). When Alice uses the expression—in answer to Edgar's earlier reproach—it significantly occurs between the doctor's dance of life and Edgar's dance of death:

C. /—/ Shall I dance for you?
A. No, thanks! You are out of the dance, aren't you?

Here both meanings are relevant.

In the final speech of this Beckettian segment with its semi-reluctant acknowledgement that the wife may flourish together with other men, Alice's situation is summarized, while at the same time her seduction of Kurt is prepared for. If Alice manages to seduce Kurt, who is younger than her, she provides a proof that she is not "out of the dance". In the last instance the seemingly petty bickering about ages and aging concerns the measure of life; it is an expression of the intense longing to count among those who are fully alive; a longing which, under the circumstances, has been perverted into a comparative formula of self-defense: 'I am more alive than you are.'

When Alice changes the topic after Edgar's reference to her charm, it may be because she finds the insinuation that she has been unfaithful disagreeable and does not wish to continue the talk along those lines. But the primary reason is an outside stimulus: it has grown dark. The last segment of the opening sequence reads:

(18) A. May we light the lamp now?
C. Very well.
A. Ring then!
C. (*walks sluggishly to the writing table and rings*).

Dramaturgically, Alice's question is inserted to motivate Jenny's entrance. Is Alice interested in the lighting of the lamp? Or is the suggestion only a pretext to terminate a situation which she finds increasingly unbearable? In the last case Jenny's entrance may be seen as a counterpart of Kurt's—just as her departure may be said to prepare for his.

Why does Strindberg not simply have Alice ring for Jenny? Why does she first ask Edgar for permission and then admonish him to ring? The reason, I believe, is primarily structural. The way the final segment is shaped, it completely corresponds to the speeches in segm. 2. A question, an endorsement, an admonition—here as there. This formal correspondence underlines the fact that the sequence is rounded off, has reached its conclusion. We have returned to the mood of the opening situation. The circle composition of the sequence corresponds to that of the whole play; here too, as has often been pointed out, we return at the end more or less to the initial situation.

In order to be able to study the structure of the opening sequence of *The Dance of Death I* in a practical way, I have broken it up into smaller units—

'segments'—whose content, form and function I have analyzed; in addition I have paid some attention to the transition from one segment to another.

A further characteristic of my analysis is that instead of allowing one interpretation at a time to prevail (the directing method), I have tried to stress the multiplicity of the text.

While a segmentation emphasizes the disjunctive components on the surface level, a thematic analysis favors the underlying, conjunctive factors. A simple scheme may clarify the situation:

surface level visually/verbally/acoustically shaped 'topics' (segmentation)	1	2	3	4	5	6	7	8	9	10
depth level the meaning of the 'topics' (thematic structure)	a	b	a	a	b	c	a	a	c	b

While the topics constantly change, their meaning can be reduced to a few, recurrent themes. Thus, in our example five segments are linked through theme a, three through b and two through c. One of the most urgent tasks of a playwright is the endeavor to make the topics thematically related and meaningful; if he does not succeed in doing this, the drama becomes superficial and incoherent.

A segmentational transition (a shift of topic) can have various causes; in the present case we may distinguish between the following:

Segm.		*Transition/cause*
A		
	———	outer composition
B		
	———	outer composition
1		
	———	stimulus, need
2		
	———	stimulus, need
3		
	———	need, association
4		
	———	need
5		
	———	need
6		
	———	chance
7		
	———	association
8		
	———	need
9		
	———	stimulus
10		
	———	stimulus
11		
	———	stimulus
12		
	———	stimulus
13		
	———	need
14		
	———	need
15		
	———	need
16		
	———	stimulus, need
17		
	———	stimulus, need

Basic for the division is the assumption that every segment has a specific place in the totality, determined by its function in this totality. This means that two segments, even if they are verbally identical, receive different designations. A special case—let us term it 'stratification'—we find in segm. 9–11. These three segments, dealing with card-game (9), company (10) and tiredness (11), could, as we have seen, be divided into 'subsegments': 9a, 10a, 9b, 10b, etc. Here the topical unity has been too strong to motivate a division into segments.

The three segments are, however, not of equal importance: while segm. 9 (and 11) could be omitted without affecting the play structure in any vital sense, segm. 10 could not be eliminated. This does not mean that segm. 9 and 11 are superfluous; on the symbolic level they have a function. But it is evident that they are not structurally as integrated as segm. 10.

What, then, is the relationship between the game of cards (segm. 9) and the dialogue (segm. 10–11) with which it is intertwined? Hardly any at all. At most one might argue that just as the card-game is at once a game with and against someone, so the association with others, dealt with in the dialogue, is determined by certain rules of etiquette (how to 'play' *with* others); beneath the polished surface the struggle for power goes on (playing *against* others). But this comparison is very general and indirect. The spontaneous impression is rather that there is a lack of congruence between the stratified segments. This may seem a serious structural flaw, and it could indeed be claimed, on the basis of Jansen's "relation de sélection", that segm. 9 is not well integrated in the play; yet at closer inspection it will be seen to connect with later segments in the play—it is highly preparatory—and, on the symbolic level, with the action as a whole.

Of the five different causes motivating a shift of segment, four may be considered genuine causes, since we deal here with changes of topic. Of a different nature are the two initial transitions, which are formal shifts, in A a change from drama-related to act-related stage directions, in B a change from act-related stage directions to sequence-related acting directions. The designations A and B indicate the special nature of these two segments; unlike all other segments in the sequence, B is related to all segments within the act, A to all segments within the play.

It is, however, the four transitions proper, all related directly to the characters, which deserve our attention in a structural analysis. Easiest to motivate are those transitions which are determined by outside stimuli. The cool air from the open doors (segm. 1–2), an extinguished cigar (segm. 2–3), the tunes from a band (segm. 9–10, 11–12, 16–17), a yawn (segm. 9–11), the growing twilight (segm. 17–18)—all these sensuous impressions influence the characters and result in comments (topical shifts) on their part.

It is true that the extensive descriptions of scenery and properties that we meet in realistic drama are expressions of the attempt to create the illusion of reality. But almost as important is probably the fact that the characters in this way are provided with a number of stimuli to which they can react. When the complete action takes place in one and the same room—as in *The Dance of Death I*—these stimuli must somehow be integrated in the stage setting. Result: detailed stage directions. Note, however, that all the stimuli listed are *incidental*; it is precisely for this reason that the characters react to them.

A topical shift can also be determined by an association. Suddenly a character comes to think of something which somehow relates to the topic at hand. Thus Alice in segm. 8 turns back to something that has been mentioned before, and in segm. 13 the doctor's party makes her think of Kurt who has presumably been invited to it.

Most frequent is the 'need' type of transition, i.e. a character's conscious or unconscious need to change the topic of conversation. The high frequency of this type illustrates the couple's attempts to disguise their own weaknesses. While Alice is responsible for seven transitions of this type (against four for Edgar) it does not, however, necessarily mean that she is more defensive than he is. Her shifts seem in fact often caused by a desire to spare him, be it more out of self-protection than altruism.

In all these cases we deal with motivated transitions: the segments succeed each other logically or plausibly. When this is not the case we have a transition by chance (segm. 6–7). There is no obvious reason for Alice to change the subject at this point. The transition forms a weak link in the structure of the sequence.

By their content the segments can be related to one another either plotwise or thematically. A plot-relation is an 'extrinsic' connection between (at least) two text elements, a thematic relation is an 'intrinsic' one. It is of course not always easy to distinguish clearly between the two.

With regard to the plot, we may further distinguish between 'prospective', 'retrospective' and 'simultaneous' relations (Van der Kun, *passim*). In a simultaneous relation the components are found together. But in the other two cases we must distinguish between the referring (prospective or retrospective) component and the component referred to (R-component); in retrospective relations the latter is found in previous parts of the play, in prospective relations in subsequent parts. To put it differently: while the prospective component precedes the R-component, the retrospective component succeeds it.

Retrospective relations can further be divided into two types, those in which the R-component is found in the 'prescenic' action (exposition) and those in which it is found in the 'scenic' action. A component may well be at once retrospective and prospective.

As an example of one of the few simultaneous relations in the sequence we may consider the artilleryman on sentry duty, whose sabre "*now and then*" reflects the setting sun. To the *reader* the simultaneity is negligible: few would think of the fact that the Sentry can be seen off and on during the conversation between Edgar and Alice. To the *spectator* this is of course quite obvious, and a director can utilize the simultaneous aspect very effectively by having the Sentry turn up at strategic moments, e.g. when Edgar points out that as "an old soldier" he will "drop dead" at once.

The retrospective components are rather unevenly distributed over the different segments, as will appear from the following, relatively complete list:

3	C has been able to smoke strong tobacco.
5	They have had a wine cellar five years earlier.
6	A and C have spent 25 years together in a miserable marriage.
7	The butcher's bill has arrived.
	C "has never been ill" but has been indisposed once.
	The doctor has diagnosed C unfavorably.
10	A has been friendly with Gerda.
	C has always been lonely.
13	K has arrived "this morning" but has not paid a visit yet.
14	K has left wife and children and gone to America.
15	K has married A off to C.
	A has been an actress.
16	A and C have been in Copenhagen many years ago, he at the American Bar, she at concerts.
17	A has sometimes been "charming" towards other men.

In all these retrospective statements—indicated by the use of the perfect tense—we deal with situations or events which belong to the prescenic action. Sometimes it concerns matters which are still relevant: the marriage is as miserable as it has always been—or worse; Edgar is still as lonely as ever—or more. But often the statements imply a contrast between then and now: they have had a wine cellar—but do not have it any more; Alice has been an actress—but is one no longer.

Unlike the retrospective components, whose order is determined by the plot, the R-components, which are related to the story of the play, should be chronologically ordered. In some cases the time is indicated:

More than 25 years earlier	K marries off A.
Nearly 25 years earlier	C and A marry.
5 years earlier	The wine cellar is empty.
The same morning	K arrives on the island.
	The butcher's bill is received.

In other cases we can only guess at the period or time by combining different statements. Thus we may safely conclude that it is about 25 years since Alice was an actress and that Kurt's divorce has taken place many years ago.

A look at the list of retrospective components gives us the impression that the sequence, as far as these are concerned, is rather firmly constructed. First the picture of Edgar's and Alice's somber matrimonial situation is drawn; then Kurt is made responsible for this situation; finally we learn that the two have had their happy moments in the past—but hardly together.

Much more frequent—as could be expected in a play opening—are the prospective components, e.g. (page references right):

A telegraph apparatus = the telegraph apparatus starts clicking (22)
B the sea is calm ~ the wind is blowing (34)
1 extinguished cigar ~ C lights his cigar (21)
2 the doors are open ~ C closes the doors (34)
3 C cannot stand strong tobacco ~ C lights his cigar (21)
4 C does not want his whiskey ~ C is drinking grog (16)
5 Kristin is cooking ~ Kristin is not cooking: has left (20, 25)
6 A does not wish to celebrate the silver wedding ~ A agrees to celebrate the silver wedding (122)
7 C "has never been ill" ~ C suffers a stroke (51)[8]
C will "drop dead" ~ C lives at the end of the play (122)
8 "everybody is riff-raff" ~ some people are not riff-raff (77)
9 A takes out a deck of cards ~ C throws the cards out of the window (101)
10 the children live in town = Judith's telegram (22)
11 C is not tired ~ C is tired (21)
12 music = dance music (17)
13 K has arrived on island = K enters (26)
14 K "left wife and children" ~ C deprived K of the children (83)
15 K married A off ~ K refused to marry A off (44)
16 C is drinking = C suffers a stroke (51)
C does not dance ~ C dances (51)
C not "out of the dance" ~ C out of the dance (51)
18 C "*walks sluggishly*" = C does not manage to dance (51)

The list clearly demonstrates how functional the segments are from a prospective point of view. As appears from the list we deal with two types of statements. Sometimes (=) the R-component (to the right) signifies a confirmation of the prospective statement, more often (~) an abnegation of it. In the former case we may speak of *true*, in the latter of *false* preparation. Though dramaturgically necessary, true preparation is usually trivial.

Much more interesting is the false preparation. We here deal with some kind of surprise, usually—but not always—with regard to the characters. Often they express views or perform actions which we had not expected from earlier statements (cf. segm. 6, 7, 8). Such changes are especially relevant when they concern a central part of the plot, as in the case of the silver wedding. We may here speak of a true change inside one of the characters. In other cases (segm. 14, 15) the surprise stems from the fact that a truth, later made manifest, has been withheld from us. We here deal with ostensible changes, amounting to a (negative) revaluation of the character who is responsible for the false statement. (In principle, we must assume that the pronouncement made in the R-component is more truthful than the prospective one.) It is interesting to see how Strindberg in Edgar's case combines the two types: at the same time as he changes for the better, his earlier duplicity is revealed to us. The discovery of the truth counteracts our sympathy for Edgar's development. Even at the end of the play we regard him with mixed feelings.

Thematically, too, the segments of course often relate to parts outside the sequence. However, we shall limit ourselves to a (selective) list illustrating the thematic relations *within* the sequence:

Segm.	*Surface level (topics)*	*Depth level (themes)*
A	fortress	imprisonment, life
	sea	freedom, death, sexuality
	battery	sexuality
B	Sentry	imprisonment
	dark, calm sea	aging, death, sexuality
	autumn	aging, death
1	extinguished cigar	materialism, sexuality, sickness
	playing the piano	life, art
2	open/closed doors	freedom, imprisonment
3	strong tobacco	materialism, sickness
4	whiskey	materialism, sickness
5	mackerel	materialism
	autumn	aging, death
	Burgundy	materialism, sickness
6	silver wedding	intercourse
	short time	life, aging
	garden plot	death
7	eyes	aging, sickness
	old age	aging
	sickness	sickness
8	doctor's	intercourse
	everybody is riff-raff	intercourse
9	game of cards	intercourse, materialism
	spectacles	aging, sickness
10	band	life, art
	colonel's	intercourse
	wives of officers	intercourse
	children in town	intercourse
11	tired	aging, sickness
12	band	life, art
13	quarantine	imprisonment, sickness
	family *vs* family	intercourse
14	(K's) divorce	intercourse
15	women friends	intercourse
16	grog	materialism, sickness
	navarin aux pommes	materialism
	concerts	life, art

17	*Alcazar Waltz*	life, art
	out of the dance	aging, death
	old man	aging
	charming to other men	sexuality
18	light the lamp	life

By means of a number of key words the column left illustrates the variation on the surface level of the sequence. In the right hand column these key words have been reduced to ten concepts (themes), expressing more or less fundamental conditions of existence. Of necessity the right hand column is far more subjective than the left one, since we here deal with interpretation. Though a precise quantification is therefore meaningless, certain tendencies can nevertheless be distinguished. Thus certain themes (aging, sickness, intercourse) seem more frequent than others (freedom, art). We may also note the distribution of the themes within the sequence. Sexuality, for example, enters very implicitly in the initial subordinate text (*Nebentext*) and returns rather explicitly towards the end in the main text (*Haupttext*). A combination of these statements suggests that Alice's inclination to be charming to other men has something to do with Edgar's dwindling potency. In segm. 3–5 there are three different examples of Edgar's present materialism, a materialism which receives its past complement in segm. 16.

We may also note that the themes can be brought together in three antithetical groups:

intercourse–sexuality–life	*vs*	aging–sickness–death
freedom	*vs*	imprisonment
materialism	*vs*	art

These fundamental oppositions can, in varying degrees, be connected with Edgar's and Alice's relation to their environment, to one another and to themselves. Certain themes we would in the first place link with Edgar; thus the complex aging-sickness-death reflects his problems, and the materialism—both in an everyday and in a philosophical sense—is connected with him. The need of art, on the other hand, belongs to Alice's domain, and the antithesis freedom–imprisonment is primarily experienced by her. The intercourse–sexuality–life cluster illustrates problems which the two have in common.

Sometimes a theme is mentioned explicitly on the surface level (cf. segm. 7). But as a rule the degree of abstraction is far greater on the depth level. By having a series of phenomena (on the surface level) illustrate one and the same thing (on the depth level), Strindberg manages to give the sequence a great amount of coherence without making it monotonous. When one phenomenon after another points in the same direction we also get an accumulative effect of great significance. Consider, for example, the category 'intercourse'. We here learn subsequently that the marriage is an unhappy one, that Alice and Edgar no longer associate with the doctor and his wife, that Edgar does not want to associate with anyone, that they no longer see the colonel and his wife, that Alice does not expect to mingle with the wives of the new officers, that the children, who "grow up without company", are far away, that Edgar despises Alice's relatives and *vice versa,* that Alice no longer has any female friends. Step by step Strindberg creates the picture of an almost totally isolated couple, who (therefore?) find it extremely difficult to accept one another, a couple, in short, who do not seem capable of any sort of intercourse. With the departure of the two servants in one of the following sequences they become completely isolated. It is time for Kurt to show up. His arrival is psychologically exceedingly well prepared for.

As our examination has demonstrated, the opening sequence of *The Dance of Death I* is not a haphazard *tranche de vie.* On the contrary, it is extremely effectively constructed. Topic is linked to topic in an often seemingly surprising but fundamentally logical way. The connection between stage directions and dialogue is skillfully utilized in the form of incidental stimuli. Retrospective and prospective components relate the different segments to other segments, both within and outside the sequence. Last but not least: the coherence on the depth level counteracts every impression of topical pluriformity. Taken together, all these circumstances contribute to the high density of the sequence. In addition to this, Strindberg has managed to structure the sequence in a dramaturgically effective way. Surprises, mystifications, climaxes etc. create an impression of mobility.

The reason why the opening of *The Dance of Death I* is masterly is not so much Strindberg's "brilliant style" (Lamm, 1926, 234) as his power to combine density with dynamics, two concepts of vital importance to any drama.

9. The Coherence of *Ett drömspel*/ *A Dream Play*

The distinction between topics and themes discussed in the previous chapter becomes especially important when applied to an almost totally theme-centered drama like *A Dream Play.* On the topical level this drama appears exceedingly loosely structured, and it is not surprising that critics have often referred to the arbitrary nature of scenes and sequences (cf. Lamm, 1926, 321). Yet since the play imitates a dream, they have argued, this is precisely what we should expect. The playwright is, in fact, being very realistic.

Undoubtedly this view emanates from the interesting but not very clarifying "Explanatory Note" preceding the play, in which is stated that "the author has tried to imitate the disconnected but apparently logical form of a dream". In accordance with this statement, especially Sprinchorn (1962*b*) has approached the play as a psychoanalyst would approach a dream. "When the dreamer is about to wake up", he writes (355), "he tries to impose a meaning acceptable to his consciousness on the disorganized material of the dream." In the same way Strindberg disguises "the true meaning of the dream" and acts as his own "dream-censor" when he lets Indra's Daughter voice her "quasi-Buddhist philosophy" toward the end of the play. Only on a level unconscious to the author himself—this is Sprinchorn's tenet—is the play truly logical and coherent.

The alternative of this is of course to regard the drama as a product of "a conscious intellect and conscious artistic planning" (Bennich-Björkman, 57). According to this latter opinion, here adhered to, there is no need to delve into the author's psyche to discover a coherence in the play; it is enough to examine the text closely.

This is actually what Strindberg himself suggests in a sequel to his "Explanatory Note", for a long time almost unknown and first published in 1965 (Müssener, 26f.):

That Life itself is a dream seemed to us earlier but a poetical figure by Calderon. But when Shakespeare in *The Tempest* has Prospero say that "we are such stuff as dreams are made on" and when, at another time, the wise Briton through Macbeth calls life "a tale, told by an idiot", then one may well begin to ponder the problem.

He who during these short hours joins the author on his somnambular walk will perhaps find a certain resemblance between the apparent medley of the dream and the variegated cloth of unruly life, woven by the "world weaver" who puts up "the warp" of human destinies and then makes "the weft" of our crossing interests and differing passions.

He who sees the resemblance has the right to say: perhaps it is that way. As for the loose, incoherent form of the drama, that too is merely apparently so. For on closer inspection the composition will appear to be rather firm—a symphony, polyfonic, fugued here and there with the main motif constantly recurring, repeated and variegated by the some thirty voices in every key. No solos with accompaniment, that is: no parts, no characters or, as one ought to put it, no caricatures, no plots, no act endings arranged for applause. The mood is severely adhered to and in the sacrificial scene of the Finale the past parades by, the motives are summed up once more, just as life with all its details is said to do at the moment of death—thus one more resemblance!

It is obvious that Strindberg here employs "dream" in two different but overlapping ways: (1) literally, in the sense of 'nocturnal dream' and (2) figuratively, as a metaphor of life. Consequently, the term 'dream play' has two distinct meanings: (1) a drama composed in such a way that it resembles a nocturnal dream, (2) a drama evoking the feeling that life resembles and therefore perhaps is a dream. Of these two meanings, the second constitutes the greater mystery, at least to Strindberg who constantly stresses the unreality of life in his post-Inferno period.[1] This being the case, we may take it for granted that the first definition is derived from the second rather than the other way about. Precisely bacause the author has the intention, not to *declare* that life is a dream but to *evoke the feeling* that it is, precisely therefore must he imitate the nocturnal dream. On the other hand he cannot abstain altogether from the first half of the simile 'life is (like) a dream', or he would play down the important metaphysical perspective. The result is a drama which broadly relates to everyday reality such as we know it but which at the same time contains enough dream elements to evoke a sense of "half-reality", to use Strindberg's suggestive term. The sensation communicated by *A Dream Play* may perhaps best be expressed thus: Is life a dream?

Consider in this light the last sentence of the "Explanatory Note":

Sleep, the liberator, appears often as painful, but, when the torture is at its very peak, waking comes reconciling suffering with reality, which however painful it may be, still at this moment is a delight compared to the tormenting dream.

This is not, primarily, a piece of dream psychology. Rather, it is an indication of a fundamental human condition, amply "repeated and variegated" in the play: man caught in his eternal dilemma of desiring precisely that which he does not possess at the moment. A similar ambivalence characterizes man's attitude to the ultimates: life and death. The sentence just quoted indicates, in fact, Hamlet's archetypal dilemma:

/—/. To die: to sleep.
No more; and by a sleep to say we end
The heart-ache and the thousand natural shocks
That flesh is heir to: 'tis a consummation

> Devoutly to be wish'd. To die: to sleep.
> To sleep? perchance to dream. Ay, there's the rub;
> For in that sleep of death what dreams may come,
> When we have shuffled off this mortal coil,
> Must give us pause./—/

However, as already implied this traditional equation of death with sleep (with or without dreams) is less meaningful to the author of *A Dream Play* than the opposite view that life is a sleep (dream) and death the awakening.[2]

In accordance with the idea that the play is to evoke the feeling that life is a dream, the traditional divison into acts and scenes is lacking; nor is there, for the same reason, any list of *dramatis personae*. Scenes and sequences are indicated only by means of blank spaces or asterisks. In the ms. notes, however, the play is divided into three acts and fifteen scenes; in the list below these indications have been retained:

Prologue: Between heaven and earth.

Act I	Scene 1	Outside the castle.
	2	The Officer's room in the castle.
	3	The Mother's room.
	4	The theatre corridor.
	5	The Lawyer's office.
	6	The church.
	7	Fingal's Cave.
Act II	Scene 8	The Lawyer's home.
	9	Foulstrand.
	10	Fairhaven.
	11	The school.
	12	By the Mediterranean.
Act III	Scene 13	Fingal's Cave.
	14	The theatre corridor.
	15	Outside the castle.

Despite this variety of locales, the play is kept together first of all by Strindberg's adherence to a unity of hero(ine): Indra's Daughter appears in all the scenes except one (Scene 11),[3] and the slight overall line of action is directly related to her. This is made clear in the Prologue, where the god Indra tells his daughter:

> Descend and see and hear ...
> then come back and tell me
> if their [mankind's] complaints and laments are justified ...

This is also wat happens. Indra's Daughter descends to (the Castle of)[4] Earth and is there reincarnated as the Daughter with the Christian name Agnes. Gradually she is made aware of the human misery. The nadir, here as in *To Damascus I,* is reached precisely in the middle of the play (Scene 8), were she experiences the most intimate kind of human relationship, marriage, as imprisonment. She now longs for freedom and prepares for her return to heaven. At the end we witness her symbolic ascension; her parting words to the Poet relate to the task initially given her by Indra:

> Farewell! Tell your fellows I remember them,
> where I'm now going, and in your name
> I shall bear their complaints to the throne.
> Farewell!

The choice of a divine protagonist is not unproblematic. We expect such a figure to know the secret of life and the Daughter's interpretation of the myth of Brahma and Maja toward the end indicates that, in fact, she does. But such a static situation is inimical to drama, where there is a need for a (human) protagonist who gradually discovers the truth initially hidden to him. For dramaturgic reasons Strindberg therefore has to stress the human aspect of the Daughter and let her grow up in the course of the play (cf. ms. outline in Johnson, 1971*a*, 105). Thus in Scene 1 she is still a little girl, in Scene 2 she is a lovable young woman, in Scene 4 she takes on more maternal characteristics, in Scene 8 she has literally become a mother, and in the final scenes she has grown wise on the basis of her experience on earth. Also her attitude to mankind undergoes a certain development. In Scene 1 she is filled with youthful enthusiasm and activity. In Scene 4 she wants to sit "observing human beings". At the end of Act I she is willing to give up this attitude of non-involvement and experience life directly, the way a human being does: she marries the Lawyer. The result, demonstrated in Scene 8, is disastrous. She now gradually distantiates herself from earthly existence and tries to re-establish contact with her heavenly Father.

Not unlike the chorus in Greek tragedy or the narrator in the novel, the Daughter takes an intermediate position between the rest of the characters on the one hand and the audience on the other. As Szondi has noted (51), her "epischen Abstand zur Menschheit"—and we may here think both of the people on the stage and in the auditorium—is indicated by the alienating third-person form of her recurrent "Det är synd om människorna", a phrase meaning not only "Human beings are to be pitied" but also "Human beings are sinful/rooted in sin". In the early part of the play, where the dramatization of human misery dominates, the former meaning prevails; the Daughter's reaction to human suffering is here largely compassionate. But gradually the sinfulness of mankind is emphasized. Thus their "*crimes and vices*" are reflected in the Lawyer's face in Scene 5, and in Scenes 9 and 12 these vices are largely connected with the upper classes. In the latter scene, which has often been considered to be badly integrated in the play, we seem in fact to be confronted with a piece of agit-prop theatre; unlike the situation in the other scenes, where mankind appears to be suffering *sub specie aeternitatis,* suffering here appears to be socially conditioned. We sympathize wholeheartedly with the revolutionary spirit of the coalheavers. At this point Strindberg inserts the first sign that the Daughter sides with the gods rather than with humanity:

DAUGHTER. Hasn't anyone thought there are secret reasons for its [life's] being as it is?

The point is well chosen. Strindberg very forcefully pits against each other the most extreme example in the play of (social) injustice and the sanctioning of this injustice. The scene by the Mediterranean is, quite logically, placed at the end of Act II. It represents the culminating clash between the two themes inherent in the key phrase "Det är synd om människorna". In Act III the second aspect—"Human beings are rooted in sin"—is increasingly emphasized on a mythic level and with the assistance of 'high' language (verse): we are now confronted with the ontological status of humanity. Yet even Scene 12 ends on a note which carries metaphysical connotations:

LAWYER./—/ Human beings aren't so bad . . . but . . .
DAUGHTER. But?
LAWYER. But the administration . . .

The Lawyer's last statement seems to be a denouncement of an unjust government or society. But since he has just defended mankind at large, it is also possible to regard the last line as a protest against the Divine Management.

Strindberg's declaration in the "Explanatory Note" that "the characters split, double" has often been applied to the trio the Officer, the Lawyer and the Poet; the three, it is usually said, represent different aspects of the author himself. This may be true but it hardly explains their function in the play. The male trio has a counterpart on the female side: next to the Daughter, the Mother and the Doorkeeper have prominent roles.

The three women have much in common. In Scene 3 the Mother's concern for her children is stressed:

FATHER. /—/ And you think of your children, first and last!
MOTHER. Why, they were my life, my justification . . . my joy, and my sorrow . . .

In the following scene this private concern is expanded and transposed to a figurative level:

DAUGHTER. Farewell. What you can do, I surely can.
DOORKEEPER. We'll see! . . . But be kind to my little friends and don't weary of their complaints.

From the context it is clear that the Doorkeeper does not merely refer to the people working at the (staged) theatre; she refers to the children of man. Both the Mother's more narrow and the Doorkeeper's all-inclusive concern return in the figure of the Daughter. Like the Mother, she has a child of her own and the Lawyer points to her duties toward this child. The Daughter at this point significantly bursts out: "I am earthbound!" A little earlier, however, she has declared that she has "higher duties", and when the Lawyer again reminds her of her child she points at all the people assembled before the castle and says: "These are my children!" In other words: she has replaced the 'lower' love for one's own kind by the 'higher' love for mankind.

The same transposition from a realistic to a figurative level we find with regard to a piece of costume linking the three women. The silk mantilla that the Mother has received from her husband and that she is now ready to lend to the maid demonstrates that "if you do something good for someone, you hurt someone else". The purpose of the mantilla is to adorn its wearer; it is an esthetic object. Quite different is the shawl that the Doorkeeper wears "*over her head and shoulders*":

DOORKEEPER. /—/ In that shawl, dear, is the agony of thirty years, my own and others! ...
DAUGHTER. It is heavy, and it burns like nettles ...

Wearing the shawl containing the sorrows of mankind is an act of *satisfactio vicaria*; it is hardly a coincidence that the period mentioned roughly corresponds to the life span of Christ; the shawl is clearly Strindberg's variant of the veil with which St. Veronica consoled Christ on his way to Calvary.[5]

Strindberg takes pains to demonstrate that the Doorkeeper and the Daughter are in complete agreement with regard to their vicarious task:

DAUGHTER (*to the* DOORKEEPER). Give me the shawl now so I may sit here observing human beings! But stand behind me to tell me what I need to know. (*The* DAUGHTER *puts on the shawl and sits down by the gate.*)

The Doorkeeper here functions as the Daughter's mentor. A little later the Doorkeeper asks if she can have the shawl back but the Daughter answers: "No, dear, I'll relieve you; I'll do your job ... I want to know human beings and life to find out if it is as hard as they say." Wearing the shawl apparently means getting to know human beings, their sins and sorrows. Again the Doorkeeper tells the Daughter: "When it gets too heavy, call me, and I'll come and relieve you."

That the Daughter is a Christ figure has often been pointed out; her very name, Agnes (*agnus dei*), indicates this and there are numerous passages in the play that suggest the connection. Her earthly father, the Glazier, corresponds to Joseph, the carpenter (Delblanc, 1979, 78). The Doorkeeper, I would suggest, is her (not too) earthly 'mother', the shawl indicating her quality of a *Mater dolorosa* and the "*bedspread with a star pattern*" on which she is crocheting indicating 'higher' love.

When the Daughter enters the church "*with a white veil over her head and shoulders*" and declares that she has "washed the shawl", it is an expression of her attempt to release mankind from sin and sorrow. The attempt proves futile. The Lawyer realizes this:

May I have the shawl, my dear ... I'll hang it up in here until I get the fire in the tile stove going; then I'll burn it with all its sorrows and miseries ...
DAUGHTER. Not yet ... I want it really full ... first ... and above all I want to gather in it your afflictions, all you have received in confidence about crimes, vices, thefts, backbiting, slander, libel ...
LAWYER. Your shawl wouldn't do for all that, my friend!

On the basis of his own experience the Lawyer here seems to tell the Daughter that vicarious suffering does not help humanity. Their difference of opinion returns later in the following lines:

POET. Wait! Wasn't it Indra who once sent His son down here to hear the complaints of mankind?
DAUGHTER. Yes, it was. How was he received?
POET. How did he carry out His mission? To answer with a question.
DAUGHTER. To answer with another ... Wasn't the lot of man better after his stay on earth? Tell me truthfully!
POET. Better? ... Yes, a little. Very little!

In the latter part of the play the Daughter appears without the shawl. And in the final scene it has been returned to the Doorkeeper:

DOORKEEPER (*enters, puts her shawl into the fire*). Perhaps I may burn up my shawl, too? (*Exits.*)

Apparently the shawl has become too heavy for the Daughter—as it has, now, for the Doorkeeper. Release from sins and sorrows—this is the conclusion—cannot be found in this life; it can be found only when death has released us from the flesh.

Also with regard to their attitude to life, the three women have much in common. Thus the Mother tells the Officer that he must "never quarrel with God", not feel "mistreated by life" and not "question everything". The Doorkeeper, similarly, is not anxious to have the door hiding the riddle of life opened. "Is that so urgent?" she skeptically asks—as though it was her task to guard the door.

More complicated is the situation with regard to the Daughter. On the one hand she echoes the Mother's view when she tells the Poet: "the work may not condemn the master. /Life's riddle still remains unsolved". And in the early part of the play she shares the Doorkeeper's unquestioning attitude: she pays no attention to he door. But from Scene 10 onwards it is she, rather than the Officer, who insists that "the door must be opened so I learn the secret".[6] Apparently she does not know it. Yet even before the door is opened she does; she now tells the Poet: "Come with me and you'll get the answer to the riddle [of life]." This knowledge explains why she is not, like the rest, startled by the fact that there is nothing behind the door:

DEAN OF MEDICINE. Why, there's nothing there.
DAUGHTER. You said it.—But you did not understand it!

She then repeats that she will tell the Poet the riddle "out in the wilderness", and in the final scene she does by relating the myth to him and explaining its significance.

What is suggested here is a development on the part of the Daughter. In the early part of the play, she is still in touch with heaven; she still knows the secret of life—why man must suffer—and she is therefore not concerned with the door. But once she chooses to lead a human life herself, once she becomes "earthbound", contact with heaven is broken; she can no longer regard life from a divine bird's eye view; she forgets what the secret is; and she sides with man in his Promethean defiance of the gods. This constitutes her second and greater Fall, the first one corresponding to her "sinking" to Earth; in Indra's words: "You have gone astray, my child." Again Maja, "the mother of the world", has succeeded in seducing a divine creature. The myth about the Original Fall is re-enacted before our eyes (Børge, 262).[7]

But the Daughter is to re-establish her contact with heaven. The story of Lina's sister (Scene 10) prepares us for this:

POET. /—/ Do you hear music and dancing up there on the hillside? Fine! ... It's Lina's sister, who has come home from the city where she went astray ... you understand ... Now they're butchering the fatted calf, but Lina who stayed at home has to carry the pail to feed the pigs! ...
DAUGHTER. There's rejoicing in her home because the one who has gone astray has given up her wickedness—not only because she has come home!

The Daughter is another prodigal son eventually returning home after her double Fall. It is, as we have noted, just before the door is opened that her contact with heaven is re-established. She now recalls the secret of life and tells the Poet that she will reveal it to him.

While the three women, then, by and large advocate acceptance of life as it is, the three men represent the opposite attitude. What unites the Officer, the Lawyer and the Poet is primarily their refusal to accept life as a vale of tears.

But there are also important differences between them, recalling those between the women. Thus the Officer feels personally mistreated by life; his wondering what is behind the door is an individual concern; and his love for Victoria, similarly, concerns beauty in the private sphere.

With the Lawyer the questioning attitude is transformed into one of protest on behalf of a whole class of people: the poor and the oppressed. Like the Doorkeeper, he tries to remedy the situation in the world by taking the burdens of others upon himself (vicarious suffering).

With the Poet we reach a metaphysical or religious level. His complaints are directed, not to the human "administration" but to the divine one, and he speaks not on behalf of a particular group or class but on behalf of all mankind.

The following slightly Kierkegaardian diagram clarifies the pattern:

	Sphere	*Stage*	*Acceptance*	*Rejection*
(1)	Individual	Esthetic	The Mother	The Officer
(2)	Social	Ethical	The Doorkeeper	The Lawyer
(3)	Global	Religious	The Daughter	The Poet

In (1) love is limited to one person or to very few; we deal with sensuous love (Eros) or with love based on kinship (maternal love); this is the lower type of love. In (2) love has become partly altruistic, that is, it concerns part of humanity (the oppressed), while the other part (the oppressor) is rejected. In (3) love has become all-embracing: all human beings are to be pitied.

The conflict between acceptance and rejection is never completely resolved in the play. The Daughter promises to forward the complaints of mankind to God ("the throne") in her concluding lines but whether she will plead her children's, mankind's, cause or not is a question that the playwright hands over to us.

But not altogether. Quite apart from the fact that a controversy between God and man may seem a foregone conclusion, it is noteworthy that Strindberg, as we have noted, has structured his play in such a way that the notion that mankind suffers meaninglessly is gradually overruled by the idea that there is meaning in the suffering (Thomsen, 94).

This overall pattern is supported in various ways by the visual and verbal imagery which to a great extent is related to the ethical and metaphysical implicaitons of a high-low dichotomy. Thus, as Delblanc (1979, 73ff.) has indicated, the frequent references to the four elements should be seen in hierarchical terms. As a result of "the union of the divine and the earthly", the myth says, the world has come into being. In the four elements the divine (high) and the earthly (low) principle can be recognized, air and fire being part of the celestial sphere, water and earth of the terrestrial one. While the Daughter belongs to the former, mankind inhabits the latter. Yet the Daughter descends from heaven; and mankind, longing to return to its celestial origin, strives to 'ascend' from the soil:

DAUGHTER. /—/ Tell me, father, why do flowers grow out of dirt?
GLAZIER (*devoutly*). Since they don't like the dirt, they hurry as fast as they can up into the light to blossom and die!

What is true of the flowers is true of man:

OFFICER. /—/ You're a child of heaven . . .
DAUGHTER. So are you!

OFFICER. Why then should I tend horses? Look after stables and have litter hauled out?
DAUGHTER. So you'll long to get away from here.

From the very beginning Strindberg draws attention to the elemental aspect. "Why is it so close, so hard to breathe", the Daughter complains as she descends to Earth, and her entering the sphere of planet "Dust" is a death through water ("I'm suffocating ... / It isn't air but smoke and water I am breathing") preparing for the imprisoning feeling in the earthy home scene ("I'm suffocating! /—/ Air, air! I can't breathe!") and contrasting with the rebirth through fire at the end of the play.

Representing spirituality and freedom, air is sadly lacking on earth. In the theatre corridor there are no windows, only a tiny "*airhole*" in the mysterious door. Yet the Doorkeeper complains of the "draft", and the Officer says he will ask the Glazier to "put in double panes" in the castle, because he is "so terribly cold"—a subtle indication of the identity between the castle and the corridor. In Scene 1, we recall, the Daughter had asked the Glazier to put in a pane in the harness room of the castle. The resemblance between the two requests indicates an essential difference. Since we expect a harness room to be dark, the Daughter's request is an expression of her alliance with light and air (windows can be opened). The Officer, by contrast, wants to keep the (cold) air out. The conflict becomes a major issue in the matrimonial scene, where the Lawyer, echoing the Doorkeeper and the Officer, admonishes Kristin, the maid, to paste up the inner windows to keep it warm inside. Note the climactic pattern: double windows are no longer enough, they have to be pasted up as well. Unlike divine beings, human ones prefer warmth to fresh air:

DAUGHTER. May I open the window? This bad air is suffocating me!
LAWYER. Then the heat will go out, and we'll have to freeze.

A withering "little flower, without light, without air", the Daughter is virtually murdered by her husband when he jealously deprives her of fresh air:

LAWYER. /—/ Paste, Kristin! Paste! Until they [the Daughter and the Officer] can't breathe!

Kristin returns in the final scene but it is characteristic that this demon of the world is not inclined to sacrifice her attribute to the fire:

KRISTIN (*with strips of paper*). I paste, I paste until there isn't anything more to paste ...
POET. And if heaven itself were rent, you'd try to paste it together ... Go!
KRISTIN. Aren't there any inner windows over there in the castle?
POET. No, not there.
KRISTIN (*going*). Then I'll go!

Beyond death, in the lofty Castle of Heaven there are only windows letting in air and light.[8] We are back where we started: in the harness room. The Daughter's attempt to furnish the Castle of Life with light and air is obviously derived from her celestial domicile. It is characteristic that as she prepares for her ascension more air is let into the play. The Kyrie of the organ pipes (Scene 6)—actually human voices—is now replaced by the lengthy song of the winds outside Fingal's Cave, carrying "the laments of mankind".

An Indian god of the air, Indra is also the god of thunder, that is, of fire. Similarly, the name of his daughter, Agnes, has been associated with Agni, the personification of fire in Indian mythology (Børge, 224). We are reminded of this in the Prologue when the Daughter says that she has "followed the flash of lightning from high Ether".

Just as in the case of air, fire can be found also on earth but it is scarce, diminutive. We find it in the Mother's flickering candle, symbolizing her tiny and brief life, perhaps also the spiritual urge upwards. We recognize it negatively in the "*fire wall*" of the theatre corridor, a wall intended to protect against fire—as the double windows are intended to protect against air. It appears again in the stove of the kitchen-bedroom scene (Scene 8); the Daughter here is "*sitting by the stove*" as she asks for fresh air; she is significantly related to both the higher elements.

Both the annihilating and the cleansing aspects of the fire come to the fore in Foulstrand (Scene 9):

to the right in the foreground one sees burned-over mountains with red heather and stumps black and white after a forest fire; /—/. To the left in the foreground, part of the quarantine building's open shed with hearths, furnace walls, and plumbing pipes.

The "*furnace walls*" here signify a development of the "*fire wall*" of Scene 4, while the "*plumbing pipes*" appear to be a 'low' counterpart of the organ pipes in Scene 6.

Foulstrand (a more literal translation would be 'Shamestrand') is clearly a place where the sinful are punished, and the infernal note is unmistakable:

QUARANTINE MASTER [*in blackface*] (*lights the stove; blue sulphur vapors rise*). Now I'm lighting the sulphur. Please step in!
SHE. My blue dress will lose its color!
QUARANTINE MASTER. Yes, it'll turn white! Your red roses will turn white, too!
HE. And your cheeks as well! In forty days!

A few moments ago He and She experienced the greatest bliss together, now they are punished for it; paradise turns into hell. Yet there is a time limit: forty days, that is, as long as Christ was tempted by the Devil in the wilderness. On closer inspection, Foulstrand is not Inferno, it is Purgatory. Like the Daughter's visit to Earth, the stay at Foulstrand "is but a test" preparing man through suffering for a higher existence.

Toward the end of the play the characters voluntarily sacrifice their earthly attributes to the cleansing fire, with the notable exceptions: the man of the senses (Don Juan) and the demon of the world (Kristin). Matter is sacrificed to spirit. And "with the help of the fire" the Daughter finally ascends "to Ether again"; alone she enters the burning castle, leaving behind her a desolate humanity: "*a wall of human faces, asking, sorrowing, despairing*".

Like fire, water is associated with cleansing. In Scene 2 the Mother insists that the undershirts of her children be properly washed also after her death—a request which points forward to the end; the death of the Mother is clearly conceived as a parallel, up to a point, to that of the Daughter—and in the early part of the play the Daughter, too, has confidence in the cleansing power of water:

DAUGHTER. /—/ Look, I've washed the shawl ... (Scene 6)

DAUGHTER. /—/ May we scrub out there [in the 'sinful' office] then? (Scene 8)

In Scene 10 handkerchiefs are linked with weeping and a human being weeps, we learn, because his eyes "have to be washed occasionally so he can see more clearly"; ironically, this variant of the recurrent suffering-is-cleansing theme is voiced by the Blind Man. When the Lawyer later announces that there will be "a big washing today; we're going to wash all the handkerchiefs", we can easily translate his statement: the world is a vale of tears but suffering is good for us.

In the latter part of the play the purging power of water is expanded to include not only man's sins but his whole life: death by water becomes a recurrent motif. It begins with the representatives of youthful love:

HE. How long do we have to stay here?
QUARANTINE MASTER. Forty days and nights.
HE. Then we'd rather drown ourselves.

It continues with "*the newlyweds*":

HUSBAND (*to the* WIFE). My happiness is so great I could wish to die .../—/
WIFE. Let's die together, right now!
HUSBAND. Die? All right! For I fear happiness! It's deceitful! (*They go toward the water.*)

After this we are ready to see more than a desire to cool off—legitimate enough if you are in hell—in the following lines:

FIRST COALHEAVER. This is hell!
SECOND COALHEAVER. Over 115 degrees in the shade!
FIRST COALHEAVER. Shall we take a dip?

By contrast, the Officer desires annihilation by fire: "at last they bring me to the crematory and burn me up", a passage preparing for the Daughter's end. And the Poet, in the first Cave scene, wants to be "set free" but "not in water". The reason is given in the second Cave scene:

POET. Do you intend to ascend ... soon?
DAUGHTER. As soon as I have burned my body ... for the waters of the sea cannot cleanse me.

The cleansing power of fire—the power to transform matter into air—is lacking in the baser element of water.

With earth we reach the basest element. This is already indicated in the Prologue when our planet is named "Dust" by Indra just as the winds later call its inhabitants "sons of dust", who "wander in dust, / born of dust / they return to dust", a phrase suggestively recalling the expulsion of Adam (the name means 'dust') from Eden: "dust thou art, and unto dust shalt thou return" (Genesis 3: 19).

Yet the mere fact that man is "born of dust" makes him attached to Mother Earth. Even the Poet, who more than other "earthlings" is connected with light and air, can be "homesick for mud". Indeed, the Daughter herself has run the risk of turning into a baser creature, she tells the Poet:

I've been too long down here bathing in mud as you do ... My thoughts cannot fly any more; there's clay on my wings ... soil on my feet ... and I myself—(*Lifts her arms.*)—I'm sinking, sinking ... Help me, Father God of Heaven! (*Silence.*)

This Father-why-hast-Thou-forsaken-me situation signifies a climactic development of the one at the end of the Prologue:

INDRA'S DAUGHTER (*on her knees as the cloud sinks*). I'm sinking!

The Daughter sinks, so to speak, first down to Dust, then into dust. The final ascension is, quite logically, preceded by a sacrifice of the most down-to-earth part of her:

DAUGHTER. Now I shake the dust from my feet ... the earth, the clay ... (*She takes off her shoes and puts them into the fire.*)

Once we realize the fundamental significance of the four elements in the drama, we can understand better various passages which may otherwise seem obscure. We can now, for example, see why the Officer's bouquet of roses turns "*dusty*" after a while. We understand why the Poet calls the mud—the mixture of water and clay (earth)—"*mon affaire*". And we realize why the Daughter prefers "fish" to "cabbage", and yet considers the waves "false and faithless". Moreover, we can see the true significance of the Billposter's fish box, green like the earth and yet belonging to water, keeping the fish imprisoned in their element as human beings are in theirs.[9] The earth-water combination returns in the song of the waves—"Green cradles, we the waves"—a reference, it would seem, to the base maternal procreative principle (Maja).

The idea that man is a hybrid and a centaur—the Officer on horseback!—split into high and low is, we have already noted, found also in the plants with their roots in the dirt and their flowers in the light;[10] this is true not only of the hollyhocks of Scene 1 but also to the blue monkshood with its poisonous roots and the strikingly dichotomous—and Beckettian—linden tree of Scene 4 with its "*coal-black*" trunk below and few "*pale green leaves*" above. The mere fact that both the hollyhocks and the blue monkshood are of "*gigantic*" stature—as is the Chrysanthemum at the end—indicate their anthropomorphic nature.

However, the flowers signify more than that. In Scene 1 they are described as follows:

The backdrop represents a forest of gigantic white, pink, scarlet, sulphur yellow, and violet hollyhocks in bloom; over their tops can be seen the gilded roof of a castle with a flower bud resembling a crown uppermost.

With all their different colors the flowers verify what the Daughter has seen from above when descending to Earth:

> I see . . . it's beautiful—with green forests,
> blue waters, white mountains, and yellow fields . . .

This is a picture of beauty. We are invited to an earthly paradise, where the castle (human life) is seen as a flower among other flowers. And we note that though there is much variety in color, there are only two types of flowers: hollyhocks (*Althea rosea*, Sw. 'stockrosor') below and a mysterious, 'royal' bud above. One 'high', mysterious and golden flower against many showy, 'low' ones.[11] Is it not a visualization of the Daughter and mankind, the contrahents of the play?

The golden bud of Scene 1 is replaced by "*a gigantic blue monkshood (Aconite)*" in Scene 4. Golden and blue: sun and sky. It is significant that the monkshood is seen in a "*bright*" but distant exterior. Just as the "*green plot*" and the "*green leaves*" of the linden tree provide a visual link with the Billposter's adoration of his green fish box (worldly values), so the "blue" monkshood suggests a contrasting concern with heavenly ones. In this respect there is a connection between the Officer's interest in the flower and in the mysterious door which is said to hide the secret of life. The Doorkeeper, too, is concerned with heavenly values, as her crocheting of a bedspread "*with a star pattern*" indicates. Her occupation reveals that she is still hoping, after thirty years, that her fiancé will return. Similarly, the Officer never ceases to hope that his fiancée will come. Their faithfulness, it would seem, is visualized in the blue color of the monkshood.

The rather inconspicuous high-low contrast in the scenery of Scene 1 has in Scene 4 developed into a horizontally split scenery suggesting earthly misery (foreground) and heavenly paradise (background): the theatre corridor is as dark and shabby as the green plot is light, airy and attractive.

In Scene 9 this development is continued. There is now nothing left of the hollyhock forest:

to the right in the foreground one sees burned-over mountains with red heather and stumps black and white after a forest fire;

This foreground is even more dismal than that of the theatre corridor; the fire wall has evidently proved inefficient. But again paradise can be seen at a distance:

The back of the stage is a beautiful shore with trees in foliage /—/. Small Italian villas /—/ can be seen among the foliage.

Behind Foulstrand lovely Fairhaven can be discerned. Yet as soon as Fairhaven becomes foreground, in the following scene, we discover that it is not the paradise it seemed to be. In Scene 12 this optical illusion is repeated in condensed form:

A shore on the Mediterranean. To the left in the foreground can be seen a white wall, over which branches of fruit-bearing orange trees are hanging. At the back, villas and a casino with a terrace. To the right, a large pile of coal with two wheelbarrows. At the back to the right, a strip of the blue sea.

The quasi-Italian villas have become genuine ones, but they are inhabited, we learn toward to end of the scene, not by the innocent but by "the unpunished". Paradise (Eden) and hell are now placed side by side; and in the background, as in Scene 4, there is a suggestion of blue. The first lines read:

DAUGHTER. This is paradise!
FIRST COALHEAVER. This is hell!

The Daughter, ironically, only sees the paradisiac part to the left—until she is made aware of its sad complement by the Coalheaver.

These scenic transformations may be compared to the more obvious ones in Scenes 4 to 6, where a number of properties remain on the stage but take on a new look when they become part of a new setting. These 'dissolves' are usually regarded as typical exponents of the dream technique employed in the play. But this is mistaking the means for the message. The true significance of all the scenic transformations and transpositions is that they evoke a feeling in us that we cannot trust our senses. This is explicitly demonstrated in the three visions of the second Cave scene. Here the Poet imagines that he sees a ship (the Flying Dutchman), then decides that it is a house or a tower of Babel until, finally, he discovers that it is a church. The idea behind this is not only that the Poet's eyesight is imperfect but also that it improves and that the last vision is truer than the first. Similarly, Strindberg's arrangement of the scenery time and again reminds us that *our* eyesight is imperfect but that it too improves when we discover that Fairhaven or any other earthly paradise is not Paradise. Again, our eyesight improves when we discover that the four-leaf clover (luck, worldly success, Victoria = victory) when found in the door leading to the sacristy (Scene 6) is actually a (Greek) cross (Bennich-

Björkman, 65ff.) matching the "*crown of thorns*" offered to the Lawyer, and that this, in turn, is the valuable remnant of what was once the Officer's bouquet of roses. Thus visual means help to make us sense that love for mankind, not Eros, is the true love and that suffering is the meaning of life.

In the final scene we are back outside the castle

but the ground at the base of the castle is now covered with flowers (Blue monkshood, Aconite). On the roof of the castle, at the top of the lantern, a Chrysanthemum bud ready to burst can be seen.

The litter and the sensuous roses of Scene 1 are gone, so is the green ground of Scene 4. Paradoxically, the ground has turned blue. We discover that there are windows in the castle and that they are all illuminated: "the flowers keep watch . . . the candles are lighted". Light, air, spirit. And awakened by the heat of the cleansing fire the Chrysanthemum opens its golden "crown" to the heavenly light.

From a budding heavenly "crown" contrasting with worldly roses we have been carried via a bouquet of roses turning into a "*crown of thorns*" to a Crown now, guarded by the faithful monkshood, ripe for the true life: "be thou faithful unto death, and I will give thee a crown of life" (Rev. 2: 10). This interpretation of the ending does not contradict the one, suggested by Strindberg himself at the end of *The Ghost Sonata,* where he has the Student pray to "wise, gentle Buddha, sitting there waiting for a heaven to grow out of the earth" that He will grant him "patience in his trials and purity of will that hope may not come to nought".

Throughout *A Dream Play* we are confronted with hoping and waiting human beings. The Doorkeeper is waiting for her fiancé to return, the Billposter has been waiting fifty years for a green fish box, the Officer a lifetime for his Victoria, the theatre people are waiting to be engaged for the next season, etc. And we find them in the 'waiting-room' of the theatre, that is, waiting in a house of illusion, in an unreal world. The fiancé never returns, the green turns out to be the wrong green, Victoria never comes. Only the hope for blue has not (yet) "come to nought".[12] A heaven growing out of the earth, that is ultimately what we are all waiting for. With this hope *A Dream Play* ends.

10. The Web of *Brända tomten/ The Burned House*

The Burned House has been called an abortive play, packed with interesting ideas which have only here and there been worked out (Lamm, 1926, 382). As a matter of fact Strindberg has given the play a shape which closely corresponds to its 'message'. At first sight it seems highly chaotic; on closer inspection a meaningful pattern can be divined; the threads come together. What is true of our experience of the play is also true of life: not until one gets old and "one's eyes can really see", as the central figure states it, is one able to interpret the "pattern", which "the world weaver has woven".

The drama comprises fifteen characters. (Of these only one is silent: the Witness, not mentioned in the list of *dramatis personae.*) This is a relatively large number considering the brevity of the drama; the reason is found in the theme of the play: the guilt-laden relationships of men.

It is further striking how one individual, the Stranger, is pitted against a collective. The drama opens with a presentation of the latter. Not until seq. 9 (90/23) does the Stranger enter, a dramaturgic convention which enables the subordinate characters to describe him. The unusual thing about *The Burned House* is that this possibility is utilized so little. We do not learn more than that the Stranger and his brother, the Dyer, were always fighting with one another as boys, that he has emigrated to America, that for many years he was considered dead because he never claimed his inheritance but that he is now said to be back. Except for the Old Woman's statement that the boys "were just so-so", we never receive any characterization of the Stranger in advance. The scanty attention devoted to him accentuates his role of outsider.

Instead we become familiar with the situation (thc suspicions of arson) and the environment (the block called the Morass) in the first nine sequences. A number of themes are also inconspicuously initiated in this opening section of the play, notably the idea that in the Morass everyone knows everyone.

After a short introductory sequence (seq. 9), the Stranger returns in seq. 12 (94/5) and from here he dominates the action. We first get a confrontation between him and his brother. It is primarily the Stranger who does the talking. The Dyer chiefly provides him with short speeches to which he can react. Actually, this section is a disguised soliloquy. Changes of subject are determined by what the Stranger discovers. Thus the sight of the burned site releases memories of the house. The discovery of "the family photograph album" on the pile causes him to ponder on the family. An apple tree in bloom leads to a long comment on the garden. When the Stranger discovers the bookcase, this too proves to have its own story. This technique is continued in the regular soliloquy of seq. 19 (113/12), where, in turn, a couple of books, the frame of a family picture, part of a mahogany bed, the leg of a dining table, the living-room clock with a globe and a cross bring back memories to the Stranger and cause him to develop his view both of his own past and of life in general.

As appears from this, the long genuine or disguised soliloquies are made possible through the rich supply of stage properties. This of course does not justify the soliloquies in any naturalistic sense—although Strindberg tries to do just that by having the Stranger state that he has the habit of talking to himself.

Which, then, are the threads running through the web of the play and which pattern do they form? The main thread, from the plot point of view, concerns the question how the fire has arisen; already the play title implies this. When the drama opens we see the ruins of "*a one-story house that has burned down*". And the first speeches make it plain that the fire has just occurred. Very soon the Mason, who is especially involved in finding out the cause, declares that the fire started "in the attic room where the student lives".

DETECTIVE. Was he home?
MASON. No, he was at the theatre.

After this the questions which continue to reverberate throughout the drama are posed:

DETECTIVE. Do you think it was arson?
MASON.They think that about all fires.
DETECTIVE. Whom do you suspect?

The idea that the house has not burned accidentally soon seems confirmed by another character:

OLD WOMAN. That's funny—then someone closed all doors and took out the keys before it began to burn! That's funny!

Through its framing clauses, this speech indicates that the Old Woman is indeed thinking in terms of arson. The Gardener, too, is convinced that "someone had set fire to it", and he has already told the police that he suspects the Student. However, with his continued excavation the Mason discovers that the fire has broken out not in but under the Student's attic room, in "the cook's closet", a circumstance which immediately causes the Gardener to pronounce a new verdict: "Then it was she!"

Note how Strindberg has the three characters voice the same idea—that of arson—each in his/her own way. The Mason, who is the oldest and (therefore) the most disillusioned person in the block, does it by means of a breakneck generalization; his wisdom of life is equivalent to disbelief in everyone. If his view is that of the misanthrope, the Gardener's is rather that of the sadist, anxious to find a scapegoat. On very loose grounds he accuses first the Student, then the Cook. Only the Old Woman has a rationally founded explanation why arson seems probable. In conclusion: with the help of three characters from the block, Strindberg pounds home the idea of arson. The question we now ask ourselves is that of the classical detective novel: Who dun it?

Now the Stranger enters:

STRANGER (*looks about*). Has there been . . . a fire . . . here?
GARDENER. Yes, the place burned down last night.
STRANGER. Good God!

Laconic though it is, the reaction is telling. Unlike the people of the block, the Stranger connects the fire not with a human instigator—but with God. To him the fire is a manifestation of Fate.

However, the inhabitants of the Morass continue to look for a criminal and a scapegoat. Not even the Mason is raised above suspicion, for he had been "seen in the attic at an unusual time". Yet he is but one of many:

DYER. And the stonecutter, the gardener, Mrs. Vesterlund, even the painter there, we're all suspected, the student, the cook, and I most of all.

In short: everyone suspects everyone. Only the Stranger seems raised above suspicion. He, the outsider, is also the only one who limits himself to the question: "Where did the fire start?"

Eventually an exploded lamp is found in the Cook's closet. The source of the fire now being established, the suspicions again turn in the direction of the Student, since it is his lamp:

DETECTIVE. How did his lamp get into the cook's closet? Was he having an affair with her?
DYER. Presumably.
DETECTIVE. If he only admits the lamp is his, we'll arrest him.

The Dyer's assumption regarding a sexual liaison seems plausible enough. But from this we cannot conclude that the Student has put fire to the house:

DETECTIVE. Well, what motive could he have had for setting fire to someone else's house?
DYER. I don't know. Spite . . . wanting to hurt . . . people can't be explained . . . maybe he wanted to hide something . . .
DETECTIVE. That was a poor method since all the nasty old facts were revealed.— Did he have a grudge against you?
DYER. Probably. I had helped him once when he needed it, and he hated me after that, of course!
DETECTIVE. Of course!

The Mason's general distrust in his fellows is shared by the Dyer. But the essential part of his testimony is the idea that the Student's indebtedness has resulted in an act of revenge: the arson. Although this hypothesis on closer inspection seems dubious—since the fire deprives the Student of his own dwelling—the Detective's agreement contributes to sanction this view and influences us in the direction of its acceptance.

Let us summarize what has appeared up to this moment. The fire has been caused by the explosion of the Student's lamp, in the Cook's closet, while he was at the theatre. Before the fire started someone has closed all the doors and taken away the keys. The evidence certainly suggests arson and the Student seems highly suspect. The question is now: What is his motive? This is the situation at the end of Act I.[1]

Act II opens with a shift in point of view. Seven of the inhabitants of the block "*stand lined up looking at the ruins*". They do not say anything. Instead we hear the Stranger's comment:

> There they stand rejoicing over the misfortune, waiting for the victim, who seems to be the main attraction. They consider it arson because they want it to be that!

Suddenly the evidence so far presented by the people of the Morass is undermined by the Stranger's opinion that what they seek is not the truth but a victim, a scapegoat. We now recall that the arguments which have so far been brought forward have been characterized by onesidedness, premature conclusions and dubious hypotheses. Once we share the Stranger's point of view, the primary question 'How did the fire start?' again becomes relevant.

The Stonecutter soon tells the Stranger that he has avenged himself on the Dyer. "And now *they*'ll go to jail!" The plural form seems puzzling. The most reasonable interpretation is that the Stonecutter has only reported the Dyer but that he is aware of the fact that the Student has been arrested. He knows that the Dyer has put the lamp in the Cook's closet; whether he has set fire to the house or not only the Mason knows, but he "shares some secret with the dyer so that fellow won't testify". The Stonecutter has no reason to report the Student, since he knows that "he's innocent but can't clear himself, for the only witness who could prove his innocence would by so doing prove his guilt—of something else". This is an allusion to the Dyer's wife, who soon confirms the Stonecutter's statement by claiming that the Student is innocent; then comes the peripety:

> STRANGER. Who is guilty? (*Pause*.)
> WIFE. No one!—It was an accidental fire!
> STRANGER. I know!

That the Wife is especially knowledgeable on this point must be due to the fact that she, not the Cook, has an intimate relationship with the Student. The hairpins which have been found in the Cook's closet and which indicate what has happened there belong to her. Although she does not explain further why she considers it an accidental fire, we are inclined to accept her view both because she expresses herself with such a conviction and because she is supported in her view by the Stranger who has always kept this possibility open and who more and more has come to appear as a prophetic figure, capable to see what others cannot see. Their agreement on this point is highly persuasive.

It may seem as though the fire motif has now been brought to an end. But the Dyer must yet be informed that he is supposed to have a share in the fire. In the final punishment of the brother, the Stranger says: "And I understand that you carried the student's lamp into the closet, I understand *that*." Note that not even now does the Stranger insinuate that the Dyer has set fire to the house. He does not even blame him for foolhardiness. On the contrary, he implies that he himself would have acted in the same way in a similar situation.

We can now reconstruct the action of the play as follows: "The Dyer placed the Student's lamp in the Cook's wardrobe, partly to suggest that the couple had a relationship, partly to make the Student suspected of intended arson. An accident, however, had occurred /—/ and the house caught fire" (G. Lindström, 1966, 63). The Wife's and the Stranger's conviction that it is an accidental fire is in agreement with this interpretation.

Yet this is no conclusive evidence. In favor of the theory of arson speaks the fact that the Mason knows something about the Dyer which he does not want to reveal; that the Dyer has paid his "insurance the day before"; and that all the doors have been locked in advance. The Dyer may have set fire to the house to take revenge on his wife and the Student, and to receive a considerable amount of money from the insurance company.

Summarizing, we may say that all the people inhabiting the Morass have guilt-laden relations to each other. It is therefore very easy to find reasons why each one of them might have set fire to the house. When Strindberg has two characters seem particularly suspect, it is because he needs to structure the play in a reasonably obvious, suspense-creating way.

The development can perhaps best be described as a game between two interpreting instances:

(1) a condemning instance (the collective and the police): arson
(2) an absolving instance (the Stranger and the Wife): accidental fire

By having instance (1) dominate in the greater part of the play and forcefully bring out instance (2) toward the end of it, Strindberg can manipulate us as recipients, first in one direction, then in the other. It is essential to note, in this context, that the two attitudes are never directly confronted with one another. To the adherents of (1) the Student still appears guilty at the end of the play; while he appears innocent to the adherents of (2), to whom we now presumably belong. By contrast, the Dyer at the end still appears to be an innocent victim to the collective, while to us he seems utterly suspect. The irony is of course, as Ward notes (249), that the Student presumably "is punished wrongly for the Dyer's crime, but justly for his own crime of sleeping with the Dyer's wife". The moral is: behind the unjust verdicts of men a higher justice is at work.

Strindberg could have developed the action differently. He could have shown how in this sordid world the innocent are condemned while the guilty are absolved. Or he could have made it quite plain that no-one is guilty. He chooses neither of these solutions—or, if you wish, both of them. By doing this he creates a situation which in its uncertainty seems highly realistic and recognizable. The question of guilt proves insoluble. "The case is canceled, the matter can't be cleared up", the Stranger states at the end. The words pregnantly summarize not only his but also our conclusion, the conclusion we have arrived at on the basis of the presented material. A conclusive solution as to how the fire has arisen is denied us. Strindberg carefully avoids any one-sided attribution of debts between Fate/God on the one hand and mankind (the individual) on the other. In the last instance it is up to us to take a stand in the matter.[2]

To complicate the situation even further he provides the fire both with negative and positive connotations. On the realistic level the fire represents of course a destructive power. The Dyer loses his house, the Gardener's garden is damaged and Mrs. Vesterlund's inn is deprived of a good day's income. Above all: a number of people suddenly find themselves without a roof over their heads. Yet it is obvious that Strindberg does not focus on these matters. The fire has primarily a symbolic meaning.

Also as a symbol, the fire may be given a negative connotation. In the later plays life frequently appears as an inferno, and it is therefore not surprising that the Morass resembles the burning Gehenna or, for that matter, Sodom, punished by sulphur and fire. However, here as elsewhere it is the positive aspects of the fire that are stressed. The fire is seen as revealer, purifier and renewer. Directly at the beginning of the play the Old Woman believes "it was time it [the house] got smoked out". The expression is telling; we deal with the extermination of a kind of vermin. The Gardener's son Alfred voices a similar idea, tempered by personal feelings of revenge, when he says: "I've had such a bad time in this house I often wished it would catch fire . . .". When the hairpins are found on the floor of the closet, the Student's secret relation to the Wife is revealed: "it was disclosed nevertheless, but fire there had to be first"; the Swedish original has here an unmistakable biblical phrasing which brings out the providential nature of the fire. The same idea is expressed, in more general terms, by the Stranger when he declares: "When it is burned, you can read in the ashes." The fire discloses the true relations, the genuine motives—however disgusting they may be. The revelations cause much sorrow. But, as the wise Stranger knows, "sorrow makes patience; patience makes experience; experience makes hope; but hope doesn't permit frustration". Like suffering, the fire purifies, creates possibilities for better soil. This is the basic idea. The fire is that of purgatory, not of inferno (Leifer, 185).[3]

The positive significance of the fire, suggested by the statement that it is "strange the heat didn't ruin the apple tree", appears above all from the fact that, while reducing the house to ashes, it makes the garden blossom. The connection fire–flowering—earlier visualized at the end of *A Dream Play*—can be interpreted causally: the flowering (the salvation) is preceded/determined by fire (suffering, purification). Behind the burned site the garden of Eden can be glimpsed. The way back to the lost paradise—this seems to be the parabolic meaning of the scenery—leads through the revelation of the duplicity inherent to mankind. In Act I the demolition of the façade has already been initiated and we can see "*a fruit orchard in bloom*" behind the burned walls. In Act II we have come a step further. The revelations have begun. Symbolically this is indicated by the fact that the walls are now "*torn down so that one can see the garden with all its spring flowers /—/ and all the fruit trees in bloom*". Not until now is the paradise fully visible. The visual contrast between the burned house and the garden soon finds a verbal counterpart; says the Stranger:

Humanity is a terrible lot, ugly, sweaty, stinking; unclean underwear, dirty socks with holes in them, chilblains, corns, ugh! No, a blooming apple tree is much prettier; look at the lilies of the field—it is as if they were not at home here—and smell how fragrant they are!

Ugliness is pitted against beauty, stench against fragrance, pigs thriving in the filth—to use another of the Stranger's misanthropic images—against flowers longing back to their heavenly origin. In short: sinful humanity is contrasted with virginal nature. When the Stranger ends Act I by proposing to his brother that they enter the garden, his proposal suggests a 'back to nature', to the lost paradise of the individual (childhood) and of mankind (Eden).

That the orchard corresponds to the garden of Eden appears in several places. As we remember from Genesis 3, God forbade Adam and Eve to eat from the Tree of Knowledge, the lovely apple tree in the middle of the garden. But Eve, tempted by the serpent, could not resist. She ate and asked Adam to eat. "And the eyes of them both were opened, and they knew that they were naked; and they sewed fig leaves together, and made themselves aprons." When God towards evening came along, "Adam and his wife hid themselves from the presence of the Lord God amongst the trees of the garden". For they were ashamed of their (relative) nakedness. God understands what has happened and takes Adam to task. But Adam blames Eve and Eve blames the serpent. All three are cursed. Adam and Eve receive "coats of skins". And both are banished out of Eden.

Strindberg's version is no coherent counterpart. Rather, fragments of the story of the Fall appear here and there, in transparent contemporary disguise. The first of these reads:

STRANGER./—/ But the day came when you had stolen apples and were weak enough not to admit it but blamed me.
DYER. Haven't you forgotten that?
STRANGER. I haven't forgotten it, but I've forgiven you.—I'm sitting looking at the apple tree, the very one, because I remember it so well. It's still over there, a pale yellow.—And if you look at it carefully, you'll find the mark of a large sawed-off branch.—It so happened I didn't get angry with you because of the unjust punishment, but got angry with the tree and cursed it.—Two years later that very branch had dried up and was sawed off. Then I happened to remember the fig tree that the Saviour cursed, but I didn't draw any arrogant conclusions.

By pointing to a particular apple tree and by mentioning its name, the Stranger indicates its connection with the Tree of Knowledge. It is significant that the tree is a pale yellow (Sw. 'vit gyllen'), belonging to the family *Cruciferae*; in this way the connection between the Fall and the Redemption is indicated, the connection between the first and the second Adam.

In *The Burned House* the Dyer comes to play Eve's dubious part. It is he who steals apples and who puts the blame on someone else. But while Eve did have a reason to blame the serpent, the Dyer falsifies reality and makes an innocent person, the Stranger, responsible for what he himself has done. While God curses the sinful trio, the Stranger curses not the sinful brother but the tree. What does this mean? Presumably that the Stranger is more inclined to protest against the existence of forbidden fruit than against the fact that someone has trespassed against this prohibition and furthermore laid the blame on someone else. The brother's guilt is less to him than the guilt of Him who has arranged the world according to the law of prohibition. The Stranger resembles Prometheus allied with man, his sinful brother, against God. But the cursing of the Tree of Knowledge receives a kind of sanction when this tree is identified with the fig tree cursed by Jesus (Matt. 21: 19–21).[4] Does this mean that the Stranger—as he himself implies—should be identified with Jesus? Hardly. There is a decisive difference between Jesus' cursing of a barren tree and the Stranger's of a fruitful one.

Another of the Stranger's memories further underlines the symbolic aspect of the garden:

STRANGER. /—/ I remember the orchard was rented out once, but we had the right to walk in it. It seemed to me then as if we had been expelled from Paradise—and the tempter was standing behind every tree! In the fall, when the apples were lying ripe on the ground, I yielded to the temptation, I couldn't resist . . .
DYER. So you stole, too?
STRANGER. Of course! But I didn't say I was innocent or accuse you!

He continues to relate how, much later, thieves had visited his lemon orchard every night. The Gardener is mentioned; he too has stolen apples as a child.

It is evident that Strindberg, by generalizing the stealing of fruit in this way, suggests that we deal here with original sin, a circumstance which is further indicated by the fact that it concerns a sin committed in childhood. The infancy of the individual is compared to that of mankind. Note, by the way, how the Stranger's sin is played down in relation to that of the Dyer. The former steals only windfalls—and he admits his guilt.

After this it is easy to see the significance of the following speeches:

STRANGER. Why are your hands so black?
DYER. Because I handle dyed things ... Or did you mean something else?
STRANGER. What would that be?
DYER. That I don't have clean hands!
STRANGER. Nonsense!
DYER. You're probably thinking of the inheritance!
STRANGER. Just as small-minded as ever! You're exactly what you were when you were eight!

This is only superficially a conversation about the inheritance the Stranger has not received and the Dyer's possible guilt in connection with this; the exact situation remains obscure. On the parabolic level, it concerns Original Sin from the childhood of man (cf. the reference to the Dyer's childhood), the Sin which has made all men unclean.

Also the third reference to Eden is put in the mouth of the Stranger. In the father's bookcase, we learn, he has found "parts of a certain aristocrat's famous memoirs—I took them out and shut the bookcase". The Stranger obviously refers to Casanova's erotic memoirs which have been concealed behind a number of respectable books in the bookcase.

STRANGER. /—/ And under that big oak over there I studied them. We called it the tree of knowledge, all right. And with that I left the paradise of childhood and was initiated, too early, into the secrets which ... Well!
DYER. You too?
STRANGER. Oh, you found them, too!

The brothers have not only stolen apples as children; they have also got hold of a forbidden book, introducing them to the mysteries of love. The parabolic pattern is now easy to see. The apple and the book are, in fact, one and the same thing. Just as God forbids Adam and Eve to partake of the knowledge of good and evil, the father of the brothers forbids them to acquaint themselves with the books in the bookcase. It is in this context interesting to see that the Dyer, too, is guilty of book-theft. On the pile of saved objects the Stranger discovers a book. It is his own book but his name has been erased: "So somebody stole it from me, and I accused a maid, who was fired as a result!"

At the end it appears that the Dyer is the thief. The emphasis, however, is not on the theft but on the duplicity and cowardliness the Dyer has demonstrated.

The bookcase testifies to the façade mentality of the family—a mentality which has served its purpose; compare the Old Woman's remark that the father was "a fine man". Among the visible books are "books of sermons, the works of great poets, books about orchards and gardening, collections of customs regulations and rules about confiscation, the national laws"—all works which suit a punishing Jehovah looking after his garden. Behind this apparent façade of law and order, care and culture, a number of objects are concealed: a cane (the attribute of punishment), a jar of cyanide (enough to poison recalcitrant individuals) and a collection of pornography (for self-satisfaction). The locked bookcase is clearly Strindberg's counterpart of the forbidden tree of knowledge. When the Stranger finds a key, opens the bookcase and discovers what has hitherto been concealed from him, it is equivalent to the eating of the forbidden fruit.

The conclusion we can draw from this is that the Stranger's revelation is more significant than it first appears. His accusations can, in fact, be interpreted on three levels. On the realistic one, it concerns of course the disclosure of the hypocrisy of his own family, notably of the father. But since the mentality of the family is a *pars pro toto* symbol of that of the species, it becomes, on the parabolic level, an accusation against all of mankind. This accusation is, however, considerably modified when the father is seen as a substitution for God; at this parabolic depth the guilt is transferred from mankind to their Creator. As in *A Dream Play,* the question posed is ultimately: "is the blame theirs / or yours"? (*SS*, XXXVI, 299).

As Sprinchorn has observed (1962*a*, xviii), a new Adam and Eve appear at the end of the play, when the beauty of the garden brings back memories of the dawn of creation. They are Alfred, the Gardener's son, and Matilda, the Stonecutter's daughter—in the notes referred to as "Eve". Resemblant of the original couple, they enter "hand in hand" and express their love of the garden:

ALFRED. I've had such a bad time in this house I often wished it would catch fire . . .
MATILDA. Well, I knew it shaded the garden and orchard too much; things should grow better now; unless they build a new and bigger house . . .
ALFRED. It's lovely and open, airy and sunny here, of course, and I've heard they're going to make it into a street . . .

In these speeches both a stage before the Fall, when only a garden existed, and a stage after it, with a house shading the garden (original sin), seem implied, maybe even a third future stage in which either the lost paradise is regained or, on the contrary, a tower of Babel is erected—compare the reference to a "tower of lies" in the notes.

In the love between Alfred and Matilda there is a paradisiac ingredient: *Amor vincit omnia*. But before long a touch of disharmony beclouds the happiness of the young couple. The seed of duplicity characteristic of the older generation has already been planted in them; their development seems sadly predestinated.

It is in this context of interest to note that Alfred is the son of Gardener Gustavsson. Does Strindberg here allude to Adam as son of the first Gardener, God? If we interpret the situation in these terms the following passage becomes metaphysically significant:

DETECTIVE. What sort of man is the gardener?
MASON. His name's Gustavsson ...
DETECTIVE. But what sort of man is he?
MASON. Listen! I'm seventy-five ... so I don't know anything bad about Gustavsson, and, if I did, I wouldn't stand here telling you!

Nothing but good about God! The Mason consistently adheres to his view that humanity is to be blamed.

This positive view of the Gardener cannot, however, be kept up. "Think of it: Father-in-law isn't what I thought he was", Matilda complains, after she has learned that the Gardener has merely pretended to be poor and tired, while in fact he is rich and lazy. "Maybe you're like that, too", she adds with dawning distrust, an ironic variation, it seems, of the idea that man is created in the image of God.

In the chamber plays houses, not human beings are the protagonists, it has been said with a certain justification (Rinman, 132)—darkening, rotting, burning or burned houses.[5] As the play title indicates, we are here concerned with the last category:

The left half of the back consists of the walls of a one-story house that has burned down; one can see the wallpaper on the walls and the tile stoves.
Behind the walls can be seen a fruit orchard in bloom.
To the right an inn with a wreath on a pole; tables and benches outside the inn.
To the left in the foreground rescued pieces of furniture and household utensils heaped in a pile.

As we have already noted, "the old house" is located in the block called the Morass, where all "hate each other, are suspicious of each other, slander each other, torment each other". And yet those who move away always come back to the Morass—the name seems adequate—until they move away for the last time, "to the cemetery up at the end of the street". "A whole lot has happened in this house", the Old Woman assures, "so much I thought it was time it got smoked out.—Ugh! What a house! The one came, and the other left, but they came back, they died here, they were born here, they got married and were divorced here." Significantly, the inn is called "The Last Nail", partly because the hearse drivers used to stop there on their way to the cemetery, partly because the criminals used to take their last drink there before they were taken to Gallows Hill.

It is evident that the Morass represents the world, a world filled with misery, from which we try to escape, and shadowed by imminent death. Usually the misery is concealed behind more or less impressive façades, but when the fire comes, they tumble down and the hideous interior is revealed. The demolished walls anticipate the demolition of the human façades and the revelation of the past to which the Stranger will soon devote himself. In this figurative sense he is the incendiary of the play.

The symbolic significance of the house is not immediately apparent. As usual Strindberg carries us from a realistic to a parabolic level. The house we see on the stage is not the house we believe it is. We too are victims of an optical delusion.

The play opens with two activities:

The PAINTER *is painting the window frames of the inn; he listens to all the conversations.*
The MASON *is digging in the ruins.*

On the realistic level, the one is patching up the paint that has flaked off because of the nocturnal fire, while the other is trying to locate the source of the fire. On the symbolic level, we deal with two contrasting activities. The Painter tries to cover up what the fire has laid bare, while the Mason on the contrary tries to reveal something. It is hardly a coincidence that the Painter is linked professionally with the Dyer, the primary exponent of the endeavor to conceal bare reality below an illusory layer of color,[6] while the Mason voices the same misanthropic view of humanity as the Stranger, the character who figuratively speaking is the one who is digging in the ruins. Directly in the opening of the drama, then, two silent minor characters illustrate the thematic conflict which the two chief characters, the brothers, are later to incarnate.

Connected with the house symbol are the interrelations between the characters. In one of the first speeches this is hinted at:

MASON. We all know each other, for there's something special about this street; the people who once move in here never get away.

The first indication of kinship is soon to follow:

DETECTIVE. Is the student related to the owner of the house?
MASON. No, I don't think so.

Note that the Mason is not certain; later it will appear that the Student may well be the Stranger's son, and in that case the Dyer is his uncle. The Mason's answer is more adequate than it originally appears.

The Mason and the Gardener, the list of *dramatis personae* informs us, are brothers-in-law. When the Old Woman, the Mason's wife, refers to the latter as "brother-in law", we understand that the Gardener is married to the Mason's sister. The Gardener has a son, Alfred, who is to marry the Stonecutter's daughter Matilda. The Hearse Driver is the Old Woman's cousin and the Stonecutter's second cousin, etc.

In addition to these blood relations there are other connections. The Old Woman has "worked for the dyer's father" forty years earlier, while Mrs. Vesterlund has cared for the Dyer himself when he was a baby. The Student teaches the Dyer's children and plays tennis with his wife.

The impression we get from this information is that the characters are all related to each other in some way or other—exactly how, we cannot make out. And this is precisely the point. Our first impression should be chaotic; the relations of the characters must seem as complicated and enigmatic as life itself. In short, the various relations form a complex, interwoven pattern; they corroborate the Stranger's view of life as a web woven by the World Weaver. In the same way the photograph album becomes "the book of our fate! Father's father and mother's mother, father and mother, brothers and sisters, the relatives, the so-called friends and schoolmates, the maids, our godparents ...". After this the demasking of the family—and the species—begins.

We can now see how Strindberg has structured the family theme. First he informs us that all the characters are related to each other. The concept 'family' hereby gains a much wider meaning than the traditional one. When the Stranger later speaks of 'family' in the conventional sense, we are prone to apply this wider meaning to his concept. The Valström photograph album in this way becomes not only *their* book of fate but that of humanity. The defects of the family (Sw. 'släkt') are those of the species (Sw. 'släkte'). When the Stranger, like a modern Caligula, pleads for capital punishment of all mankind, his view is well prepared for by the playmaker.

Although the misanthrophy does not disappear, there is an important change when the Stranger accepts the idea that he is related to the rest, that he too is an imperfect human being.[7]

STRANGER. /—/ When one has seen enough of the blue mists, one turns one's eyes inward to look into one's own soul. There's really something to look at there ...
WIFE. What?
STRANGER. Oneself! But when one has seen oneself, one dies!

The same uncertainty concerning the cause of the fire, is met with regard to the Stranger's possible paternity. The Student, we learn, is "a foundling, born to unknown parents". Shortly after this we hear that the Stranger had "a child in the orphanage". When the Student claims that his parents are no longer alive, the Stranger points out that he is lying, "but without knowing it".

STRANGER. /—/ I know your father.
STUDENT. I don't believe it!
STRANGER. So much the better for me!

Clearly, the Stranger at this point regards himself as the Student's father. A little later he asks himself: "Is he my child? /—/ And I'm his ... what else? Besides ... who knows?" The Stranger is now less certain and since his hesitation is part of a soliloquy, we may assume that he is truthful. A little later he has switched to a point of view contrary to the initial one; to the Stonecutter's question whether he knows the Student he replies:

STRANGER. Very little, but his mother was a maid in your house. She was both good and beautiful; I courted her; during that time she bore a child.
STONECUTTER. Aren't you its father then?
STRANGER. No-o! But since paternity may not be denied, I suppose I'm sort of a stepfather!

But if the Stranger here speaks the truth, why should he merely question the paternity in his soliloquy? The conclusion must be that he is uncertain about the true situation. He feels unjustly treated by the maid and by those who have testified against him. The Stonecutter is one of them. To deny the paternity is to take revenge on him.[8]

One of the more puzzling elements of the play is a number of references to the monument which is to be erected in memory of the bishop at the cemetery.[9] Many people want to take part in this ceremony. About the bishop we learn that he wrote books and that "he collected insects; /—/ He had cork slabs that he stuck needles in with flies on them". This is hardly a flattering portrait. The migration to the bishop's grave contrasts with the last journey of the anonymous dead man, without a wreath on the coffin and with "only *one* carriage". This is, in part, the significance of the references to the bishop.

But the attention bestowed on him also relates to the admiration the Stranger's and the Dyer's "respected family" has enjoyed, although they have all been "swindlers"—as well as to the celebrations of "the worst of our country's rulers", which make the Stranger experience the world as a "madhouse", an experience which in turn results in his attempt at suicide. The message is clear enough: the most respected in society deserve the least respect. The bishop, the Valström family and the ruler—all of them exemplify the façade mentality, the humbug.

One of the controversial elements of *The Burned House* is the protagonist. G. Lindström (1966, 63) calls the Stranger "the most elusive character in the play /—/ an inaccessible, shadowy figure". And Lamm (1926, 389f.) finds him irritatingly righteous in an unrighteous world, irritating because he is so similar to Strindberg himself. However, this similarity will not bother those who, unlike Lamm, are not familiar with Strindberg's biography. Lamm's analysis of the Stranger is also dubious in several respects. Thus he considers the Stranger's eagerness to unveil the shortcomings of his fellows an expression of his malicious joy. But if this is true, the Stranger is not as righteous as Lamm postulates.

As we have already noted the Stranger is not flawless. He has stolen apples. He has opened the locked bookcase and studied the tempting memoirs. He has unjustly accused a maid of having stolen his book about Columbus: "maybe that led to her fall". He is also responsible for the Painter's fate, he who longed to become an artist. Finally, he has escaped to America "because of debt".

However, the Stranger's list of sins is not very burdensome. The stealing of apples and books are expressions of the collective original sin. His actions toward the maid and the Painter were undertaken in good faith. Only the last point seems obscure. An explicit reason is never provided, but it is natural to combine the escape to America with the paternity case. On dubious grounds the Stranger has been judged father of the Stonecutter's maid's child. And he is said to have seduced "someone else's wife". As a matter of fact, it is suggested, that the maid has been unfaithful to him. Even so, the Stranger is not altogether rehabilitated. As we have seen, he is not certain that he is not the father of the child. And he has in any case let himself be seduced by the wife, and this, too, is a form of adultery. Moreover, if the Stranger had considered himself innocent, he would have no reason to tell the Student the opposite. As far as one can see, the escape to America was determined both by personal feelings of shame and by a need to leave a corrupt society.

If we compare the Stranger to the other characters, we can state that—apart from the still innocent Alfred and Matilda—he is less guilty than they are. At the same time he is (therefore?) far more anxious to reveal the crimes and the duplicity. The others are primarily eager to identify the incendiary, to find a scapegoat, someone who can take over their sins. The Stranger does not accept this attitude; according to him, everyone must be responsible for his own deeds and openly admit his shortcomings.

The Stranger's exceptional position is indicated in different ways. Unlike the static inhabitants of the Morass, he is a man who has traveled around, a man who knows the world and mankind. This alone makes his pronouncements on life weighty. But more essential it is that he also in another respect has a wider knowledge than the rest:

OLD WOMAN. /—/ And for many years they thought their brother Arvid in America was dead /—/ but, as I said, they say now he's back, though no one has seen him—

DYER. You are Arvid?
STRANGER. Yes! (*Pause.*)
DYER. So you're not dead?
STRANGER. Yes, in a way!

PAINTER. Is—it—Mr. Arvid?
STRANGER. Has been and is, if being perceived is being.

LADY. They say you've been on the other side . . .

STRANGER. I've been across the river, but I don't remember anything, but—that everything there *was* what it seemed to be! That's the difference!

DYER. Are you haunting the ruins?
STRANGER. Ghosts thrive on ruins.

As appears from this collection of quotations, the idea that the Stranger fundamentally differs from the rest is kept up throughout the play; not only has he been across the sea, he has also been across the river (Styx). The thirty year stay in America somehow seems to combine with the days he spent in the mortuary, "as someone dead", after his attempt at suicide, motivated by the misery of the world. About this decisive event in his life he says:

When I regained consciousness, I thought I was in someone else's body; /—/ But in death I had gained new skills . . . I saw right through people, read their thoughts, heard their intentions. When I was in a group, I saw them all naked . . .

The experience of death has given him an extraordinary power. As he himself implies, the Stranger has a certain affinity to "the Saviour". Like Jesus, he can penetrate people's souls and like Him he seems able to perform miracles. He is the only one who prays to "the Eternal One", and his attribute is a "tie pin" bought at "Charing Cross"; note how Strindberg, by the indication of place, as it were, turns the tie pin (Sw. "kråsnål") into a cross (Sw. 'kors'), a cross which the Stranger tries to hand over to the Student. Above all: like Jesus, the Stranger has 'died'—on Maundy Thursday!—and again 'arisen' from the dead. His return to the home of his childhood can be compared to the revelation of Christ to the disciples. Relevant in this context is the Stranger's remark "I have never felt related to you", a statement which could have been made by Indra's Daughter.[10]

Is the Stranger a Christ figure, then, in the sense that his pupose is to save his fellows? On this matter the play is not very lucid. There is a touch of cool rationality about the Stranger which does not seem to harmonize with the Christian gospel of love. A "technician" by profession, the Stranger's view of life is marked by a scientific distance which may recall that of Swedenborg. About his *vita nuova* he says:

I took life calmly in a cynical way; that's how it should be, I thought! And the worse it was, the more interesting it became . . . I now considered myself someone else, and I observed, studied this other person and his fate, which made me insensitive to my own sufferings.

Time after another this *flaneur* mentality is emphasized through the use of the active/passive word 'interesting':

STRANGER. You certainly haven't changed.
DYER. Have you?
STRANGER. Have I? That's interesting!

STRANGER. Just as suspicious and evil-minded as ever! That's interesting.

STRANGER. My family? I've never felt related to you, never have had any feelings for my fellow men or for myself; I just think it's interesting to look at people . . .

STRANGER. /—/ Shall we go into the orchard for a while to look at the apple trees?
DYER. Yes, we can; then we'll get to see what happens afterward.
STRANGER. Now comes what's interesting!
DYER. Maybe not so interesting, if you get mixed up in it.

STRANGER. /—/ But your husband is a still more interesting case: he has lied together a whole character for himself.

The Stranger here appears as a cool observer of life. People are at most interesting as cases. He himself remains an outsider, a "stranger". Life is to him a spectacle:

I've seen life from every point of the compass and all points of view, from above and from below, but always as if it had been staged especially for me; through that I've finally reconciled myself with part of the past, and have come to excuse other people's and my own so-called faults.

This is a strange way of reconciling oneself with life. As Lamm points out (1926, 385), a contrary view—that life passes on regardless of the individual—would be more natural to him who wants to reconcile himself with life. Should we then interpret the Stranger's words as an expression of his egocentricity, his hubris? In that case we must conclude that this hubris is never punished in the play, an idea which is difficult to accept.

But the Stranger's words can, I believe, be interpreted in another way. By his idea that everything is staged especially for him, the Stranger only means that nothing happens by chance. There is a Director behind everything that happens in life. The Stranger does not have any exclusive rights. Anyone may have the same feeling that everything is staged for him/her especially. The need to experience life in such subjective terms is universal.

Possibly, his view could seem a bit enforced. And we may well wonder whether the Stranger's observing attitude is not a pose. Is he not far more engaged than he pretends to be? Does he not feel related to the rest? Do they not concern him as fellow men? Certain passages in the play seem to suggest this.

Thus we may note that his turning up after thirty years is according to the rule of the Morass: "the ones who move away always come back all the same, sooner or later". In his case the return is caused by something which kept drawing him back: "I had to see my childhood home again"—an emotional reason. That he wants to reconcile himself with the past appears from the fact that he is going to put a wreath on his parents' grave—although he is not at all indebted to them. When he learns that Vesterlund has been false to him, he gets very upset—after thirty years! Where is the cool observer now? His way of expressing himself is also often very emotional. The family consisted of "swindlers", we live in "the world of illusions and fools", you ought to "put a rope around everyone's neck", etc.

As Steene (1973, 110) has pointed out, the Stranger's arrogant view of the world is partly "a rationalized attitude". While the rest are worse than they want to appear, he is better. His façade is the armour of an oversensitive person. His attitude to his fellow men is certainly that of the revealer and punisher but he can also be forgiving. He enjoys the love of the young couple. He consoles the Wife by speaking of the hope for something better. He even shows indulgence with his brother: "Go in peace, Brother!"

In short, the Stranger is, as he himself indicates, a divided person. As a consequence of this, his revelatory eagerness, like Gregers Werle's, may seem dubious. If we could be convinced that he is driven by love for his fellow men—well, then he becomes far more acceptable as a protagonist and as an object of identification than if he merely returns to the past in order to avenge himself. Up to the end, the Stranger remains a character with both components inside himself. As a psychological portrait this is convincing but dramaturgically Strindberg might have settled for a happier solution.

The tragic protagonist is ethically superior to the average person—in this respect the Stranger does not differ markedly from the classical pattern. But in addition to this—and this is remarkable—he has a knowledge surpassing that which we consider possible for a human being. His experience of life beyond death should not, however, be understood literally. He *has* not been on the other side, he only feels it that way. But this feeling is enough to give him a new perspective on existence. The distinction is possibly unessential. Essential it is that the Stranger, not only with regard to the other characters but also with regard to us—the audience—with his special knowledge of life beyond, comes to play the part of the initiated, of Master.

11. *Sein* and *Schein* in *Spöksonaten* / *The Ghost Sonata*

A few weeks after its completion Strindberg sent *The Ghost Sonata* to his German translator, Emil Schering. In the letter accompanying the manuscript, dated March 27, 1907, he comments on the theme of the play:

It is *schauderhaft* like life, when the scales fall from the eyes and one sees *Das Ding an Sich*.

There is form to it, and content, the wisdom which comes with the years, when experience has accumulated and the power to survey is there. This is how "the World Weaver" is weaving human destinies, all these secrets are found in *every* home. People are just too conceited to admit it; most of them boast of their imagined happiness, and usually they try to conceal their misery. The Colonel plays his autocomedie to the end; the illusion (Maya) has become reality to him—the Mummy is the first to awaken, but she cannot wake the others ...

I have suffered as though I were in Kama Loka (Scheol) while writing and my hands have (literally) been bleeding.

What has kept my soul from plunging into darkness during my work is my religion (= *Anschluss mit Jenseits*), the hope of something better and the firm conviction that we live in a world of illusion and folly from which we must struggle to free ourselves.

On the contrary, things seem brighter than before, and I have been writing with the feeling that these are my "last Sonatas". (*ASB*, XV, 354)

As Strindberg clarifies in this letter, *The Ghost Sonata* is a play not so much about individuals as about mankind; and its fundamental theme is the conflict between reality (*Sein*) and illusion (*Schein*), between seeming and being, a conflict which operates both on the human and the metaphysical level (Törnqvist, 1970*a*). We could also put it this way: Like the other chamber plays, *The Gost Sonata* is not primarily a play describing relations *between* human beings—in the fashion of traditional intrigue drama. It is rather "ein episches Spiel über die Menschen" (Szondi, 54), a metaphysical drama just as *A Dream Play*. It is also, in a sense, a play *within* the central intelligence, the Student; it is primarily *his* vision of life we partake of, just as in *The Father* we partake primarily of the Captain's vision, in *To Damascus* of the Stranger's vision and in *A Dream Play* of that of Indra's Daughter. All four—the Captain, the Stranger, Indra's Daughter, the Student—and especially the last two, function much as the chorus in Greek tragedy or the narrator in a novel. Placed somewhere between the rest of the characters and the audience, their purpose is to serve as objects of identification. In their experience of life Strindbergian drama finds its objective correlative.

The play is structured as follows:

[*Act*]	*Seq.*	*Page/ line in* *SS* XLV	*On stage*															
I	A	149/1																
	1	149/24	DL	CW	OM													
	2	150/1	DL	CW	OM	M												
	3	150/9	DL	CW	*OM*	M	*S*											
	4	151/28	DL	CW	*OM*		*S*+											
	5	157/1	DL	CW	OM													
	6	157/4	DL	CW	*OM*		*S*											
	7	158/4	DL	CW+	*OM*		*S*	C										
	8	159/27	DL		*OM*		*S*	C										
	9	161/4	DL		*OM*		*S*	C	F									
	10	161/22	DL	CW	*OM*		*S*	C	F									
	11	164/1	DL	CW	OM		S	C	F	YL								
	12	164/5	DL	CW	*OM*		*S*	C	F									
	13	165/17	DL	CW	*OM*		S	C	F	YL								
	14	166/8	DL	CW	*OM*		*S*	C	F	YL	D							
	15	166/28	DL	CW	*OM*		*S*	C	F	YL								
	16	167/10	DL	CW	*OM*		S	C	F	YL		J						
	17	167/27	DL	CW			S	C	F	YL								
	18	168/1	*DL*	CW			S	C	F	YL			*A*					
	19	168/16	DL	CW			*S*	C	F	YL		*J*	A					
	20	172/6	DL	CW	*OM*		S	C	F	YL		J	A	B				
	21	172/20	DL	CW	*OM*		S	C	F	YL		J	A	B	Ma			
	22	173/1–12	DL	CW	*OM*	M	*S*	C	F	YL		*J*	A	B	Ma			
II	B	174/1																
	23	174/6						C		YL								
	24	174/8						C		YL		*J*				*Be*		
	25	176/1						C		YL		*J*				*Be*	*Mu*	
	26	176/24						C		YL		*J*				*Be*		
	27	178/11			*OM*			C		YL		*J*				*Be*		
	28	179/10			*OM*			C		YL		J						
	29	179/16			*OM*			C		YL								
	30	179/22			*OM*			C		YL								
	31	184/1			*OM*			*C*		YL								
	32	187/25			*OM*		*S*	*C*		YL								
	33	188/30			OM		S	*C*	F	YL								
	34	189/12			*OM*		S	*C*	F	YL			A					
	35	189/23			OM		S	*C*	F	YL			A				*Mu*	
	36	193/10			OM	M	S	C	F	YL			A				Mu	
	37	193/12			OM		S	C	F	YL			A			*Be*	*Mu*	
	38	194/5			*OM*		S	C	F	YL		J	A			Be	*Mu*	
	39	194/28–195/22					*S*	*C*	*F*	YL		*J*	*A*			*Be*	*Mu*	
III	C	196/1																
	40	196/7					*S*	C		*YL*							Mu	
	41	201/22					*S*	C		YL							Mu	*Co*
	42	202/1					*S*	C		*YL*							Mu	

[*Act*]	*Seq.*	*Page/ line in SS* XLV	*On stage*					
	43	205/6		*S*	C	*YL*		Mu *Co*
	44	205/24		*S*	C	*YL*		Mu
	45	210/5		S	C	*YL*	Be+	Mu
	46	210/7		S	C	YL		Mu
	47	210/8		S	C	YL	Be+	Mu
	48	210/10		*S*+	C			Mu
	49	211/5–7	Böcklin's *Toten-Insel*					

+ designates exit not indicated by Strindberg.

Abbreviations

DL = The Dark Lady
CW = The Caretaker's Wife
OM = The Old Man, director Hummel
M = The Milkmaid, an apparition
S = The Student, Arkenholz
C = The Colonel
F = The Fiancée, Beate von Holsteinkrona
YL = The Young Lady, Adèle
D = The Dead Man, the consul
J = Johansson
A = The Aristocrat, baron Skanskorg
B = Beggars
Ma = The Maid
Be = Bengtsson
Mu = The Mummy, Amalia
Co = The Cook

As appears from the scheme, Strindberg has not always clearly indicated the exits of the characters. This is especially remarkable at the end of the play, where the solution suggested here is, in fact, only one of three possible solutions. Alternatively, we may imagine that the Student remains on the stage also during the final sequence. More awkward but formally acceptable it is to let also Bengtsson remain during seq. 49. The question of whether or not the Student should be visible when *Toten-Insel* is reproduced, is connected with the question of to what extent we regard the final vision as an expression of his subjective experience. The alternative we have selected emphasizes, rather, the universal significance of the final tableau and testifies to the playwright's endeavor to influence the audience directly. Presumably the kind of ending Strindberg had in mind was so obvious to him that he forgot to explicate it.

Similarly, there are other inadvertencies which can best be accounted for as carelessness resulting from Strindberg's fast way of writing (Falck, 81 f.) and his negligence as a proof-reader. Thus "the Caretaker" figures in the list of *dramatis personae* although he does not appear in the play; while on the contrary the Cook, the Maid and the Beggars appear in the play but not in the list of characters. It is also remarkable how little attention Strindberg pays to the Dark Lady—considering the fact that she is on the stage throughout Act I. Why does he not let her and the Aristocrat take part in the homage paid to the Student in seq. 20? Has he forgotten to indicate an exit on their part after seq. 18? Or do they continue their conversation whisperingly while the rest hail the Student? What about the Caretaker's Wife? Does she remain on the stage until the end of the act or does she exit shortly after her conversation with the Young Lady in seq. 11? We may also wonder whether the guests at the ghost supper remain on the stage when the Student recites the Song of the Sun at the end of Act II (seq. 39) or whether the asterisk in the middle of this sequence indicates their exit. Strindberg does not clarify these matters and it is evident that our sequence scheme to some extent is based on interpretation.

Only three of the characters—the Student, the Young Lady and the Colonel—appear in all the three acts. It is also noteworthy that the number of characters diminishes with each act: if we exclude the Beggars of the first act, we have in Act I twelve characters, in Act II nine and in Act III six. The gradual reduction harmonizes with the shrinking space which seems indicated in the series street, round room, hyacinth room.

Of great interest is the frequent use of mute sequences and characters: no less than ten of the forty-nine sequences depend on pantomime. In Act I seven of the characters (plus the Beggars) are mute, while two only have a few lines to speak. In fact, there are only three proper speaking parts: the Old Man, the Student, Johansson. In Act II five of the characters are mute, or nearly so, while five have speaking parts. In Act III there are three speaking parts against three mute ones. A glance at the distribution of silent/spoken sequences with regard to the different characters reveals that several of the speaking parts have long moments of silence. Thus the Colonel speaks only in six sequences, while he remains mute in thirthy-six; for the Young Lady the corresponding figures are 5–31, for the Mummy 6–10.

On the whole, the unity of place is (loosely) adhered to in the play. We find ourselves either outside or inside a bourgeois apartment house. Moreover, every act is spatially linked to the next one; thus in Act I we can look into the round room (as well as into the hyacinth room), the playing area for Act II, and once inside the round room we look into the hyacinth room, where Act III takes place; not until the end of the play is this unity destroyed through the introduction of Böcklin's *Toten-Insel.*

Also with regard to time, the three acts are kept together. Act I opens on a Sunday morning, Act II plays in the afternoon and evening of the same day, Act III a few days after Hummel's funeral about a week later. Again the introduction of *Toten-Insel* means a disruption of the temporal unity.

However, through the spatial arrangement of Acts II and III—we see just about the same people from opposite directions—Strindberg creates the illusion that hardly any time at all has passed between these acts. Also in other parts of the play an uncertain sense of time is created. Thus the ticking of the clock and the many pauses during the ghost supper contribute to the impression that the fictive time is much longer than the playing time.

Parabolically, the play covers a whole life or even, in a sense, the history of mankind. We can thus speak of no less than three different time levels in *The Ghost Sonata.*

It has been a matter of dispute whether the play has a unity of action or not. Usually the Old Man, Hummel, being the most active character in the play, is considered the protagonist. But in that case his disappearance at the end of Act II becomes problematic. Those who adhere to this view have also concluded that Act III signifies an unnecessary repetition of what we have already witnessed (Szondi, 56).

It is, however, not necessary to view the action in this way. It is noteworthy that the vampiristic Old Man of Acts I–II has a counterpart in the Cook of Act III; this character was, significantly, added at a late stage, presumably in an attempt to strengthen the unity of the play. The connection between Hummel and the Cook could be interpreted in different ways; it stresses, we could argue, the idea that evil is an intextricable part of life; or we could even, in this play about spectres, see the Cook as a reincarnation of Hummel: after his death, he avenges himself by haunting the house in the form of the huge Cook. If we focus on the Young Lady, rather than on Hummel, we can state that the play mainly deals with the possibility of saving her from the (symbolic) house. In the first two acts the Old Man tries to save her, in the last one the Student. But also the Student, the observer of the house and its people and the only outsider in the play, has a unifying function. Schematically the action is as follows:

Acts I–II		Act III
	The rescue of the Young Lady	
Rescue attempt by the Old Man	→	Rescue attempt by the Student
Revenge attempt by the Old Man	→	Revenge attempt by the Cook
	The Student studies life	

An excellent example of the combination of old and new techniques we find in the exposition. As G. Lindström (1964*b*, 169) has pointed out, Strindberg resorts to several well-known types of exposition. In Act I he has the Student, who knows nothing about the house, be informed by the Old Man; we get here a dialogue of questions and answers. At the beginning of Act II this type of exposition is repeated in the gossip between two servants; here Bengtsson informs the new-comer Johansson, who functions as a kind of stand-in for the Student ("it was always my dream to enter this house"). The ghost supper parodies another classical type of exposition: the meeting of old acquaintances. In Act III we find yet another kind: two people in love who have recently met.

It is the first of these types—the conversation between the Old Man and the Student—which Strindberg handles in an unconventional way: Hummel's description of the people in the house is supplemented by the dumb shows of the characters he is commenting on.

According to Szondi the development of modern drama is characterized by an increasing resort to epic devices as a result of the fact that interest in inter-human relations has been replaced by a (psychoanalytically determined) concern for intra-human aspects. In *The Ghost Sonata*—so runs his argument—people need an epic presentator since their own versions are altogether subjective and unreliable (Szondi, 55). As the Colonel puts it: "What's the point of talking—we can't fool each other anyway."

However, the Old Man is far from being the objective guide Szondi would have us believe. On the contrary, he more than anyone else illustrates the deceit referred to by the Colonel. It is true that Hummel's speeches carry a strong epic note: he is chiefly commenting on the people dwelling in the house. But the point is that he has very intimate, guilt-laden relations to them; presumably this is precisely why he feels such a need for commenting on them: he is actually constantly justifying himself to the Student. When this gradually becomes clear, his authority as objective narrator is considerably undermined; it is in fact virtually impossible to make out to what extent Hummel can be trusted.

In a letter dated October 22, 1908 Strindberg refers to *The Ghost Sonata* as a fairy tale playing in modern times (G. Lindström, 1963*b*, 96). As Mays has demonstrated, the play can indeed be read as a "parodied fairy tale". Here is the courageous young hero, who sees what others cannot see because he is a "Sunday child". He falls in love with a beautiful lady who lives in a 'castle' which seems like a paradise to the hero. A benevolent 'magician' helps him to find his way into the castle. In the second act we discover that there are 'trolls' inside who keep the young 'princess' prisoner. The magician is prepared to fight with them. In the last act hero and princess seem happily united but the play does not end the way we expect. The hero is disillusioned: "Where is honor and faith? In fairy tales and children's plays!" Yet the paradise of the fairy tale can be found just the same—beyond life. There are the stable values lacking in life. The bold knight of the fairy tale who saves the princess from the dragon has his counterpart in *The Ghost Sonata* in the young man who 'saves' the young woman from the hell of life in exchange for a heavenly paradise. The immanent happiness of the fairy tale is replaced by a transcendent one in Strindberg's play.

The play title, as Strindberg notes in a letter to Schering dated April 1, 1907, alludes to "the *Gespenster* Sonata (we may call it so after Beethoven's Ghost Sonata in D minor and his Ghost Trio, hence not *Spuk*)" (*ASB,* XV, 355). What is here referred to is the Piano Sonata No. 17 in D Minor (Op. 31, No. 2), usually called "Der Sturm", and the Piano Trio No. 4 in D Major (Op. 70, No. 1), usually called "Geister-Trio".

Strindberg's interest in "Der Sturm" has been discussed by G. Lindström (1962). The D Minor Sonata is played during the 'ghost hour' in *There Are Crimes and Crimes,* where it voices the pangs of conscience suffered by the protagonist. Strindberg sometimes referred to this sonata as "the conscience drill". The ghosts in *The Ghost Sonata*--the Milkmaid and the Consul—have a similar function; both have been 'murdered' by Hummel and their return from the dead is an expression of his pangs of conscience.

Another, less esoteric attempt to explain the play title we find among those critics who believe that Strindberg has above all been concerned with "the concept of chamber music transferred to drama" (*SS*, L, 11). The subtitle "chamber play opus 3" seems to support such a view. Thus Steene (1973, 113) argues that the play is

> divided into three movements (Scenes) according to the musical form ABA. Scenes 1 and 3 concern the Student's confrontation with the world of the play; scene 2 in which the Student takes no active part deals with the guests at the ghost supper and their unmasking. Finally, the Student brings the play to a close by a restatement and summing-up ("the coda") of its major themes: he tells the story of his father's "ghost supper" when he (the father) revealed the truth and was destroyed by it; and he concludes that death is the only relief from the pain of living.

Reasonable though this may seem, the connection between the *temporal* qualities determining the movements of a sonata and the *spatial* arrangement in Strindberg's play is exceedingly loose.

Other critics have seen the three acts of the play as rhythmically related to musical movements. Thus Sprinchorn (1962*a*, xx) finds that

> The three scenes of the play correspond to the three movements of a sonata, the principal theme being introduced immediately in the first scene with the secondary themes quickly following. The first and longest scene /—/ is a brisk allegro, its mood sustained by the youthful buoyancy of the Student and by the grasping eagerness of the Old Man as they lay their plans for entering the house of elegance. In sharp contrast is the second scene or movement, the largo. To its slow tempo and its long silences the ghost supper takes place. The final scene is a quiet andante, which stresses the principal theme of the sonata and brings it to a close with a brilliant coda that restates all themes.

How personal this interpretation of the three 'movements' is appears from the fact that Berendsohn (541 ff.) has used different designations for the last two parts: allegro furioso, largo; while Vowles (1967, 175 f.) wishes to identify the whole play with the second movement of the Piano Trio: largo assai ed espressivo.[1]

As a matter of fact, the variations of tempo within each act are so great that every designation must be misleading—except, perhaps, the designation 'coda' with regard to the Student's final monologue. In a sonata one distinguishes between an expository part, presenting the theme, an executive part and a repetitive part similar to the expository one and ending in a coda, which often (particularly with Beethoven) grows into a second execution.

This scheme bears, it would seem, a certain kinship to *The Ghost Sonata.* It is, for example, obvious that Act III opens in a light and hopeful mood, recalling the situation at the beginning of Act I, while the second part of this act, the coda, signifies a furious repetition of what has earlier taken place (the 'murder' of the Young Lady corresponding to the drowning of the Milkmaid and the 'murder' of Hummel) and an execution (development) since the Student, not Hummel, is now the agent.

When Strindberg notes that "the significant theme" forms an important part of what he means by "the concept of chamber music transferred to drama" (*SS,* L, 11), he seems to be saying much the same as Hummel, when he states that "though the tales are different, they all hang together on a thread, and the theme recurs regularly". The fundamental theme of the play, we have already noted, is the antithesis between being and seeming, between *Sein* and *Schein.* The events which take place, the activities of the characters, the existence shown to us—all are but variations, concretizations of this basic theme. In this arrangement we find the essential reason why we may legitimately speak of a 'musical' structure in *The Ghost Sonata.*

The prescenic action in *The Ghost Sonata* is complicated and, on several points, obscure. It therefore seems legitimate to attempt an unravelling of the various human destinies with which we are confronted. The following presentation of the characters (in order of appearance) is based on the facts presented in the text plus an interpretation of these facts. Needless to say, the facts may be combined and interpreted also in other ways.

The Old Man. The 80-year-old director Jacob Hummel—the name is false—became engaged to Beate von Holsteinkrona when he was twenty, but when she allowed herself to be seduced by the Colonel, the engagement was broken. To avenge himself Hummel seduces the Colonel's wife, Amalia. She gives birth to his daughter Adèle. When the Colonel learns about what has happened, he beats his wife. Amalia divorces him, perhaps in the hope that Hummel will marry her and take care of their daughter. But Hummel "gets the women to leave when he's tired of them" or he alternatively loses his women. Amalia therefore remarries the Colonel.

Among the many women with whom Hummel has had a liaison, Bengtsson's cook is one. For two years Hummel has been a sponger in

Bengtsson's kitchen. He also seems to have drowned the little Milkmaid while staying in Hamburg as a usurer and "bloodsucker". He has ruined his youth friend, merchant Arkenholz, a circumstance which seems to have led to Arkenholz' insanity and premature death. He has caused the death of the Consul by running him into debt, literally and figuratively. He has turned Johansson into a "slave", chief servant among the servants (the Beggars) with whom he surrounds himself.

Hummel also has a son, "a scoundrel" who tortures the life out of him. (We never learn who the mother is.) At the end of the drama we get to know that this son has had a homosexual relationship with the man who carried the mace at Hummel's funeral and that Hummel has borrowed money "from his son's admirer". The Old Man has thus utilized his son for his own egoistic purposes. Is this why he regards the son as a scoundrel? The courageous Student appears to be a healthy contrast to Hummel's own son.[2] By having the Student inherit him "alive", Hummel deprives his own son of the inheritance.

Hummel claims that he is "very rich", and Johansson describes him as a powerful man: "he looks at houses, tears them down, opens up streets, settles squares" and "he always keeps in good with policemen".

As we have seen, Hummel has much on his conscience. He is a hardened liar, Don Juan, tyrant, usurer, "horse thief in the human market", "vampire" and murderer. All in all, his crimes indicate his complete recklessness toward his fellow-men. Indeed, Hummel bears a certain kinship to the Devil himself.

Is Hummel, then, altogether evil? His assurance that he "has not always been like this" and that "one is always related to them [people] in some way" suggests at least that he has not always been the way he is now. Although he is undoubtedly the most guilt-laden character of the play—he is presumably also the oldest one and the connection does not seem coincidental—it is not he but the Colonel who has initiated the chain of crimes. Nothing prevents us from seeing Hummel as a once innocent young man, who has gradually lost faith in his fellow-men after the Fiancée and the Colonel have deceived him. With this interpretation his brutality against the Colonel becomes understandable.

However, Hummel is not always negative about others. He admits that the Consul could be compassionate. He points out that the Fiancée, once young and beautiful, is still attractive. And his comment on the Young Lady is *con amore*: "Have you ever seen such a masterpiece?" Admittedly, he is at this point anxious to get the Student interested in the Young Lady. Hummel himself adheres to the view that his recklessness is primarily determined by his love for his daughter: "That was my mission in this house: to get rid of the weeds, expose the crime, bring the accounts to a conclusion, so that the young people may have a fresh start in this home, which I have given them!"

But other reasons are also possible. Confronted with the Student and the Young Lady, Hummel may well in them relive his own youthful self and that of the Fiancée—just as he recalls the Mummy as a young woman when he regards the marble statue of her. From a quite different point of view, his altruism vis-à-vis the young couple may be seen as resulting from his pangs of conscience. "You see, I have *taken,* all my life; now I have a longing to give, give", he confesses to the Student. The demand for the good deed that will wipe out the crimes committed in the past and reconcile the Powers, begins to feel urgent to the aging man. He now wants to play the role of benefactor to the Student, the son of the man against whom he has trespassed: "before I die, I want to see you happy ... Our destinies are linked through your father—and other things ...". But Hummel does not see, or refuses to see, that the means he employs—the one-sided demasking of others—is in fact a new crime, hubris, which is punished according to the law of retribution.

The Student. The young Arkenholz, we have already noted, occupies a special place in the play: that of observer, interlocutor, catalyst (Kjellin/Ramnefalk, 93 f.) Assisted by the Old Man, he regards the house and its inhabitants from the outside in Act I. In Act II he has entered the house. In Act III he learns about its many deficiencies. Not until all this has happened, is he ready to take an active part in the play.

The Student obviously represents man(kind). Innocent and hopeful he enters life (the stage), different from all those who have been there for some time and who are marked by it. The contrast is strengthened by the fact that the Student is the only character who (initially) is independent of the house and its inhabitants. Gradually he gets to know life, outwardly and inwardly. On the basis of his experience he makes up the balance.

It is evident that the play is structured in such a way that the Student's experience of the house (of life) is more or less synchronized with our own. It is true that he is absent from the great demasking during the ghost supper, but from his final monologue we conclude that he has learned about it. At the beginning of Act III he can nevertheless cling to his initial optimism, because he still regards the Young Lady as untainted by the duplicity characterizing humanity at large.

The Student is surprisingly versatile. He is interested in sports, mathematics, music, he sings, writes poetry, studies languages. In short, he has a great lust for life. His interest in languages has a symbolic meaning, for "languages are codes and the one who finds the key understands all the languages of the world". Arkenholz is seeking the meaning beneath and beyond the words or, to put it differently, a language which *expresses* thoughts instead of disguising them. In the last instance he studies life. Rather conventionally, he dreams of a beautiful young wife, pretty children and wealth. But he also harbors more unusual qualities. At the collapse of the house he has proved active and courageous. And as a Sunday child he can see what others cannot see.

The Student's name, Arkenholz, has been explained in different ways (G.

Lindström, 1963*b,* 81; H. Lindström, 1979, 32). Suggestive is Sprinchorn's (1962*a,* 226) idea that the name refers to the biblical ark made of wood (Germ. 'Holz'), indicating how the Student is another Noah, as it were, trying to save people from catastrophes. It is indeed a kind of deluge that we witness at the end of the play. "Alas for all of us. Saviour of the world, save us; we perish", the Student exlaims after he has declared that a curse rests on all creation.

At the very beginning of the play, the Student is linked with two other biblical figures. When he says that he has "bandaged up injured people and kept watch over the sick all night", we associate him both with Jesus and with the compassionate Samaritan—especially since he refers to the Milkmaid as the "good Samaritan". The expression is a key to the whole sequence which, as Northam (1966, 41) has first observed, recalls the passage in John 4: 7–14, where Jesus meets a woman of Samaria at Jacob's well. "Give me to drink", he asks her. "Give me a drink of water", the Student asks the Milkmaid. When he begs her to bathe his poor eyes with the "fresh water", it directly alludes to the following words by the Samarian woman: "from whence then hast thou that living water? Art thou greater than our father Jacob, which gave us the well, and drank thereof himself, and his children, and his cattle?" (John 4: 11–12). The 'conversation' between the Student and the Milkmaid takes place next to the street drinking fountain; close by we see 'father Jacob' Hummel, seated in his wheelchair. The antithesis in the biblical text between Jacob's earthly water, which only temporarily quenches the thirst, and Jesus' living water which does so eternally, is here latently present in the contrast between earthly existence on which Hummel's power rests and the heavenly one for which the Student finally hopes.

The Milkmaid. Her fate is linked with that of Hummel, as Bengtsson informs us:

> Later on I ran across this man [Hummel] in Hamburg under another name. He was a loan shark or bloodsucker; but he was also accused of luring a girl out on to the ice to drown her, because she had witnessed a crime he was afraid would be discovered . . .

That Hummel also managed to drown the Milkmaid appears from the fact that, when she appears for the second time, "*she stretches up her arms like a drowning person and fixes the glance of the old man*".

What kind of crime, then, witnessed by the Milkmaid, had the Old Man committed? Why a milkmaid? Is she Swedish or German? And why does she wear summer clothes if she was drowned in the winter?

What we would expect is that Hummel, who "has been a Don Juan" and who "gets the women to leave when he's tired of them", has seduced the girl, and that this has led to undesirable consequences (Fraenkl, 53). But Bengtsson's way of expressing himself is in that case somewhat strange; it gives us rather the impression that the Milkmaid has witnessed how Hummel has seduced another woman. Hummel himself also declares: "on such issues, as I'm referring to, one does not take any witnesses along; nature itself has provided man with a sense of shame, which tries to conceal what should be concealed". The vagueness of Bengtsson's way of expressing himself is possibly determined by the fact that it underlines the parallel between the relationship the Milkmaid-Hummel and Hummel-Johansson; the latter has committed an error which only Hummel knows about.

As Berendsohn (543) has pointed out, the Milkmaid has a distinctive function: "She frightens her murderer Hummel, but is helpful to a good young man. The Student's goodness could hardly be better illustrated." This leads us straight to the symbolic significance of the Milkmaid.

The theme of food takes a prominent place in Strindberg's writings. In a very fundamental sense, food to him means life. "Scarce or spoilt food is a threat to life. To feed at the breast or to hand out food is a holy, life-giving act of love" (Delblanc, 1968, 94). The sucking vampire has her antipode in the suckling mother. Hummel and the Cook are the vampires of the play. But where do we find the opposite, nourishing character? Ironically enough in the character who is but a vision: the Milkmaid. Undoubtedly Strindberg has turned the young girl into a milkmaid precisely because he wanted to indicate that she represents the nurturing, loving force in life. When he provides the Cook with "a coloring bottle with scorpion letters on it", he gives her an attribute which blatantly contrasts with the Milkmaid's white bottles.

The Caretaker's Wife. Her husband has received his post as caretaker of the house in 'payment' for the Consul's sleeping with his wife. The Dark Lady is the result of this adultery.

The Dead Man. The information about the Consul is rather controversial. The Consul, vain and charitable, has become indebted to the usurer Hummel. In vain he tries to repay his debts by cheating the state. When he does not succeed, he commits suicide. This is why the Mummy can tell Hummel: "you murdered the consul /–/, you killed him with promissory notes". We even get an indication of how the Consul has died; when the Mummy sends Hummel away to the closet, she does it with the words: "There's a cord hanging in there that can represent the one you strangled the consul with up there."

The Dark Lady. She is an illegitimate daughter (cf. the Young Lady) of the dead Consul and the Caretaker's Wife. The following line by Hummel indicates that she knows who her real father is: "now his daughter in another man's marriage is wondering about inheriting". In the short, cryptic conversation between her and the Aristocrat the nature of their relationship is indicated. The lines read:

THE ARISTOCRAT. Well, what can we do about that?—We'll have to wait!
THE LADY. But I can't wait!
THE ARISTOCRAT. Really? Then go to the country!
THE LADY. I don't want to.
THE ARISTOCRAT. Come this way; otherwise, they'll hear what we're saying.

The Aristocrat has apparently made the Dark Lady pregnant and now she wants to marry him before this becomes visible. But since the Aristocrat is not divorced from his wife, he cannot remarry yet. The death of the Consul also makes marriage inappropriate for the time being. This being the situation, the Aristocrat suggests that the Dark Lady go away to give birth to the child somewhere else. It seems obvious that he wants to escape the disgrace of marrying a servant's daughter whom he has made pregnant. His attitude is similar to that of the Consul and Hummel.

The Colonel. He incarnates duplicity. He has deceived his wife (provided that they were married at that time) with Hummel's fiancée. He has had the Young Lady grow up in the belief that she is his daughter. Just as Hummel he has once been a servant and a sponger but an aristocratic mask—moustache, false teeth, wig and corset, a dubious title which is no longer valid and a false noble name—has disguised this circumstance.

The Colonel has so long cherished false ideas about himself that he can no longer give up his role-playing. This appears from his refusal to believe that the wife has deceived him. It also appears when he complains to Hummel that the Student is not "a nobleman and an equal" after the latter has demonstrated that he himself is merely "the servant *x y z*".

The Mummy. How old she is "nobody knows". She must be at least 55 and may be 75. She apparently did not marry the Colonel until she was 35—although she had him believe that she was 19. Both Hummel and the Aristocrat have been her lovers. With the former she has the daughter Adèle. The Colonel seems to have believed for quite a long time that he is Adèle's father (which explains the choice of name)—until the Mummy has told him of the true situation in a fit of anger.

The Mummy has tried to leave her husband but she has always come back. What is true about the people of the house at large, is true also of her marriage to the Colonel: "We have broken up and left each other infinitely many times, but then we're drawn together again", for "crimes and secrets and guilt bind us together". None of the characters in the play is so guilt-ridden as the Mummy. It is as though she has ceased to live after having committed adultery with Hummel. Since then she hides herself in the dark closet, crying over her crime. She cannot stand cripples (Hummel) and sick people (the Young Lady), because they remind her of what she has done. And she imagines that she is a parrot.

With the parrot we associate three qualities: vanity, speaking ability and imprisonment. It is therefore not surprising that Strindberg has settled for this "talkative bird" in his conretization of deformed mental life or—with a more interesting interpretation—of language as a dubious means of communication. The closet, clearly, functions as the Mummy's cage.

According to Bengtsson, the Mummy is crazy because "when people are together tormenting each other for a long time, they go crazy". Bengtsson here seems to refer not so much to the matrimonial monotony as to the general tendency among people to accuse and remind one another of errors in the past. It is from all this that the Mummy tries to escape. She imagines that she is dead—because she does not have the strength to live, and that she is a parrot—because she does not have the strength to be a human being.[3]

But not even as a parrot can she completely forget the past. Polly's "Is Jacob there?" prepares us for Amalia's "Is it you, Jacob?", the first words spoken by the Mummy "*in her normal voice*". Having repented for twenty years, the Mummy finally recovers; the 'parrot sickness' is transferred to the unrepentant cripple.

The Mummy, in short, appears in two forms: the crazy Polly and the sensible Amalia; to these we may add a third one: the marble statue which she adores, her innocent self.

One more aspect of the parrot language should be noted. There is an old Swedish game known as 'Jacob, where are you?', in which a blinded person (the master) has to catch the other (the servant Jacob), assisted by the sounds he receives in answer to his question: "Jacob, where are you?" When the servant has been caught, the roles are reversed.

When we first hear the Mummy ask "Is Jacob there?", she finds herself in the cupboard. It is a hide-and-seek situation hinting at the hide-and-seek between master and servant, innocent and guilty which stands central in *The Ghost Sonata* with its surprising reversals of roles. When the Old Man finally answers the Mummy's question with his "Jacob is there", it indicates that he acknowledges that he is caught. The game has come to an end.

The Young Lady. "A victim of the discord which a mother's 'crime' has produced in a family, a victim too of the complaisance of the day, of circumstances, of her own defective constitution" (*ASD,* III, 304)—thus Strindberg characterizes Miss Julie. The description admirably fits Miss Adèle. Remarkably passive, Adèle does not perform any actions which contribute to a profund characterization of herself. The most enigmatic character of the play, she is primarily characterized by what others have to say about her.

We have earlier claimed that the Young Lady is ignorant of the fact that Hummel is her father. This at any rate is the conclusion we must draw, when she refers to "director Hummel's" funeral at which she has evidently not been present. Presumably she has not heard Hummel's revelations in Act II—she then converses with the Student in another room—neither that the Colonel, who wants to keep up appearances, has never told her the truth. Nor does the Student reveal anything. The Young Lady, we must conclude, dies without having learned her own identity.

At the beginning of the play her aristocratic occupations are emphasized: she rides on horseback, cares for her hyacinths, goes to the Opera, reads books, plays the harp. At the end of Act III we get quite a different picture of her everyday occupations. We now learn that she mostly has to serve the servants, perform all the dirty chores they refuse to do or which they perform carelessly. The Young Lady's life, in other words, is not the way it seems to be; she is, to paraphrase the Mummy's remarkable words, essentially better than the façade causes us to believe.

The Aristocrat. In the list of *dramatis personae* it says: "called Baron Skanskorg"—a subtle hint that his nobility is as illegitimate as that of the Colonel and his name, with its military associations, as false as Hummel's. In view of this, the designation 'the Aristocrat' appears highly ironical.

The Aristocrat, who has been the Mummy's lover, is the recently dead Consul's son-in-law. This is why he is dressed in mourning. He is about to be divorced, possibly in order to marry the Dark Lady. His wife "is giving him a stone house to get rid of him" (cf. Hummel's present to the Young Lady and the Student). As far as we can make out, the Aristocrat has married for money; Hummel seems to refer to this when he metaphorically calls him "the jewel thief". The Aristocrat lives "up above" in the house, and it is his bed clothes—"a blue silk quilt and two white pillows"—which are aired on the balcony.[4]

Johansson. He is "an educated man" and has been a bookdealer. In punishment for a crime he once committed, only known to Hummel, he is enslaved by the Old Man. "Instead of having me locked up, he made me his slave", Johansson bitterly comments.

Bengtsson. For a generation the Colonel's servant, he has earlier served Hummel. But Bengtsson, who must be quite old, was once an independent man, and in those days Hummel "for two whole years" was a sponger in his kitchen. Later Bengtsson has met Hummel in Hamburg, where he has heard about his drowning of the Milkmaid. The reason why Strindberg has placed the crime abroad is, I suppose, that in this way it seems more plausible that the other characters are ignorant of it. Bengtsson's knowledge of the crime explains why Hummel wants to get him dismissed. When revealing Hummel's secret crime, Bengtsson functions as a *deus ex machina.*

Bengtsson is not the man he appears to be. Although he has received a medal "because of his great merits", he has "very great" flaws—"but one doesn't get a medal for those".

The Fiancée. The 79-year-old Beate von Holsteinkrona represents the high nobility. She is a secular canoness, a privileged person. Sixty years earlier—she was then 19—she became engaged to Hummel (hence the subjective designation 'the Fiancée'), a circumstance which she seems to have forgotten altogether. While still engaged, she has allowed herself to be seduced by the Colonel. A beauty in her youth, she is still "an attractive old woman" although she "*looks crazy*".

The Cook. She is "big and fat" from all the meat-stock she has been drinking—leaving the fibers and the water to the family she is serving. It is not surprising that the Young Lady is pining away.

The Cook has been interpreted in at least three different ways. To Lamm (1942, 312) she is simply an accident, a proof that Strindberg could not keep his own household problems outside his work. It is indeed quite likely that Strindberg has added this character to his play as an act of revenge on the housemaid who left him two days before the drama was completed.[5]

But this explanation is not enough. For must we not assume that Strindberg would never have included the Cook in the play unless he found that she fulfilled a function there? Lamm's biographical motivation signifies a distrust of Strindberg's dramaturgic competence.

More satisfying is Delblanc's (1968, 110) suggestion that the Cook is "a punishing representative of the lower classes", who "repays the upper classes with the means at her disposal". The idea of class struggle is, in fact, voiced by the Cook herself, when she tells the Student and the Young Lady (both representatives of the upper classes): "You suck the strength out of us, and we out of you." To Delblanc, the Cook is both a realistic and a symbolic figure; in the latter capacity she is "a projection of the social guilt weighing on the bourgeois society of *The Ghost Sonata*". The Cook, in other words, has both an objective and a subjective reality; she has half-reality. It is a separate problem whether the subjective aspect should be sought within the social rather than, say, the religious sphere; to this question I will return later.

To Leifer (181, 187) the Cook is partly a representative of "the evil of existence", partly of that which is "low and earthbound within the Young Lady". In the latter case, the Cook is again viewed as a projection, this time not of the guilt of a whole social class but of "what is evil, 'sick'" within an individual. It is obvious that by combining the Cook with the Young Lady—turning them into a Calibariel—Leifer tries both to integrate the Cook in the play and to give an explanation for the Young Lady's obscure illness.

The symbolic signifiance of the house in *The Ghost Sonata* has long been recognized. It is obvious that it stands for existence. But this symbolic aspect is often forgotten when various aspects related to the house are discussed.

As a symbol of existence the house is inhabited by a varied group of people. Among the inhabitants various ages, social classes and relationships are found. And the house is modern: it is the situation of modern man Strindberg describes.

When we first meet the Student, the house still appears attractive to him and to us. Entering the house, he believes, is like entering paradise. His innocent faith gains support by the attractive and seemingly stable house front with its paradisiac ingredients:

Through the round room's open windows can be seen when the shades are raised a white marble statue of a young woman, surrounded by palms, brightly lighted by sunlight. In the window to the left pots of hyacinths (blue, white, pink) can be seen.

But what we and the Student see is merely a façade. Once inside the house the situation changes. He now experiences the house as "strange", later as "rotten"—like the state of Denmark: there are numerous echoes from *Hamlet* in the play.[6] Finally the realistic fiction is done away with: "Jesus Christ descended into hell—that was his journey on earth, this madhouse, this reformatory, this charnelhouse, the earth." Similarly, the Student enters 'hell': his moving inwards—from the street through the round room to the hyacinth room—is an inverted pilgrimage from Paradiso via Purgatorio to Inferno. By synchronizing this movement with his increasingly negative attitude to the world, Strindberg implies a relationship between life experience and denial of life. To make sure that the Student's changing view of the house is not interpreted as his individual reaction, Strindberg also has Johansson independently share his experience. The servant first declares that it has always been his "dream to enter this house"; later he is forced to conclude that "it is a terrible house". In Act III this movement is repeated with coda-like swiftness. At the beginning the Student, now in love, believes that he has entered paradise. Soon he learns that he finds himself in purgatory: the hyacinth room is referred to as "the room of ordeals": like life it is beautiful to look at but full of flaws.[7] He then comes to the conclusion that life is an inferno.

The hyacinth room testifies to the desperate attempts of the Young Lady of "keeping the dirt of life at a distance". The attempt proves to be in vain. The room is located, it seems, between the round room—the disillusioned domain of the aged—and the kitchen, the domain of materialism.[8] Purity—this is the conclusion—cannot be found in life; it must be sought in the hereafter: "*The room disappears, Böcklin's* Toten-Insel *becomes the backdrop*."

The destruction of the house at the end is well prepared. The day before, the Student has already experienced the fall of a house:

THE STUDENT. /—/ I was drawn to that obscure little street where later on the house collapsed ... I got there and stopped in front of the building which I had never seen before ... Then I noticed a crack in the wall, heard the floors splitting; I dashed over and grabbed a child who was walking right below the wall ... The next second the house collapsed ... I was saved, but in my arms, where I thought I had the child, was nothing ...

This description should be compared to another. When Hummel asks the Student whether he has noticed the house we see on the stage, the latter answers:

I've certainly noticed it ... I walked by here yesterday when the sun shone on the windows and, imagining all the beauty and luxury there must be in there, I said to my companion: "How lucky it would be to have an apartment there, four flights up, a beautiful young wife, two handsome children, and an income of 20 000 ..."

Although he does not explicitly say so, we cannot help getting the impression that when the Student saw this house the day before, it was the first time he paid attention to it. This has a certain significance in the symbolic context, since it is precisely the Student's unfamiliarity with the house (of life) that motivates his infatuation with it.

The Student, then, has the previous day discovered two houses: the one we see before us and the one which collapsed. Symbolically, however, it is one and the same house—existence—a circumstance which Strindberg seems to imply by having the Student refer to "that obscure little street" while the stage directions for Act I speak of *"a side-street running towards the back"*. It is as though one front of the house on the stage has already collapsed, while the other one follows suit at the end of the play.

On closer inspection it also becomes clear that the Student's undertakings the previous day correspond to his way of acting in the play itself, where, in Act I, we see him admiring the house, dreaming to enter it; where, in Act II, he enters the house and begins to discover the crevices in the walls; and where, in Act III, he tries to save, not a child but a young woman from a symbolic collapse. When the Student toward the end calls the Young Lady "a poor little child, child of this world of illusion, guilt, suffering and death", it is not only to stress the fact that she is a representative of mankind, a child of man; it is also to clarify her identity with the child the Student has earlier tried to save. Northam (1966, 43) sees a connection between the child and the Young Lady already in Act I; the child "passing under the wall" corresponds to the Young Lady as she first enters under the wall of the house. Embroidering upon this idea one may also note the Student's reaction when he first sees the Young Lady: he *"covers his eyes with his hand"*. It is as though he cannot trust his own eyes after the vision of the child the day before.

The essential connection between the child and the Young Lady does not appear until the end of the play. Northam (1966, 47) interprets it as follows: "the young and innocent girl has been rescued from the collapse of the House of Life, but only spiritually; the Student's arms remain empty". Northam is, of course, right in seeing a connection between the two 'manoeuvres of rescue'. But the nature of this connection is open to discussion. If one does not believe, as Northam does, that the Young Lady is innocent, another interpretation seems more relevant. The child which the Student believed he had saved did not exist, i.e. the innocence ascribed to or symbolized by the child cannot be found in reality, only in our illusory views of it. As the Student puts it: "Where is anything that fulfills its promise? In my imagination." Branded by original sin, we are all guilty. The Student discovers that the Young Lady, far from being an innocent child is "sick at the very source of life", that is, she is not radically different from the rest of the inhabitants of the house. The child he thought he had found in her suddenly disappears. He is left empty-handed, deprived of the illusion that purity is to be found in this life.

What, then, causes the house to collapse? About Hummel we learn that he demolishes houses. Just as the house is built of stones, so Life consists of individual lives. This is why the house is "full of defects". Hummel's attitude to his fellow-men is succinctly summarized by his servant. The Old Man, Johansson says, is "sowing a little word, loosening one stone at a time, till the house falls down—metaphorically speaking". By revealing the shortcomings of the various inhabitants, Hummel indirectly demonstrates the rottenness of life.

The same revelatory eagerness characterizes the Student at the end of Act III. When he assumes that "the world would go to pieces if one were completely candid", he actually foreshadows the end, which demonstrates how his candid outburst not only kills the Young Lady but also causes the house (the world) to collapse.

As the obvious materialist of the play, Hummel, not unlike the biblical Tempter, boasts: "Everything that can be seen, I own, it is mine!" But he is not the only one. The wife of the Aristocrat, we learn, presents Skanskorg "with a stone house to get rid of him". Not even the Student, as we have seen, is indifferent to material comfort.

At other times 'house', especially when the plural is used, seems to stand for the life of the individual. Thus Hummel speculates in houses; this corresponds to his own euphemistic: "I am interested in the destinies of other people." He "looks at houses, tears them down, opens up streets, settles squares, but he breaks into houses, too, creeps in through windows, plays havoc with human destinies, kills his enemies, and never forgives". All these accusations are verified in the course of the drama. When Hummel arrives uninvited at the ghost supper, it is an example of his breaking into a house. And his first acquaintance with the Student is via a window:

THE OLD MAN. Listen . . . I think I've heard your voice . . . I had a friend when I was young who couldn't say window, he always said winder—I've only met one person who pronounced it like that, and that was him. The other is you.—Are you possibly related to Mr. Arkenholz, the merchant?

But the Student has never said "winder"! Hummel here reveals himself as a liar. He has simply picked up a word, which the Student's father apparently pronounced in a strange way, in order to get the Student into his net (to use Johansson's expression).

Since the house represents life, it is not surprising that it reflects the hierarchy characteristic of human society. In *A Blue Book I* (1908) Strindberg writes in a piece entitled "Through constraint to freedom":

The teacher continued: In this world you are constrained for you are all dependent on each other, press upon each other like the stones of a vault, from above, from below, from the sides; guard each other, spy on each other. Freedom thus does not, may not exist in this building called state and society. Since the foundation-stones must carry the greatest burden, they are of gray stone, while the rest are light bricks. There are also some luxurious bricks, which do not carry anything, just adorn, while they are supported by others; still, they adorn, feel embarrassed and dispensable, but they serve as adornment, and this they get to hear. (*SS,* XLVI, 49)

Here three social classes—upper, lower and middle class—appearing also in *The Ghost Sonata* are metaphorically described. Among the luxurious bricks we find the Consul, the Baron, the Secular Canoness and, at least seemingly, the Colonel and the Young Lady. Among the light bricks we find director Hummel, merchant Arkenholz and the Student. The gray stones are represented by Johansson, Bengtsson, the Milkmaid, the Cook, the Caretaker's Wife, the Dark Lady, the Beggars and the Maid.

This being the situation, one would expect that the class struggle would take a prominent place in the drama. We have recently noted how this theme is clearly brought forward in the Cook's remark: "You suck the strength out of us, and we out of you." The dependency of the lower class is also indicated in a few places. Thus the Caretaker's Wife seems to have 'bought' her husband a job by 'selling' herself to the Consul.[9] Johansson, Hummel's servant, "slaves for [his] food, which isn't the best". And Hummel surrounds himself with beggars who keep pushing his wheelchair and who as reward only get "a hint there'll be something at his funeral". The last clause should possibly the interpreted figuratively: the death of the bourgeois class means bread for the working class. When the Beggars, admonished by Hummel to pay respect to the Student, *"uncover their heads but do not shout 'hurrah'",* this may be interpreted as a refusal to obey the orders of the 'tyrant'.

By contrast, the representatives of the upper classes devote themselves to the drinking of punch, the cultivation of hyacinths, horse-riding, playing the harp, visiting the Opera, etc. It is significant that the Student desires an apartment "four flights up", where the bricks of luxury are found.

Yet it is obvious that Strindberg has not drawn a black-and-white picture. The representatives of the lower classes are not altogether likeable, those of the upper ones not altogether unattractive. Of importance in this context is the fact that the social status of the characters at times is rather uncertain. Thus Johansson and Bengtsson have declined on the social ladder, while the opposite is true of Hummel. The Colonel has climbed from lower class to (false) upper class, and it is likely that the Baron has done the same. The Mummy's social status is unclear. The Dark Lady, daughter of the Consul and the Caretaker's Wife is a social hybrid. And so is, to an even greater extent, the Young Lady, daughter of a former servant, now director, brought up by a former servant, now (false) nobleman and colonel.

It could, of course, be argued that *The Ghost Sonata* is an attack on bourgeois society and that the dreams of Buddha that "poor earth is to become a heaven" concern a social Utopia. But this thesis would only seem convincing if it could be demonstrated that the collapse of the house at the end is equivalent with the collapse of a socio-economic system.

Yet it is obviously not the socio-political question which is central to the play but the religious one. The collapse of the house makes room not for an earthly Utopia but for *Toten-Insel.* And the characters are not so much representatives of different social classes as of humanity, erring and suffering in a number of ways. Their varying fates form a meaningful backdrop for the Mummy's central lines: "We are poor human beings, we know that; we have sinned; we have done wrong, we *like everyone else*" (my italics).

It is significant that at the end of "Through constraint to freedom", the house is given a metaphysical rather than a social significance. Having stated that we may speak of a socially determined longing for freedom and that it is up to "the management" to see to it that the citizens do not carry heavier burdens than they are obliged to, Strindberg continues:

> But behind this general longing for freedom, there is another more profound one, often confused with the former type. It is the pining of creation for liberation from the shackles of the flesh, most pregnantly expressed by Paul: "O wretched man that I am! Who shall deliver me from the body of this death?" But this freedom can be gained only through the patient acceptance of the constraint of this world. Hence, through constraint to freedom! (*SS*, XLVI, 49)

There is apparently a conflict within the author himself between his socio-political and his religious conviction. While he feels the need to revolt against earthly authorities, he is inclined to subordinate himself to heavenly ones. The same ambivalence we find in the Student's final monologue.

It is hardly surprising that the social criticism plays a limited role in *The Ghost Sonata.* If each individual has been given a task in life—as Strindberg wished to believe—and if his salvation depends on whether he accepts this task or not, there is no reason to admonish the lower classes to revolt. To the older Strindberg religion is no opium for the people.

The people of *The Ghost Sonata* belong to a sickly species. Hummel is a cripple; Amalia is mummified; the Colonel wears a corset; besides being sickly, the Young Lady is so thin that she drops her bracelet; the Cook, by contrast, is abnormally fat.

Hummel comments on his 'sickness' as follows: "You see I'm a cripple; some say it's my own fault; others blame my parents; I prefer to blame life itself with its snares ...". Is his invalidity a result of self-inflicted ("my own fault") or inheritied ("my parents") syphilis? Hummel's statement *can* be interpreted in this way.[10]

Hummel's son is homosexual and his daughter, we have noted, is sickly. If we accept the idea that the Old Man suffers from syphilis, it seems natural to ascribe the same sickness to his daughter.[11] This would throw light on the following passage:

THE YOUNG LADY. /—/ You can never win me.
THE STUDENT. Why not?
THE YOUNG LADY. You may not ask that question.

It would also explain the Student's conclusion: "Why didn't you want to be my bride? Because you're sick at the very source of life ...". In line with this, the beautiful, aphrodisiac hyacinths which poison the Student may be seen as a warning of the Young Lady's venereal disease.

The expression "sick at the very source of life" may, however, also be combined with a few words belonging to the preliminary annotations for the play: "the Daughter has Cancer". Our conclusion would then be that the Young Lady suffers from cancer of the uterus, an interpretation which seems supported by the fact that the Cook—representing her base self—carries a soy bottle "with scorpion letters on it" in her hand; the associative chain scorpion–crayfish (Sw. 'kräfta')–cancer (Sw. 'kräfta') would be natural to a Swede.

Whether we prefer the interpretation of the first or the second type of illness, it is obvious that the bad health from which the characters suffer is a symptom of their spiritual infirmity. In line with this view the Young Lady's illness may well be seen as a symbol of original sin (Leifer, 189)—in a very direct sense, we may add. Conceived in sin, she is the product of a fall, hence: "sick at the very source of life". It is in this context interesting to note that Strindberg places a well (the street drinking fountain) on the stage in Act I and behind this a paradisiac vision: "*a white marble statue of a young woman* [the Young Lady's mother], *surrounded by palms, brightly lighted by sunlight*". This is clearly a picture of Eve in the garden of Eden before the Fall.[12]

When the Student tells the Milkmaid that he has witnessed the collapse of a house and that he has "bandaged up injured people and kept watch over the sick" all night, the word "sick" seems surprising in connection with the accident that has just occurred. When he utters this word, he is standing next to the Milkmaid who has just 'purified' herself in the street drinking fountain, in front of the pure marble statue. Here, it seems to me, Strindberg draws attention to two marked stages: woman before and after the Fall. The Milkmaid's washing prepares for the Young Lady's attempt to keep the dirt of life at a distance, to find a cure for the sickness at the source of life: original sin.

The Milkmaid and the Dead Man are the two ghosts of the play. Their function is similar to that of the Ghost in *Hamlet*: they bear witness to secret crimes which must be expiated. Shakespeare makes this quite clear by letting his Ghost address Hamlet. By contrast Strindberg's ghosts are mute.

Both plays begin with a ghost scene. The Milkmaid testifies to Hummel's murder just as the Ghost indicates Claudius' secret murder. Both visions appear three times, under different circumstances. It should be noticed that the Milkmaid makes her first entrance before the Student—just as the Ghost appears to the guards and to the audience, before Hamlet sees it. This is very functional, since in this way she is experienced as a flesh-and-blood reality by the spectator. The connection with Hummel, who is already on the stage, also becomes more evident in this way. Not until we notice that she does not say anything and learn that only the Student sees her, do we understand that she is a vision or, better, a mental reality.

Between the Milkmaid's first and second appearance, the dead Consul makes his entrance; he too has been 'murdered' by Hummel. At her first appearance, the Milkmaid is seen only by the visionary Student, who is also the only one who sees the Dead Man. (The audience sees what he sees—a subjectivist trait.) In both cases he relates his experiences to the Old Man, thereby reminding him of his crimes against these two people. We may therefore be inclined to see the Student as a representative of Hummel's better self. When the Milkmaid appears for the second time, she is seen both by Hummel and the Student. At her last appearance—during the ghost supper—she is seen only by the Old Man. (The Student on this occasion remains in another room.) These variations are due to the fact that Strindberg wants both to provide dramatic suspense and to illustrate a change within Hummel, whose evil is gradually revealed both to himself and to us. Hummel's reactions make this clear. After the Milkmaid's first appearance, he asks the Student to whom he, the Student, has been talking; and when the latter astonished says "Didn't you see that?", he does not reply; after a pause he significantly changes the topic of conversation. Already at this point Hummel feels that he is in the grip of supernatural powers or, to put it in psychological terms, that he is beginning to suffer from pangs of conscience. When he later learns that the Student has talked to the Milkmaid, he "*shudders*". And when she appears for the second time and is seen also by Hummel, he "*collapses with horror*". The third time she is "*unseen by everyone but* THE OLD MAN, *who shudders*". Gradually Hummel's sense of guilt awakens.

It is evident that the visions have been incorporated into the play as a theatrically effective means of dramatizing inner processes. There is also a point to the fact that the Strindbergian ghosts, unlike their Shakespearean counterparts, do not differ conspicuosly from the living characters who, Berendsohn (539) points out, are the true ghosts of the play.

This paradox applies also to the beginning of the play as compared to the final vision of Böcklin's monumental *Toten-Insel,* the logical outgrowth, as it were, of the death screen of Acts II–III (Bayerdörfer, 523 f.). The painting shows an island with high, craterlike rocks, surrounding a group of tall cypresses. In the walls of the rocks, openings similar to those of sepulchral chambers can be seen. On the shore below, center, there is a staircase of white marble; here the recently dead are received. "*A black boat with a black rower, carrying a white coffin with a white figure standing next to it*" (*Toten-Insel, SOS,* I, 295) approaches the staircase across the still water.In the final picture of *Toten-Insel,* we have, I would propose, a spiritual counterpart of the solid façade at the beginning of the play. Thus the marble staircase of the house—the entrance to Life—corresponds to the marble steps of the island, the entrance to Death; the windows of the house to the sepulchral openings; the white marble statue inside the house, "*surrounded by palms*" to the erect white figure in the boat, surrounded, as it were, by the cypresses of the island; the Dark Lady, "*in black*", "*standing motionless on the stairs*" to the black rower in the boat; the fresh water of the street drinking fountain, in which the Milkmaid, "*in summer clothes*", mirrors herself, to the still water around the island, in which the reflection of the white figure in the boat can be seen.

The idea of having one decor in this way form a pendant of another, Strindberg may well have received from Böcklin, whose Isle of Life and Isle of Death were copied at Strindberg's request and put up on either side of the stage of his Intimate Theatre in Stockholm (Falck, 53). In his prologue at the opening of this theatre, Strindberg spoke of "the journey from the Isle of Life to that of Death" (Falck, 65 ff.)—an adequate summary of the action in *The Ghost Sonata.*

That the final tableau of the play should also be seen in the light of Swedenborg's concept of the beyond, appears both from the play called *Toten-Insel,* which Strindberg began (but never finished) shortly after the completion of *The Ghost Sonata,* and partly from the little piece entitled "Higher forms of existence; *Die Toten-Insel*" appearing in *A Blue Book III.* The first station where man arrived after death, we here read

> consisted of islands, swimming in something which could be air or water. /—/ On every island there was a castle, where guardians,helpers and teachers dwelled. Good people, who had come out of the ordeal reasonably well, were now living here. They had mostly suffered in life, had been dragged down by sins and crimes but had then come to feel such a loathing for evil that they had turned in the direction of good. Liberated from the base human body and from what is evil and untrue, they were all beautiful and pure. They were half transparent, so that they could not conceal anything or lie. /—/
>
> This was the station of rest, or the summer vacation after the first death; and the days seemed as short to them as a feast. (*SS,* XLVIII, 1034 ff.)

It is to this paradisiac existence that the Milkmaid belongs—hence her "summer clothes"; it is to this existence that the Young Lady is journeying forth in the final tableau. The house of earthly existence has collapsed and in its place we see its spiritual counterpart, "a home without dust", *Toten-Insel*, the station of rest.

As Northam has demonstrated (1966, 41, 48), the connection between the beginning and the end of the play is also underlined by the sound effects. When the curtain rises for Act 1, we can hear the ringing of the bells of "*several churches at a distance*". While the Milkmaid washes her hands and looks into the water of the street drinking fountain, using it as a mirror, "*a steamboat bell can be heard ringing, and now and then the deep notes of an organ in a nearby church break the silence*". By these acoustic means, Strindberg from the very beginning creates a strange and solemn mood.

The sound effects return at the end. When the Young Lady feels death approaching, she "*rings the bell*" and the servant enters. As she dies behind the black screen of death, the Student prays for her:

> Poor little child, child of this world of illusions, guilt, suffering, and death, the world of everlasting change, disappointments, and pain! May the Lord of Heaven have mercy on you as you journey forth . . .

We then see how "*the room disappears*" and how "*Böcklin's* Toten-Insel *becomes the backdrop*". The Student's prayer that the Lord of Heaven be merciful to the Young Lady as she journeys forth clearly relates to the voyage depicted on Böcklin's painting. To the visual impression Strindberg adds an acoustic one: "*soft, quiet, pleasantly sad music can be heard from the island*". Here, just as at the beginning, the idea of a voyage is combined with that of celestial music—but this time in an explicitly metaphysical fashion. Without knowing it we have all along been on our way to another reality.

The fundamental theme—or leitmotif—of *The Ghost Sonata* is found in the conflict between illusion and reality, between *Sein* and *Schein*. In the antithesis between mask and face, façade and interior, word and deed, in the depiction of the dead as living and the living as dead—everywhere we are confronted with the fundamctal idea that the world is not what it looks like and mankind not what it seems to be. To make this basic idea dramatically effective Strindberg turns his protagonist, the Student, into an observer who only gradually gains insight into the true state of things. Originally influenced by the character who incarnates the materialistic *Schein*, Hummel, the Student eventually comes to see reality as it is. From another point of view we may say that in the Student Hummel sees himself as a young man; or to put it in another way: the Student incarnates an earlier stage in Hummel's life—while Arkenholz' development in the play suggests that he may turn into another Hummel. Together the Student and Hummel, the young man and the old man, give a picture of Man, of the fate of Man.

In the last instance, *The Ghost Sonata* is an allegorical drama, a parable, depicting the pilgrimage of man, a *Stationen* drama, in which each station (act) corresponds to an inner state of mind. After the three earthly stations, which we may well connect with youth, middle age and old age, the fourth and final station, "the station of rest" as Strindberg calls it, awaits us: *Toten-Insel.*

At the end of the play we realize, with the Student, that life should not be understood literally but metaphorically; as Strindberg puts it in a remark from about this time: "'Alles Vergängliches ist nur ein Gleichnis.' Thus Goethe ends his *Faust* at the age of 80. After a very varied life, rich in experiences, I begin to take Goethe at his word at the age of 60" (*SOS,* II, 203).

12. Theme and Structure of *Pelikanen / The Pelican*

The Pelican, Strindberg's chamber play opus 4, has a simple plot and a fairly complex thematic pattern.[1] The structure of the play is as follows:

[*Act*]	*Seq.*	*Page/ line in SS* XLV	*On stage*				
I	A	215/1					
	1	215/5	E				
	2	215/10	*E*	*M*			
	3	221/7	*E*		*F*		
	4	228/15	E				
	5	228/18	*E*			*A*	
	6	234/5	*E*			*A*	*G*
	7	236/1					
	8	236/7–241/25	*E*			*A*	
II	B	242/1					
	9	242/2					G
	10	242/5			*F*		*G*
	11	254/23			*F*	*A*	*G*
	12	256/21–258/9	*E*		*F*	*A*	*G*
III	C	259/1					
	13	259/2					G
	14	259/4	*E*				*G*
	15	261/7	*E*			*A*	*G*
	16	262/1	*E*			*A*	
	17	264/6	E				
	18	264/12	*E*		*F*		
	19	271/1	*E*				
	20	272/1	*E*				*G*
	21	277/23	*E*		*F*		*G*
	22	278/21–280/11			*F*		*G*

Abbreviations

E = Elise, the mother, a widow
M = Margret, a servant
F = Fredrik, the son, a law student
A = Axel, the son-in-law, married to Gerda
G = Gerda, the daughter

From the scheme we may gather that the stage is left empty twice, that there is only one 4-character sequence in the play and that Strindberg once permits a soliloquy, a non-naturalistic trait. We may further note that Margret, the cook, appears only once in the beginning—an indication of her expository function—and that Axel already disappears for good in seq. 16, a suggestion of his thematically somewhat peripheral part. These observations, and others of a similar kind, may set us on the track of essential structural and thematic characteristics, a few of which will be considered in the following.

Outwardly *The Pelican* falls into three parts, lacking a designation but here referred to as acts, since in a note on the cover of the longhand draft Strindberg observes (*SS*, XLV, 345) that the play can be regarded either as a three-act drama or as a one-acter.[2] This difference is of significance chiefly to the spectator, who will be confronted with a production either with or without intervals.[3]

Intermissions or not—the choice affects our experience of the time span of the scenic action. Our spontaneous impression is that this action covers a few hours of one and the same evening. This impression is communicated by the unity of environment: not only do we find ourselves in the same room all the time; the storm in Act I is with us also in Act III.

However, with this interpretation the distribution of meals becomes problematic. At the end of Act II, Gerda invites the men to a meal. At the beginning of Act III, Axel tells Elise: "... and since we don't get enough to eat in this house, Gerda and I intend to eat by ourselves". But if Axel and Gerda have just eaten, why should they eat again? From Axel's way of expressing himself we must conclude that a certain time has elapsed between Acts II and III. Thus understood, various developments—Fredrik's drunkenness, the deterioration of Axel's and Gerda's marriage, Elise's sense of being closed up—become rationally more acceptable.

While the time of scenic action, in other words, seems spread out over two non-consecutive nights, separated by a time lapse of unknown duration, the unity of mood and environment creates a feeling that everything happens in one and the same evening. This clash of two time concepts results in a sense of unreality, or better, half-reality. It adds to our feeling that the play is both a realistic drama and an existential parable, both a description of everyday people and of archetypal figures, an impression communicated also by the fact that the characters bear both a Christian name—i.e. have individual status—and a socio-biological designation: the mother, the son, the daughter, the son-in-law, the servant. The dead husband/father is the notable exception. Like the Count in *Miss Julie,* he is ominously nameless.

As a consequence of the central role played by the dead husband, the prescenic action is fairly extensive. When the curtain rises the following has happened:

1. Elise has profited from her husband's good income, while the rest of the family has led a bare existence.
2. Elise has become Axel's mistress and has lent him money.
3. Gerda has fallen in love with Axel and he has pretended to return her love.
4. The husband, knowing that Axel is his wife's lover, has turned hostile against him.
5. Gerda, unaware of the relationship between Elise and Axel, has sided with the mother and him against the father.
6. Fredrik, more aware of Elise's true nature, has sided with the father.
7. The husband has died from a stroke, provoked by Elise and Axel.
8. Axel, hoping for an inheritance, has married Gerda.

This list raises a number of questions. Why does Axel go so far as to marry Gerda, once Elise's husband is dead? Why does he not, eventually, marry Elise instead? After all, this would only improve his financial situation. And how can Elise accept his marrying her daughter, when she herself is in love with him and free to remarry? The great difference of age, we must assume, prevents marriage—but not adultery.[4] So Elise and Axel settle for a *ménage-à-trois*. More difficult to accept is the fact that the wedding takes place shortly after the death of the bride's father. The months separating funeral and wedding in *Hamlet* are here reduced to days. Granted that Gerda is eager to marry Axel and Axel eager to share in the inheritance—even so, it is not likely that they would dare to break so radically with a firmly established convention.

I mention these circumstances mainly to indicate that this kind of reasoning, which is legitimate when we deal with purely realistic drama, is not very rewarding when applied to Strindberg's post-Inferno plays, where almost everything has primarily a metaphorical significance.

The scenic action, which has been analyzed by Holm (180f.) in terms of Freytag's well known Cone, revolves around two discoveries: Axel's discovery that there is nothing to inherit and Fredrik's discovery that Elise has committed adultery and spiritual murder. Both discoveries are connected with the letter which the dead husband/father has left for his son. For the development of the plot, this letter is thus of central importance. Strindberg's handling of it is as follows.

The letter is discovered by Axel in seq. 5. While Elise peruses its entire content, Axel and the recipient (r) are informed only of the part centering around the murder, let us call it *a*. In seq. 9, similarly, Fredrik acquaints himself with the entire content, while Gerda and the recipient are informed not of the 'murder' but of the adultery, let us call it *b*. To secure a sense of progression and suspense, Strindberg in other words informs us step by step. With his *a+b* knowledge the recipient at the end of seq. 9 knows as much about the content of the letter as Elise and Fredrik, and he knows more than Axel and Gerda. Moreover, aware that Fredrik and Gerda are familiar with the letter—let us call this knowledge *c*—he knows more at this point than

Elise. His knowledge is in fact equivalent to the son's. Fredrik's accusations against the mother in seq. 18 therefore do not come as a surprise to the recipient—as they do to Elise. When she, the protagonist, is as fully informed as we are, the play virtually reaches its conclusion. What remains are the consequences of the newly gained information: a triple suicide.

The situation can be formalized as follows:

seq.
5 E learns $a+b$. A and r learn a.
9 F learns $a+b$. G and r learn b.
18 F and r know $a+b+c$. E learns c.

Structurally significant is also the way in which the characters are emotionally related to one another. When the play opens, Axel and Gerda still side with Elise against the dead husband/father and his 'confidant' Fredrik. When it closes, Elise is completely isolated. Axel deserts her, when he discovers that she has nothing more to offer him. Gerda turns against her, when she becomes aware of her true nature. In Fredik's case the change is less obvious, since he is hostile toward the mother from the beginning. To him it is, however, important that his suspicions are confirmed. The letter from the deceased fater—much as the Ghost in *Hamlet*—provides him with the information he needs to overcome his passivity and take action. He now puts fire to the house and pronounces judgement over the mother.

From a somewhat different point of view, the main action may be said to consist of the revolt of a number of victims against their oppressor. Margret is the first to revolt, when she declares that she is about to leave for good. The dead husband avenges himself by means of his unusual testament; instead of being a benefactor he turns out to be a creditor. Axel, feeling betrayed, begins to bully his former mistress. Finally Fredrik and Gerda take up arms against their mother.

In agreement with this, we find a striking hubris-nemesis pattern in the play. Elise is punished according to the law of the Old Testament, which demands an eye for an eye. Her isolation at the end is a punishment for the isolation she has forced upon her husband. And Fredrik's 'murder' of her is a retribution for her 'murder' of her husband, his father.

Elise has deprived her family of all the essentials of life. She has always kept her house cold because, as she repeatedly says, "we can't afford to burn up our money". Once her power has dwindled, she is forced to feed the fire—like a servant. But not being used to it, she is not very successful. Left alone in the living room, she is "freezing to death, and the fire in the stove's going out".

Similarly, at the beginning Elise tells Fredrik to turn on "only a couple" of lights, because they must save on electricity, while later, when feeling forsaken, she herself "*turns on all the electric lights*". Now Gerda enters and "*turns off all the electric lights but one*":

MOTHER /—/. Don't put out the lights!
GERDA. Yes, we have to economize!

Gerda here retributively takes over the mother's former role.

Elise has served her family porridge with blue skim milk, while she herself has grown fat on the skimmed-off cream. When Gerda, in seq. 12, refuses to eat porridge and treats Fredrik and Axel to "a sandwich and a steak" in the kitchen, a reversal of roles is indicated. She, not Elise, is now the lady of the house. The men, not the mother, are invited to the hearty meal. The retributive pattern becomes manifest in Axel's remark to Elise in seq. 15: "you should reduce a little for the sake of your health, as the rest of us have had to do". It is now the mother's turn to be invited to porridge and skim milk, while Axel and Gerda are to have a more substantial meal. The roles have definitely been reversed.

The most obvious example of nemesis is the fact that Elise is forced to sleep on the very chaise longue where she has 'murdered' her husband. It is significant that as soon as Fredrik has 'murdered' her with words,[5] Elise *"throws herself head first on the chaise longue with her face hidden"*. The son has 'killed' his mother on the very spot where she 'murdered' his father. The *"purplish red plush cover"*, turning the chaise longue into "a bloody butcher's bench",[6] at the end grows into *"the red glow"* of the fire. The furies have avenged themselves.

In short, just as in the early part Elise denies her environment the essentials of life, so in the latter part she is herself denied these things. The retributive pattern could hardly be more symmetrical. Strindberg has written a tale about a possessor self-dispossessed.

We can now see that the frequent references to food, far from being a testimony to Strindberg's failure to keep his household problems outside the play, form an integral part of a larger thematic pattern, which structurally helps to keep the play together. Taking these references at their face value means misunderstanding their true metaphorical function. Thus Fredrik's and Gerda's hunger is not so much physical as emotional: it is a hunger for love. And their physical shortcomings are above all a frightful piece of evidence of what lovelessness can do to your *soul*. Their constantly feeling cold is caused less by the lack of proper heating than by Elise's icy nature. And Elise's "freezing to death" tells us, not that the temperature has suddenly dropped, but that *she* now feels lonely, forsaken, unloved. In these metaphors Strindberg has seen a possibility to express inner processes in a theatrically effective way. Theatre, we must remember, is a physical medium asking for stageable imagery.

The mother, it is usually claimed, is a monster, a witch; in Germany the play is significantly known under the title *Scheiterhaufen. The Pelican* is above all a rejection of the traditional idea of "mother love"—to mention another satirical Strindberg play title.

This is largely correct—though a simplification of the matter—in the sense that Elise is indeed *the* mother rather than *a* mother. To regard her as an exceptional case is to disarm the play of its explosive power. It is true that mothers do not normally murder their husbands, steal money, make their children starve. But since these things are merely theatrical metaphors of an underlying mentality—egotism, lovelessness—Strindberg has actually only made concrete (and exaggerated) an attitude inherent in all mothers. And not just in mothers. Toward the end of the play, in seq. 20, Elise states:

> Do you know about *my* childhood? Do you have any idea of what a bad home I had, what wickedness I learned there? It's inherited, I think from above, from whom? From our first parents, it said in the children's books, and that seems to be right ... So don't blame me; then I won't blame my parents, who could blame theirs, and so on! Besides, it's like this in all families, but the rest of them don't show it to outsiders ...

Although Elise here, of course, pleads her own cause, her speech bears the stamp of truth and is, in fact, the most significant objective statement in the whole play. It is noteworthy that Gerda does not question it. "If that's how it is", she replies, "I don't want to live, but if I'm forced to, I'll go through this miserable life deaf and blind in the hope there'll be a better hereafter ...".

The point I wish to make is that our view of Elise is not the same from beginning to end, not because she changes but because of the way in which Strindberg distributes—manipulates—the information about her.

From the very beginning we tend to take a negative view of her. Gradually our negative impressions multiply until the mother comes close to being an incarnation of evil. Unlike the classical tragic protagonist, Elise appears baser rather than nobler than the average person. We sympathize with her victims, not with her. Strindberg has reversed the traditional situation.

Close to the end comes the big surprise, when the mother is characterized as a representative specimen of *homo sapiens*. If *she* is a vampire, so are we, all the way back to Adam and Eve. Actually, already in seq. 18 Fredrik alludes to original sin, when he states that the mother is so evil that "she's to be pitied", a statement which reads like a spelling-out of the key phrase in *A Dream Play*: "det är synd om människorna", men are sinful and (therefore) to be pitied.

Let us now return to the beginning of the play, where Elise sits listlessly in her living room, dressed in mourning. Outside it is a stormy night. Inside, in the room behind her, there is a horrible smell of carbolic acid, to obliterate the even more horrible smell of the dead husband. Trying desperately to repress her feelings of guilt, Elise insists that the door be kept closed. Once we see her as a representative of mankind, this situation takes on an existential character, suggesting man's imprisonment in life, his awareness of his shortcomings and his concomitant fear of death.

MARGRET. Why do you stay here, ma'am? Why don't you move?
MOTHER. Our landlord won't let us move, and we can't . . .

'Moving' here carries both psychological and metaphysical connotations. Psychologically, it indicates Elise's inability to free herself from the haunting memories of her own guilt (Rothwell, 32).[7] Metaphysically, it indicates man's fear to depart from life. "Our landlord won't let us move" can be transcribed: it is not for man but for God to decide when we are to die. Compare this to the following speech by Margret:

. . . I won't stay here very long . . . I came here as if I were condemned to watch over the children . . . I wanted to leave when I saw how the servants were mistreated, but I couldn't or I wasn't allowed to . . . /—/ my hour of release will soon come, though not quite yet . . .

Margret's situation is much the same as Elise's. She too voices the idea that life is a condemnation and death a release. Her exit prepares for that of the mother.

We can now see that the unity of place adhered to in *The Pelican* is primarily determined by the theme of the play. The spatial monotony is an adequate expression of Elise's feeling of imprisonment.[8] It makes her final exit from the living room—from life—all the more striking. Also to Fredrik and Gerda death signifies an escape from the confinement of life; says Gerda: "Everything had to burn up, otherwise we could never *get out of here*" (my italics).

As a major unifying factor we must regard the many leitmotives illustrating Elise's vampirism and feelings of guilt: the references to food, temperature, fire and sleep; the constant attention paid to stage properties like the chaise longue and the rocking chair, both connected with the dead husband; Fredrik's intermittent screaming in the background, recalling the husband's "horrible cries" outside Axel's home on another rainy night; above all: the leitmotif found in the play title.

According to a well-established tradition, the pelican nourishes its young ones with its own blood. In classical iconography this circumstance has turned the bird into a symbol of Christ sacrificing himself for mankind.[9] In Strindberg's play this aspect is not irrelevant but it is overshadowed by another one: the idea that a mother, who figuratively speaking nourishes her children at her own breast incarnates a love similar in kind to that of the pelican. The question is now: Does the pelican symbolize altruistic love in general or does it symbolize the variety known as maternal love? To answer this question we must examine the motif more closely.

Already in seq. 2 the idea that maternal love is altruistic is put forward by Elise: "The whole world knows how I have sacrificed myself for my children", she tells Margret. Yet her son, we have just learnt, has been a bottle baby and when at school he and his sister have not had enough to eat. There is apparently a discrepancy between Elise's true nature and her own conception of it. Parading as a pelican, she is in fact a vampire, a blood-sucker. Far from sacrificing herself to others, she sacrifices others to herself. This is made clear in seq. 5:

MOTHER. The verses to me, you mean? Well, I suppose no other mother-in-law has received verses like that at her daughter's wedding ... Do you remember what they said about the pelican, who gives its lifeblood to its young? I wept, I really did ...
SON-IN-LAW. At first, yes, but then you danced every dance. Gerda was almost jealous of you.
MOTHER. That wasn't the first time—she wanted me to come dressed in black—in mourning, as she said, but I didn't pay any attention to that. Am I to obey my youngsters!

Elise's deeds speak louder than her and Axel's words. Again she is revealed as a vampire rather than a pelican. At the wedding she, not Gerda, has been the bride. Instead of sacrificing itself for "its young" (Sw. "ungarne"), as the pelican does, she has refused to obey her "youngsters" (Sw. "ungarna"). Strindberg's choice of identical words underlines the ironical contrast between Elise and the pelican.

Equally ironical is Fredrik's observation, in seq. 9, that "the woman who gave us life was a big thief". The only thing Elise has *given* her children is—life, a doubtful gift in her case, since Elise is a 'taker', not a 'giver'.

Elise may be evil but at the beginning of the play we tend to see her as a deviation from the norm, symbolized by the altruistic pelican. Egotistic mothers exist—and Elise is one of them—but our concept of maternity is hardly affected by this circumstance.

To effect a revaluation of our traditional view of motherhood, Strindberg not only forces us to accept the idea that Elise represents the norm; he also undermines the symbol of love:

MOTHER. /—/ Look at me. I've reached a certain age ... though I've worked, slaved, and done my duty to my children and my house. Haven't I?
SON. Ha!—Like the pelican who never gave its heart's blood—the zoology books say it's a lie.

If it is not true that pelicans love their children, what proof do we have that mothers do—except their own opinion? Or that altruism exists at all? Axel's rhetorical myth-making is destroyed by Fredrik's scientifically grounded description of reality. Neither Elise nor the pelican can be trusted; they are not what they seem to be.

For a brief moment, in seq. 18, Elise sees herself the way she is. She awakens—only to fall asleep again, the truth being too brutal to be bearable. In seq. 20, she echoes her initial illusory view when telling Gerda: "I'm your mother and have nourished you with my blood." But by now we know that this is a lie. So does Gerda. Unlike her brother and the recipient Gerda does not question the existence of (maternal) love—the pelican—only the idea that Elise is a pelican.

However, in his final speech Fredrik is to recant:

> I think he [father] was the pelican who stripped himself for us: he always had wrinkled trousers and a worn velvet collar while we walked about like little artistocrats . . .

How are we to understand this? Is not Fredrik's earlier rejection of the pelican myth his moment of truth, his awakening? And is he not now deluding himself again? Is his development not identical with Elise's and Gerda's: from sleep through awakening back to sleep? Is his reference to the pelican at this point not a pathetic testimony to his need to believe in the existence of love at all costs? And is he not in this respect a true child of man?

Alternatively, we may regard his statement as a reversal of the traditional roles. As earlier in *The Father*, the father here turns out to be the true mother. Only paternal love is altruistic—this seems to be Strindberg's provocative counter-statement. The parents obviously represent binary oppositions:

father	$\sim$	mother
altruism		egotism

The surprising thing is that this realization on the part of the children does not lead to any rejection of the mother. Fredrik's final words are: "I don't see her—it isn't fun without Mother—there she comes!—Now the summer vacation begins!" Love for the mother seems in the last instance to be biologically determined, a longing, now at the moment of death, to return to the warm protection of the womb. Unless we prefer to see the children's concern with their "poor mother"—the expression occurs three times in the last few speeches—as an indication of compassion and forgiveness, in the spirit of Indra's Daughter and, ultimately, of Christ's words to the repentant sinner: "Today thou shalt be with me in paradise."[10]

If we compare the statement 'the mother loves her children' with the statement 'the pelican loves its young ones', we notice that 'the mother' can refer either to an individual—in this case Elise—or to a class (all mothers), whereas 'the pelican' in our context refers only to a class. By introducing the pelican and linking it first with the mother, then with the father, Strindberg stresses the archetypal nature of these characters, widens the scope of the play and involves the recipient. This is the primary function of the symbol.

As we have seen, the pelican theme cannot be reduced to a simple formula: a represents b. The same is true of the other themes. If this were so, there would be no play. The significant structuring of the themes—this is the stuff that the chamber plays are made on.

13. The Modernity of Strindbergian Drama

What do we mean when we speak of 'modern drama'? Modern—in relation to what? Clearly, the adjective is problematic because of its relativity; what was modern yesterday is traditional today and will be old-fashioned tomorrow.

Even to critics writing in roughly the same period, 'modern drama' means different things. For Lamm (1948) it begins with Scribe and Hebbel. Since Scribe's best known play, *Un verre d'eau,* was produced as early as in 1820, this means that Lamm uses 'modern' in a very wide sense. Why he chooses to draw the line where he does remains unclear. He admits that what he calls modern drama is both in form and content an outgrowth of the *drame bourgeois;* his starting-point therefore seems arbitrary—as does his selection of dramatists; thus a playwright like Büchner, who largely belongs to the 1830's and who nowadays strikes us as being much more 'modern' than both Hebbel and Scribe, is not discussed in his book.

Much more common—and certainly better grounded—is the idea expressed by Gassner that modern drama begins with the new concern for illusionism and environment in the 1870's, Zola's *Thérèse Raquin* (1873) being a mile-stone.[1]

What Szondi means by 'modern drama' appears partly in the title of his book, which includes the dates 1880–1950. It might seem from this as though Szondi shares Gassner's view and that he merely prefers to settle for a safer date as to the start of naturalism. But this is not the case. Szondi is not at all concerned with the illusionistic tradition Gassner favors but with the counter-tradition: the breaking away from illusionism. His reason for selecting the date 1880 is that he considers Ibsen's and Strindberg's plays of the 1880's part of a modern tradition, anticipating later 'epic' developments. Unlike Lamm and Gassner to whom 'modern' is largely a period label including both illusionism and non-illusionism, Szondi uses the term not merely as a period concept but also as a stylistic concept; to him 'modern' means not just plays written between 1880 and 1950—the last date is of course arbitrary—but more specifically: those plays breaking away from the classical idea of absolute dramatic values, notably the demand for interhuman relations. In addition to, or instead of, traditional man-to-man relations we now, in the wake of positivism and modern psychology, get interiorized drama demonstrating intrahuman conflicts. Dramatic values tend to turn into epic ones.

Strindberg stands at the beginning of this transient period, a period marked to an unusual extent by religious, political, social, moral, esthetic and theatrical reorientation. With regard to the dramatic form, this reorientation can be traced from Strindberg's early dramas, still in the classical, romantic and *bien faite* tradition, over his naturalistic dramas to his symbolistic and pre-expressionistic ones. Clearly, these movement labels are simplifications, and for all their difference, each of the plays bears a very obvious stamp of their author: whether it is a one-acter or a five-act play, a naturalistic or an expressionistic piece, a Strindbergian drama is as recognizable as a Beethoven composition.

Traditionally, critics speak of the pre-Inferno (1869–92) and the post-Inferno plays (1892–1909).[2] This distinction, which applies also to the form of the plays, is certainly meaningful. As I have indicated, there are indeed important differences between the two groups of plays.

In the pre-Inferno plays, Strindberg still dramatizes primarily interhuman conflicts; he is still a fairly plot-oriented playwright; and he relies to a great extent on illusionism. In the post-Inferno plays, the conflict is largely extrahuman, dramatizing a struggle between the protagonist and what Strindberg called the Powers; the dramas are primarily theme-centered; and illusionism has given way to "half-reality".[3]

Instead of a break we may, however, speak of a gradual transition. Evidence of this can be found both in Strindberg's theoretical statements and in the plays themselves. Thus in 1889 Strindberg hails the idea that "only the demands of taste and of the modern spirit are allowed to determine the artistic form" (*SS,* XVII:2, 302); although he pleads for artistic freedom he is nevertheless prepared to adjust to the demands of naturalism. Som twenty years later, he is no longer concerned with what others consider an adequate play structure, only with what he himself finds appropriate: "No predetermined form is to limit the author, because the theme determines the form" (*SS,* L, 12). As Strindberg himself points out, the concentrated form characterizing the chamber plays signifies a continuation of the tradition established already in the late 1880's. Even "the concept of chamber music transferred to drama" (*SS,* L, II) can be traced back to *Miss Julie,* where the dialogue, according to the Preface, "wanders, gathering in the opening scenes material which is later picked up, worked over, repeated, expounded, and developed like the theme in a musical composition" (*ASD,* III, 306); actually this description fits the chamber plays even better than *Miss Julie.*

Commenting on *The Father,* Brandell (1971, 177ff.) has observed that the play owes its strength and its modernity to the fact that in several respects, notably with regard to the question of paternity, we are left in ignorance of the true circumstances. We share, as it were, in the Captain's own uncertainty; his state of mind is made ours. The same is true in a much more radical way of *To Damascus I,* where the inner life of the hero is extended to the audience by means of various devices. This does not, however, mean that Strindberg in this play completely abstains from depicting outer reality, nor that what happens to the Stranger should be understood merely figuratively. The point is precisely that here, as in the other post-Inferno plays, characters, episodes, scenery and dialogue function both on a realistic and on a symbolic level, that the objective and subjective viewpoints overlap.

Especially in these later plays Strindberg appears as a master 'weaver', a playwright concerned more with texture than structure, working according to the formula form-determined-by-theme. As we have seen, the web imagery takes a central place in *The Father* and it might be argued that in the course of the play we virtually witness how Laura spins the Captain into her web, that the imagery, in other words, has its counterpart in the play structure. Much later Strindberg explicitly established the connection between theme and structure in his Explanatory Note for *A Dream Play*; and again he resorts to the same imagery: "on an insignificant basis of reality the imagination spins and weaves new patterns: a blending of memories, experiences, free inventions, absurdities, and improvisations" (*SS*, XXXVI, 215). In *The Ghost Sonata* the Old Man, the 'narrator' in the play, assures the Student that although his "tales are different, they all hang together on a thread, and the theme recurs regularly". Similarly, in a letter to his translator Schering, who had started to write plays himself, Strindberg remarks: "Don't forget the leitmotif! Weave the fates of men together, warp and weft" (May 16, 1907). The most elaborate statement we find in *The Burned House,* where the Stranger says:

When one's young, one sees the web set up: parents, relatives, friends, acquaintances, servants are the warp; later on in life one sees the weft; and the shuttle of fate carries the thread back and forth; and sometimes the yarn's forced into twists and turns, and the web's done. In old age when one's eyes can really see, one discovers that all twists and turns form a pattern, a cipher, an ornament, a hieroglyphic, which one can now interpret for the first time: That is life! The World Weaver has woven it!

It should be clear from these quotations that Strindberg is very much equating life with his own play structures; or to put it more precisely: he is endeavoring to shape the plays in such a way that they reflect his own conception of life. This is especially true of the later plays: *To Damascus, A Dream Play,* the chamber plays. When we experience these plays for the first time, they appear like a welter of "twists" and "turns", a difficult "cipher", a mysterious "hieroglyphic". When we experience them again we begin to distinguish a pattern. The power to survey which according to the Stranger comes with old age has a kind of counterpart in our gradual power to get below the surface and discover the correspondences which are found there.

This process on our part—as readers or spectators—is important. Strindberg has fully realized that it is not enough to *declare* that life despite its apparent confusion forms a meaningful pattern. What matters is the emotional transference of this idea to the reader or spectator. Not until he *experiences* life (as it is imitated in the plays) in this way, can he profoundly accept it. As usual Strindberg strives to include the recipient in his own sphere of experience.

An important consequence of this dramatic method is that we cannot properly determine the coherence—or even the meaning—of a Strindbergian play until we come down to what we might call its thematic level. Not until we realize that the topics in these plays are only superficially "different" and that the various "tales" all "hang together" on a thematic thread, can we evaluate these dramas in a new way. Initially we tend to experience characters, episodes, scenery and dialogue in a realistic fashion but gradually—and this is where the thematic pattern, the texture, becomes of utmost importance—Strindberg makes us sense that they are something more. Characteristic of the Strindbergian drama—especially in the post-Inferno period—is the gradual progression from letter to spirit, from outward to inward reality, from the singular to the universal. When we turn back to our point of departure—the opening of the play—we discover that what we first took to be the truth has another deeper significance. By structuring his dramas in this way, Strindberg makes us partake of his own view that what we call reality is actually at best a half-reality, often a lie and most likely a phantom, a mirage. The true reality is behind the letter and presumably beyond life. When we arrive at the end of these plays, we discover that our view of reality has changed. In this lies the true structural power of Strindbergian drama.

Appendix. Translating Strindbergian Drama. *Spöksonaten* in English

Strindberg's plays in translation are texts not only for actors, directors and spectators, texts to be transformed into visual and aural reality in the theatre. They are also texts for readers.[1] Unlike the situation in the theatre, where the director functions as a go-between, a reader of the translated plays is only once removed from Strindberg. Few English-speaking theatre critics would know any Swedish; similarly, much of the work devoted to Strindberg in drama departments in different parts of the world is done by people who have no knowledge of Swedish and who are therefore totally dependent on translations.

In this situation the risk is imminent that Strindberg's text is criticized for what are actually shortcomings—unavoidable or not—in the translation. Faithfulness toward the original text must certainly be a primary demand. But since play translations are usually undertaken with a production in mind, it is equally important that the lines are idiomatic and easily speakable. A third criterium may be added: the text must be easy to grasp, since in the theatre we have little time to ponder. Generally speaking the target language plays a more important role in drama translations than in translations of novels.

It is obvious that the three critieria just mentioned, to a certain extent compete with one another and that the balance between them must be settled from case to case. The problems involved will be examined here with regard to one Strindberg play, *Spöksonaten,* translated into one and the same language: English. (I ignore the fact that some of the translations discussed below are intended for a British audience, others for an American one.)

To my knowledge *Spöksonaten* has so far been published in nine different English translations.[2] All of them will be considered below. They are, in chronological order (for further details, see the list p. 252 ff.):

(1) *The Spook Sonata.* Tr. Edwin Björkman. New York 1916.
(2) *The Ghost Sonata.* Tr. Erik Palmstierna and James Bernard Fagan. London 1929.
(3) *The Ghost Sonata.* Tr. Elizabeth Sprigge. Garden City 1955.
(4) *The Ghost Sonata.* Tr. Max Faber. London 1960.
(5) *The Ghost Sonata.* Tr. Evert Sprinchorn. New York 1962.
(6) *The Ghost Sonata.* Tr. Michael Meyer. New York 1964.

(7) *The Ghost Sonata.* Tr. Arvid Paulson. New York 1965.
(8) *The Ghost Sonata.* Tr. Carl Richard Mueller. San Francisco 1966.
(9) *The Ghost Sonata.* Tr. Walter Johnson. Seattle 1973.

In the following, references to these translations are made only by means of the figures left.

The first question a translator should ask himself is: Which edition am I going to use? The reliability may differ considerably and it is not always easy to know which text is the best one. *Spöksonaten* is a case in point. As with most other Strindberg plays, there is so far no quite reliable edition of this play. Traditionally, Landquist's edition of Strindberg's collected works (*SS*) is used by translators. In this particular case, however, a more reliable text is Lindström's school edition of *Spöksonaten* (1963). Unfortunately, translators seldom inform their readers of which edition they have used; this is true also of the *Spöksonaten* translators; in all cases I have assumed that Landquist's edition (*SS*, XLV) has been used.[3]

A question which is relevant with regard to translations of plays is: How has the translation come about? Is the published translation based on a production? This is obviously the case in (6), which also proves to be very actable; in the other cases information is lacking on this point.

Already the play title provides us, as we have seen, with two alternatives: while (1) has chosen to call the piece *The Spook Sonata,* all the others have preferred *The Ghost Sonata.* In (6) there is a certain vacillation in the sense that "spook supper" appears twice in the text—while the expression "ghost supper" is used the third time. An interesting comment on the alternatives is given in (3):

I have called this the most famous of Strindberg's Chamber Plays /—/ *The Ghost Sonata,* in spite of the tempting alternative *Spook* sometimes used before, because I believe "ghost" is a truer translation of the author's "spök" than "spook". The latter word has, in English, a facetios flavour—one inevitably thinks of "spooky"—which the Swedish word has not and, fantastic, in part even grotesque though the play is, it is very far from being facetious.

A similar view, this time biographically motivated, appears in (5):

Strindberg did not want his play called *The Spook Sonata.* To his German translator he insisted that the play be "called *The Ghost Sonata* after Beethoven's Ghost Sonata in D Minor and his Ghost Trio. Hence not Spook Sonata" (letter to Schering, April 1, 1907).

Although the situation is hardly as simple as the commentator—by translating Strindberg's "Gespenstersonaten" and "Spuk" into English—claims, one can agree with the view that the author's information to Schering supports the alternative "ghost".

As we have earlier noted, the drama contains a number of inadvertencies. It is also obvious that certain lines call for particular movements/gestures not indicated in the acting directions. The principal question, then, is: Should a translator keep these inadvertencies/lacunae or should he emend? The question is touched upon in the "Translator's foreword" with which (7) opens:

I have /—/ added casts of characters (not infrequently omitted by Strindberg in his manuscripts) and have inserted additional stage directions wherever urgently needed—details that Strindberg, in his feverish and impassioned absorption in the fundamental labor of the play itself, often neglected or left to the discretion of the publisher and the stage director.

This principle is more or less adhered to by all the translators. Thus most of them omit the Caretaker from the list of characters while the Cook, the Maid and the Beggars are included. Practical concerns here motivate the corrections.

The translators rarely omit anything of Strindberg's text. To the few examples belong the omission in (7) of the initial stage direction "*det är en klar söndagsmorgon*" (it is a bright Sunday morning) and in (8) of the line "Väl, så är det skrivet!" (Well, thus it is ordained!). There is, of course, no reason for leaving these passages out.

The same moderation is not shown with regard to additions. Although the three parts of the play have not been given any designations by the playwright, most translators prefer to call each part "*Scene*".

Sometimes the text is provided with "additional stage directions" (7). Thus (5) provides the line

Men hon [klockan] hyttar först, innan hon slår! – Hör nu varnar hon: "Klockan kan slå".

with the addition (by the dash): "*The clock can be heard preparing to strike the hour.*" In Strindberg's text the speaker—the Old Man—may well be imagining that the clock is about to strike; in the translation he is clearly not. In any case the translator should have indicated, in some way or another, that the stage direction is an addition.

Most disturbing are the additions containing evaluations. In the original we find the following acting directions:

GUBBEN *i tamburen /—/ smyger sig fram och lyssnar.*

GUBBEN *har försökt resa sig och taga ordet, men har fallit ner i stolen och krympt ihop, krymper allt mer och mer under följande.*

In (5) this is rendered as follows:

The Old Man appears in the hallway /—/. He moves silently forward on his crutches, like a black spider, and eavesdrops on the servants.

The Old Man has tried to rise and speak but has collapsed in his chair and shriveled up, and, like a dying insect, he shrivels up more and more during the following dialogue.

Unlike the playwright, the translator here openly sides against the Old Man. The picture of him becomes too diabolic. The translator has taken over the role of the director.

With regard to the order of presentation, Strindberg's stage directions sometimes seem capricious; this is, for example, the case in the long passage opening the play. Here (1) and (3) have chosen to change the order of presentation to some extent. In this way the stage directions are easier to grasp but the associative Strindbergian order of presentation has a thematic-symbolic value which is lost.

Without a considerable knowledge of the Swedish language and culture no translator ought to deal with *Spöksonaten.* In all the translations one can find faults based on lack of knowledge in these respects.

Although Strindberg never explicitly says so, it is obvious that the play is set in Sweden. When the references to Swedish habits are very special, a translator is faced with the question: maintain or change? In the opening of the play the Student tells the Milkmaid:

Ja, jag har inte sovit i natt, och du tror naturligtvis, att jag varit ute och rumlat ... /—/ Druckit punsch, va? – Luktar jag punsch?

Well, I didn't get any sleep last night, and you think of course that I was out living it up ... /—/ Drinking punch, eh?—Do I smell of punch?

We here deal with a very national drink, relished by Swedish students around the turn of the century. Two translators (6, 9) translate "punsch" with "punch"—which leads the thoughts of an English-speaking audience to 'punch bowl', i.e. a much weaker drink than the Swedish one. Presumably aware of this, others (1, 3, 7) speak more generally of "liquor". Three (2, 4, 5) avoid a noun. And one (8) proposes a drink—whiskey—which is as natural to American students today as it was rare to Swedish students around the turn of the century.

Typical examples of (old) Swedish mourning ritual we find in the remark that the windows "*äro behängda med vita lakan*" and that the Caretaker's Wife spreads fir twigs outside the entrance. Three approaches can be distinguished here: (*a*) the original is faithfully translated, (*b*) the original is faithfully translated and complemented with a note explaining the significance of the national custom, (*c*) explanation is included in the running text, for example:

(2) *hung with white sheets*
(3) *hung with white sheets**
*Sign of mourning.
(8) *hung with white mourning sheets*

Of these solutions, only (*b*) seems recommendable. (*a*) means that the English-speaking reader is not put in a position to understand what to his Swedish counterpart is a matter of course; in a play where 'ghosts' haunt the stage, where the characters speak like parrots, etc., it may be difficult for a foreign reader to know what is realistic and what is not; thus, with regard to another typically Swedish phenomenon—the wallpaper door leading to the Mummy's closet—(5) sees reason to point out that this "is *not* one of the bizarre elements in the *Sonata*"; if no explanation is given concerning the white sheets and the spreading of fir twigs, there is a risk that these ingredients, too, are considered bizarre elements. As for (*c*), it is of course incorrect not to point out that we deal with an addition by the translator. Our conclusion, then, is that a translator should provide necessary information but keep it apart from the author's own text. It could be objected: This may be recommendable for stage and acting directions, but what about the dialogue? Here again the *reader* may be assisted by a note but the *spectator* is helpless. Should a translator not in these cases insert the needed explanation in the running text? Maybe. But even in these cases I would prefer an explanatory note and have the director change the dialogue as he pleases.

Sometimes a Swedish reader, too, would need an explanatory note. Lady Beate von Holsteinkrona is referred to as "stiftsfröken"; few people would know that by this is meant "an unmarried noblewoman who belongs to an order providing her with an income designed to cover the base necessities of food, shelter, clothing, and keeping up appearances" (9). The word is difficult to translate. The closest equivalent seems to be "secular canoness" (1, 2, 9). Mislead by the first part of the compound ("stift" meaning 'diocese'), two translators turn the old lady into "a pillar of the Church" (3, 8), while (5) makes her "very active in the church" and (7) "active in her church"; in the last case this representative of old Swedish aristocracy has—*mirabile dictu*—been enrolled in American sectarianism.

A similar vagueness concerning the place of action is found in another context in (8). "Your father robbed me of seventeen thousand crowns", it says with a pronounced allusion to Sweden or at least Scandinavia. But a little later it is pointed out that the Consul "cheated the state out of another fifty thousand pounds" ("50 000 kronor"), which—quite apart from the incorrect rendering of the amount—makes the reader believe that we deal with a British consul or that the action is set in Britain.

A time reference, not without interest, is lost when the original's "*en modärn husfasad*"—an indirect critique of contemporary life—in (6) is rendered by "*a fashionable house*"; also the symbolically pregnant "*fasad*" (façade) has here been left out. It may be objected that "*modärn*" is not very informative unless we know in which period the play is set; a comment by the translator is called for here.

Strindberg's Caretaker's Wife "*sopar farstun*". In the translations she is sweeping "*the doorstep*" (3), "*the stairs and the sidewalk in front of the house*" (5), "*the front step*" (4, 6), sometimes quite correctly "*the vestibule*" (2, 7), "*the hallway*" (1) or "*the entrance*" (9). On the balcony rail we see a blue spread and "*två vita sängkuddar*" (two white pillows); (5) translates with "*pillowcases*". The Milk Maid wears "*bruna skor*" (brown shoes); in (7) they are "*black*". The Mummy "*stryker*" Hummel on his back; in (9) she "*strikes* HUMMEL'S *back*"—instead of "*strokes*", a misleading misprint. In these last examples we deal with carelessness rather than lack of knowledge.

With regard to local references—and there are many more in *Spöksonaten* than have been mentioned here—we may pose a principle question: To what extent and in what way should a translator explain these words/expressions, more or less incomprehensible to a foreign audience? If we examine the translations of *Spöksonaten* from this point of view, it is striking how different the approaches are. Some translators (1, 6, 8) provide very few explanations, others (5, 9) quite a number. It is difficult to distinguish any selective principle. Thus quite a lot of biographical information is given, interesting enough but rarely necessary for an understanding of the text. While words/expressions such as "*reflexionsspegel*", "Sursum corda", "Cor in aethere" are usually left unexplained. In the last two cases the translator can, of course, defend himself with the argument that these Latin expressions are as incomprehensible to the average Swede as to the average Englishman or American. Occasionally the explanation is incorrect. Thus it is not easy to understand what "*reflexionsspegel*" is with the assistance of the following note: "Set at an angle inside the window, so as to show what is going on in the street" (3). "Solsången" (The Song of the Sun), two translators explain (1, 5), is taken from the *Edda,* a misunderstanding which may have contributed to the choice of metre in (5); they are corrected on this point by (7).[4]

Even theatres have their national conventions. The entrance of the house is placed by Strindberg "*till vänster på fonden*", to the left upstage; (5) instead places it "*at the right*"—quite illegitimately since he further adheres to the Strindbergian references to stage areas. So does (7) but in his case we deal with a consistent principle, accounted for in the foreword:

> For the purpose of conforming to American stage custom, I have reversed the author's directions—Right and Left—to their opposites. Thus they are given here from the viewpoint of the actor on the stage.

When none of the other translators reverse the stage directions, it may be because they also think of the reader of the play. The remark at any rate calls attention to the fact that playwrights and translators rarely indicate whether their stage directions are from the viewpoint of the actor or of the spectator.

As could be expected, the translators rarely reveal lack of knowledge of the Swedish language. However, in the following examples this is the case. When the Student asks "Var finns heder och tro? I sagorna och på barnföreställningarna!" (Where is honor and faith? In fairy tales and children's plays!), it is obvious that there is an intimate relation between tales and children's plays: in both cases we deal with an illusory picture of reality. "Barnföreställningarna" is correctly rendered with children's plays by (9), while (1) and (3), who evidently confuse the preposition "på" with "i" incorrectly translate with "childish" resp. "children's fancies". Misleading are also the alternatives "children's games" (5) and "games that children play" (6).

Class circulation plays an important part in *Spöksonaten* and when Johansson, now serving Hummel, declares that he has been "bokhandlare" (bookdealer) we get a measure of his social decline. When (2) translates this phrase with "used to be in a bookshop", this perspective disappears.

The Cook's "Nu går jag, men stannar ändå, så länge jag vill!" (Now I'll go, but I'll stay anyway, as long as I want to!) is in (5) translated as follows: "I'm leaving now, but that doesn't mean I haven't stayed as long as I wanted to." In other words: Strindberg's Cook remains while that of the translator leaves. The point implied by the original—the idea that the Young Lady cannot free herself from the vampire in the kitchen until she dies—is lost.

Bengtsson's remark that Hummel "höll på att få oss i fängelse, när vi kallade kokerskan tjuv" (nearly got us into prison, when we called the cook a thief) is by (6) exaggerated into: "he had us put in prison"; what is grotesque with Strindberg becomes comical in the translation. Comical, too, is the same translator's rendering of the Student's description of his father:

FRÖKEN. Var han sjuk?
STUDENTEN. Nej, han var frisk, men han var galen! Nåväl det bröt ut en gång, och under följande omständigheter . . .

By (9) this is correctly translated as follows:

YOUNG LADY: Was he sick?
STUDENT: No, he was well, but he was crazy! Well, it broke out once—under these circumstances . . .

(6) translates the last speech:

STUDENT: No. He was perfectly well; just mad. He only showed it once; I'll tell you how.

The translator here has read the Student's speech in an unnatural way, as though the word "en" were strongly emphasized.

Sometimes a translator ascribes to a certain character a role which actually belongs to another one. When Strindberg has it "som han [Hummel] måste bort klockan tre, så gjordes middan färdig klockan två", we must imagine that it was the Cook, with whom Hummel had excellent relations, who prepared the dinner. There is simply no point in the idea of having Hummel cook for himself, or for the whole family, the way (8) has it: "Since he had to be away at three, he prepared dinner at two." When the Young Lady's reference to the "coloring bottle with scorpion letters on it" is put in the mouth of the Cook (1, 2), the reason, I suppose, is carelessness; if not we have yet another example of translators doing the job of the director.

Not seldom the vagueness of the original is determined by a wish to maintain suspense through mystification. The following passage offers an example:

GUBBEN. /—/ Där kommer fröken ...
STUDENTEN. Överstens dotter?
GUBBEN. Ja! Dotter!

In (9) this is rendered quite literally as follows:

HUMMEL: /—/ There comes the young lady ...
STUDENT: The colonel's daughter?
HUMMEL: Yes! Daughter!

Note that Hummel does not explicitly state that the Young Lady is the Colonel's daughter, well aware that she is his own daughter. But all the translators, except (9), render the last speech with an unequivocal "Yes! His daughter!" or something to this effect. Hummel is more honest in the original than in the translations.

When a translator does not understand a passage, he can either try to render it as literally as possible or else change (emend) it so that it becomes more comprehensible in the translation than in the original. How he chooses presumably depends on his view of the original. Is it a mediocre or a subtle text, is it carefully composed or loosely structured? The difficulty with *Spöksonaten* is that for all its merits it contains certain inadvertencies. These may give a translator the feeling that emendations are called for. Two examples may throw light on this problem.

Early in the play we find the following puzzling exchange of speeches:[5]

GUBBEN. Är ni sportsman?
STUDENTEN. Ja, det var min olycka ...
GUBBEN. Så skall det vändas i lycka!

THE OLD MAN. Are you a sportsman?
THE STUDENT. Yes, that's my misfortune ...
THE OLD MAN. We'll make it your fortune!

The Old Man's question has to do with his desire to get the Student attached to the Young Lady, who enjoys riding a horse; she is, in other words, a sportswoman. If the Student now proves to be a sportsman, the chances of coupling them seem favorable. But beyond this literal meaning, the word "sportsman" has a figurative one, both in Swedish and in English: an honest, chivalrous person. This suits both the Young Lady and, even more, the Student, the Sunday child who can see what others cannot. His sportsmanship was demonstrated the preceding night when he distinguished himself as a "brave rescuer" of human lives. But purity, chivalry and courage have no place in this world of sin and guilt. The Student discovers that at the end of the play: "Where is honor and faith? In fairy tales and children's plays! Where is anything that fulfills its promise? ... In my imagination!". Already at the beginning he has the feeling that his sportsmanship distinguishes him from his fellow men who have very little of this quality. That is why he can reply: "Yes, that's my misfortune." Hummel's "We'll make it your fortune!" forebodes his attempt to turn the Student's exceptional sportsmanship into a norm.

If this interpretation is correct, the conclusion must be that it is essential to keep the word "sportsman" in a translation; and this is so in four cases (1, 2, 4, 7). But (3), who has obviously found the lines incomprehensible, translates "sportsman" with "gambler": in this way the Student's "Yes, that's my misfortune" is given a logical motivation. "Gambler" returns in (5), (6), (8) and (9). By reading the lines superficially, these translators have come to exchange the pregnant "sportsman" of the original for a word which has the opposite connotations: duplicity, frivolity, greed, recklessness. A less adequate characterization of the Student is hardly thinkable.

A nice example of how Strindberg's habit of thinking in metaphoric terms may puzzle the translators is the following:

GUBBEN. Kanske förmögen?
STUDENTEN. Inte alls . . . tvärtom! Jag är utfattig!
GUBBEN. Hör nu . . . jag tycker, jag hört den rösten . . . jag hade en ungdomsvän, som inte kunde säga fönster, utan alltid sa funster – jag har bara råkat en person med det uttalet och det var han; den andra är ni – är det möjligt att ni är släkt med grosshandlar Arkenholz.

But the Student, as we have already noted, has never said "funster"! Most of the translators seem to be of the opinion that Strindberg has been careless, judging by their emendations:

(1) HUMMEL. Wealthy, I suppose?
STUDENT. Not at all—on the contrary—poor as a durmouse!
HUMMEL. Look here . . . It seems to me as if I recognised your voice. When I was young, I had a friend who always said "dur" instead of door.

The same 'improvement' is used by (2) and (4), whereas (3) prefers a vague paraphrase:

OLD MAN. Do you know, it seems to me I've heard your voice before. When I was young I had a friend who pronounced certain words just as you do.

Not until (5) do we get a satisfactory solution:

THE OLD MAN: It's strange ... but I can't help thinking that I've heard your voice before ... When I was a young man I had a friend who couldn't pronounce window, he always said winder.

That this is not just an easy way of sticking to a literal translation but the result of a convincing interpreation appears from the introduction (xv) where the passage is commented on:

If this were a realistic play, there would be no explanation, just as there would be no explanation for the appearance of the Milkmaid as an apparition visible at first only to the Student. On the other hand, if the apparition can be accounted for as a symbol, so can the window. For Hummel is described later as a thief who enters through windows to steal human souls, and here we see him as he first steals into the Student's life by means of a "window".

One would perhaps expect later translators to be influenced by this interpretation—and the solution that is a result of it—and this is the case in (8), but in (6) and (5) and later in (9) we come across different attempts at emendation. The solution in (6) is of the same kind as in (1, 2):

STUDENT: /—/ I'm ab-absolutely penniless.
OLD MAN: Wait a moment! I seem to know that voice. When I was young I had a friend who couldn't say absinthe, he always said ab-absinthe.

In (9) a vague formulation à la (3) is chosen:

HUMMEL: Listen ... I think I've heard that voice of yours before ... I had a friend when I was young who spoke like you—he's the only other person with the same pronunciation ...

In this last case the translation is supplemented by a note in which we are told that a more literal translation would have been "who couldn't say window, but always said wendow"; it would of course have been much better if this alternative had been used in the play text.

Sometimes a translator is forced to resign. The two vocative forms in Swedish ('du, ni') create possibilities which inevitably get lost in an English translation. The change of vocative form is subtly utilized in the third act of *Spöksonaten.* Here the Student and the Young Lady address one another with an impersonal "ni"—they have just met—until, after a crescendo-like antiphony, they find one another in an ecstatic "du":

FRÖKEN. Ja, Gud så stort! Vilkens tanke var det?
STUDENTEN. Din!
FRÖKEN. Din!
STUDENTEN. Vår! – Vi ha fött något tillsammans, vi äro vigda ...

THE YOUNG LADY. How heavenly! Wonderful! Whose thought was that?
THE STUDENT. Yours!
THE YOUNG LADY. Yours!
THE STUDENT. Ours!—We have given birth to something together—we are married ...

But the short moment of communion is soon gone. The misery of life makes itself felt and separates the two again. The renewed distance is indicated by a return to the "ni" form. Not until the end, when the Young Lady is dying, does the Student revert to the intimate form of address: "Sov du sköna, osälla, oskyldiga, utan skuld till dina lidanden . . ." (Sleep, beautiful, unhappy, innocent girl, without blame for your suffering . . .). Neither the gentleness of the "du" nor the coolness of the "ni" can be communicated by the "you" that replaces both.

Ambiguities and puns are also often untranslatable. "Är han klok?" (Is he sane?), the Student asks, referring to Hummel, and Johansson answers: "Ja, vad är *det*?" (Well, what's that?). Most translators have rendered "klok" with "in his right mind", etc., but two (3, 8) prefer "wise". Both alternatives are legitimate. The point of the Student's question is that it is phrased in such a way that wisdom and madness conjoin; cf. his remark about the father: "he was well, but he was crazy". This ambiguity inevitably disappears in all the translations, but the passage becomes unnecessarily trite when (1) translates: "Is he in his right mind?—Who can tell?". Here the universal problem has been reduced to a question concerning Hummel's mental state.

Ambiguous it is, again, when the Student declares that "prestaven hade älskat den avlidnes [Hummels] son" (the mace bearer had loved the dead man's son). "Älska" can here be taken either in a spiritual or in an erotic sense. The Young Lady's reaction—she "*fixerar, för att utleta meningen*" (stares fixedly at him trying to understand what he means)—reveals that she hesitates between these two meanings. Again Strindberg creates a situation in which the meaning of the words is questioned, in this case the meaning of 'to love'. The Young Lady's reaction becomes incomprehensible and the Student's description uninteresting if the ambiguity of his phrase is not preserved. How do the translators solve this?

(1, 2) translate "hade älskat" with "had been rather too friendly", i.e. the ambiguity is replaced by a euphemistic phrase in the spirit of the Victorian period. In this way the Student seems slightly prudish and the reaction of the Young Lady is difficult to account for. Several translators (3, 6–8) use the expression "had been in love with", which is so straightforward that the Young Lady's difficulty to understand seems hard to grasp. Far too direct is the alternative "had been the lover of" (5). As so often the literal translation—"had loved" (9)—proves to be the best one.

Surprising words, expressions, compounds are often due to an attempt on the part of the playwright to give his play an extra dimension. When the Old Man states that baron Skanskorg hopes to get rich and that he is getting divorced from his wife who presents him "ett stenhus" (a stone house) to get rid of him, we may be surprised at the classification stone house. Why not just house? The reason may be that around the turn of the century, when wooden houses were still the rule in Sweden, a stone house had a greater social prestige than nowadays. But more essential it seems that the word—or the material—elsewhere in the play connotes materialism. Note that the house we see on the stage—a symbol of life—apparently is a stone house. The house Skanskorg hopes to get from his wife is essentially identical with this house; just as his expectations are comparable to those of the Student and Johansson, who both dream of entering the staged stone house. The parallels indicate that we are ultimately dealing with the illusory hope of man that happiness can be gained from worldly success.

This being the case, it makes a difference whether "stenhus" is rendered as "apartment-house" (1), "big house" (2), "stone mansion" (3), "mansion" (4, 7), "town house" (5), "fine house" (6), "great mansion" (8) or—"stone house" (9). Again the most literal translation is the most adequate.

We here touch upon a problem of great importance, especially to translators of Strindberg, whose superior handling of the language consists above all in his ability to combine words and phrases in such a surprising way that situations, words and thoughts gain in depth. The surprising combinations often mean deviations from the linguistic norm. In such cases translators are inclined to substitute normal and trivial expressions for strange but meaningful ones.

The names of the *dramatis personae* can often form a problem to a translator. *Spöksonaten* offers certain examples. A name like Skanskorg, meaning literally 'entrenchment-basket', may imply the Aristocrat's attempt to secure a social position. But it would definitely not be recommendable to translate the name into English. There is no reason, however, to reduce the original's "kallad baron Skansborg" (called baron S.) to "Baron Skansborg" (3, 5, 7, 8); there is an implication in this "called" that Skanskorg is not what he seems to be.

That Strindberg has christened his student Arkenholz may, as we have noted, have something to do with the biblical ark. There is at any rate no reason to spell the name Arkenholtz (1–4).

Nor is there any reason for changing the speaker-labels and substitute "Hummel" (1, 7, 9) for Strindberg's "Gubben" (The Old Man). The appelative here corresponds to the other designations in the play and underlines the important generation motif.

Extremely important for an understanding of Strindberg's plays is a certain sensitivity to significant correspondences in the text; inadequacies in the translations are often due to an inability to discover such correspondences. As we have earlier noted, the sound effects at the beginning and end of *Spöksonaten* correspond with each other; the organ music from a nearby church has a counterpart in the sighing of the harp strings, the chiming of distant church bells in the "*soft, quiet, pleasantly sad music*" from the distant Isle of the Dead. It is therefore unfortunate when the ringing of the bells in (3) is said to come not only from distant but also from nearby churches; when in (5) we hear "*the deep notes of the organs in the nearby churches*"; and when in (7) the final sound effect is sentimentally described as "*the soft strains of ecstatic music, mournfully ending on a note of peace*". None of these translators seem to have sensed the connection between the beginning and the end of the play.

A special problem is presented by the literary, notably biblical, allusions which appear in several places in *Spöksonaten* (Bandy, 200ff.) The opening conversation between the Student and the Milkmaid offers an example; as we have noted, it relates both to the story of the good Samaritan and to Jesus' conversation with the Samarian woman at Jacob's well. When the Student declares that he has "bandaged up injured people and kept watch over the sick all night", we are reminded of the Samaritan who, having compassion on the man who had been maltreated by robbers, "went to him, and bound up his wounds, /—/ and took care of him" (Luke 10: 33–34). None of the translators emphasize the biblical allusion by using the expression "binding up wounds"; they all prefer more common expressions such as "dressing wounds", "bandaging wounds".

A biblical allusion which has usually been preserved in the translations is found at the end of Act I, where Hummel admonishes the crowd:

> Applaud him, fellow citizens. It's Sunday, of course, but the ass in the pit and the grain on the field absolve us ...

In Luke 14: 5—as (9) points out in a note—we read:

> Which of you shall have an ass or an ox fallen into a pit, and will not straightway pull him out on the sabbath day?

Most translators use the phrase "ass in the pit", but (9) prefers "well"—surprisingly enough, since he is well aware of the biblical allusion. (6) and (8), on the other hand, seem to be ignorant of it; the former translates "the ass at the well", the latter "the ass at the draw well". The lack of biblical knowledge has resulted here in 'emendations'; the translators have assumed that Strindberg has carelessly written "i brunnen" instead of (the intended) "vid brunnen", that he has been referring to the ass as a working animal—even on the Sabbath day.

It is of course essential that the reader/spectator is aware of the fact that the words following upon Hummel's suicide—the Mummy's "Det är fullbordat!"—are identical with Christ's last words on the cross (John 19: 30). The allusion can be interpreted in different ways. To some it may ironically underline the contrast between the Christ figure and the diabolic Hummel. To others it may indicate that these figures in spite of everything have something in common. Whichever way we interpret the allusion, we must agree that it adds a dimension to Hummel's death.

Several translators faithfully stick to the corresponding biblical phrase and translate "It is finished!". Still closer to the Bible stylistically, yet diverging from King James, is (6) with "It is accomplished!". In the trivial "It is over!" (5), "Now it is done!" (7) and "It is done!" (9), one looks in vain for Strindberg's elevated Christ parallel.

A more cryptic biblical allusion is found at the end of the play, where the Student prays:

Du vise, milde Buddha, som sitter där och väntar att en himmel skall växa upp ur jorden, förläna oss tålamod i prövningen, renhet i viljan, att hoppet icke må komma på skam!

Wise, gentle Buddha, sitting there waiting for a heaven to grow out of the earth, grant us patience in our trials, purity of will, that the hope be not put to shame.

In Rom. 5:3–5 we read:

/—/ vi till och med berömma oss av våra lidanden, eftersom vi veta att lidandet verkar ståndaktighet, och ståndaktigheten bepövad fasthet, och fastheten hopp, och hoppet låter oss icke komma på skam.

/—/ we glory in tribulations also: knowing that tribulation worketh patience; and patience experience; and experience, hope: and hope maketh not ashamed.

It is this faith in the sense of suffering that the Student at the end of the play tries to embrace. When Strindberg uses the definite form "hoppet", it is due to the fact that he is quoting from the Bible. But apart from this, the form is highly meaningful in the context, since we are dealing both with Buddha's hope and the hope of mankind.

With regard to the phrase "att hoppet icke må komma på skam", the translators are, in other words, faced with two problems. On the one hand the biblical reference should be indicated, on the other the double meaning of "hoppet" must bc retained.

As for the first point, we may note that, unlike Strindberg, none of the translators have cited the Bible literally. The reason for this is undoubtedly that the English translation of the Bible is more archaic than the Swedish one; quotations from King James would have emphasized the biblical nature of the phrase too much.[6] But several translators have given the phrase an archaic touch by using such words as "thy" and "come to nought".

As for the second point, we may note that four translators combine the hope with Buddha: "thy hope(s)", "your hope(s)"; one combines it with humanity: "our hope"; and three maintain the vagueness of the original: "this hope", "hope".

The special problems related to the translation of biblical allusions can schematically be described as follows:

Bible in Swedish		Bible in English
↓		↓
Spöksonaten	→	*The Ghost Sonata*

As appears from this diagram, the translator has a double loyalty. The more faithful he is toward one party, the less faithful he will (probably) be to the other. The difficulty consists in finding a favorable balance, so that the biblical allusions are indicated but not emphasized.

The language in *Spöksonaten* in many ways differs from that of present day Swedish. Here a translator is faced with the question: Should he settle for the kind of English spoken around the turn of the century or should he choose present day English (British or American)? We find here great divergences between the oldest translation (of 1916) and the youngest one (of 1973). Even the original text is in this respect problematic; when staging Strindberg's plays in Sweden the language is usually slightly modernized. From this we cannot, however, conclude that a translator should modernize the text; rather, that he should let director and actors do this.

So far we have focussed our attention on the *meaning* of the original text and how it has been preserved in the translations. We will now concentrate our attention on problems related to the form. To what degree can the style of *Spöksonaten* also be found in the translations?

In modern prose drama the dialogue is almost always characterized by simple vocabulary and syntax, resemblant of what we find in everyday spoken language. *Spöksonaten* is no exception. What distinguishes Strindberg's dialogue from that of many other playwrights is that it provides a maximum of information and suggestion with a minimum of words. A comparison with the translations reveals that though the natural tone is usually retained, there are more words and there is less information. As for the power of suggestion, this is usually in reverse relation to the number of words: the more laconic a speech is, the more suggestive it is. As an example we may select a short passage, the meaning of which we have discussed earlier:

STUDENTEN. Är han klok?
JOHANSSON. Ja, vad är *det*?

This exchange of speeches is rendered as follows:

(1) Is he in his right mind?
Who can tell?

(2) Is he in his right mind?
Yes, what is *that?*

(3) Is he a wise man?
Depends what that is.

(4) Is he compos mentis—you know, 'all there'?
I'm sure I don't know, sir . . .

(5) He's not crazy, is he?
What does it mean to be crazy?

(6) Is he sane?
Depends on what you mean by that.

(7) Is he quite right in his head?
Well—just what does that mean, exactly?

(8) Is he a wise man?
That all depends on what you mean.

(9) Is he sane?
Well, what's that?

As we have earlier noted, none of the translators have been able to transfer the ambiguity of the Student's question; they have all been forced to make a choice. As a result of this the suggestive element disappears. At the same time it has been difficult to maintain the laconic phrasing of the original; only one of the translators (9) has managed to limit himself to the same number of words (seven) as the author; three need nine words, one ten, one twelve, one thirteen, one fourteen and one sixteen, i.e. more than twice as many as Strindberg. As for the naturalness, it is again (9) who comes closest to the original.

One of the hardest tasks for a translator is finding the right stylistic level, the right tone. In *Spöksonaten* the style varies considerably and a translator must be sensitive here to subtle nuances. The play opens with the following 'dialogue':

STUDENTEN. Får jag låna skopan?
FLICKAN (*drar åt sig skopan*).
STUDENTEN. Har du inte slutat snart?
FLICKAN (*ser på honom med fasa*).
/—/
STUDENTEN. Vad ser du på? Ser jag så faslig ut? – Ja, jag har inte sovit i natt, och du tror naturligtvis, att jag varit ute och rumlat . . .
FLICKAN (*som förut*).
STUDENTEN. Druckit punsch, va? – Luktar jag punsch?
FLICKAN (*som förut*).
STUDENTEN. Jag är orakad, jag vet det . . . Giv mig en dryck vatten, flicka, ty jag förtjänar det! (*Paus.*) Nå! Då måste jag stå och tala om, att jag förbundit sårade och vakat över sjuka hela denna natt; jag var nämligen med om husraset i går kväll . . . nu vet du det.

(9) translates this passage as follows:

STUDENT. May I use the dipper?
GIRL (*pulls the dipper toward herself*).
STUDENT. Haven't you finished soon?
GIRL (*looks at him with horror*).
/—/

STUDENT. What are you staring at? Do I look so terrible?—Well, I didn't get any sleep last night—I suppose you think I was out living it up . . .
GIRL (*as before*).
STUDENT. Drinking punch, eh?—Do I smell of punch?
GIRL (*as before*).
STUDENT. I haven't shaved, I know . . . Give me a drink of water, girl, I deserve it! (*Pause.*) Well! Then I'll have to tell you—I bandaged up injured people and kept watch over the sick all night; you see, I was there when the house collapsed last night . . . now you know.

Strindberg's Student on one hand makes use of every day words like "faslig", "rumlat", "va", on the other of literary forms like "giv", "ty", "denna". It is not difficult to see the reason for the two styles. Strindberg has a double purpose. On the one hand he is anxious to demonstrate at once that we deal with realistic characters in a contemporary setting. (That the Milkmaid is a vision we do not realize immediately.) The Student must therefore speak like a Swedish student around the turn of the century. On the other hand it is important that we soon sense that the Student also represents the goodness and innocence of childhood. To clarify this, Strindberg has him not only perform actions in the spirit of Jesus and the good Samaritan but also describe these actions. As a result of this double purpose, we get a transition from the everyday jargon of the initial speeches to the mixed style of the last one. This is how (5) translates the last speech:

I haven't had a chance to shave, I know that . . . Come on, let me have a drink of water. After last night, I think I've earned it. (*Pause.*) I guess I have to tell you the whole story. I've spent the whole night bandaging wounds and taking care of the injured people. You see, I was there when the house collapsed last night . . . Well, that's it.

Presumably (5) has found it disturbing that the Student suddenly begins to express himself rather solemnly; he has therefore settled for a homogeneous portrait of the young man by keeping the everyday jargon throughout. The consequence is that the biblical allusions and the symbolic significance of the situation are almost impossible to discover.

A comparison between the number of words used in Strindberg's version of this speech compared to the translations in (9) and (5) gives the figures: 48–52–70. The elevated tone of the original has to a great extent been preserved in (9), even if the translator has seen no chance of keeping the solemn quality of such words as "ty", "denna", "dryck".

If the loftiness has been set aside in (5), examples of the opposite—raising of the stylistic level—can also be found. This is the way the Student describes his father in the final monologue:

Men en dag höll han en stor bjudning – det var om aftonen; han var trött av dagens arbete, och av ansträngningen att dels tiga, dels prata skit med gästerna . . .

In (9) this passage is rendered:

But one day he gave a big party—it was in the evening; he was tired after the day's work, and from the effort partly to keep still, partly to talk nonsense with his guests . . .

The Young Lady reacts strongly to the Student's words; she "*fasar*" (shudders). All the translators reproduce her reaction, of course, but the word which causes it, the vulgar "skit", is translated as "rot" (1, 2), "rubbish" (3), "nonsense" (5, 7, 8, 9) or "spiteful gossip" (6)—all eufemisms compared to the expletive of the original. As a result of this, the Young Lady's reaction seems exaggerated; in the translations she appears more prudish than in the original.

It is exceedingly difficult to find a good equivalent for a series of words, whose ideological connection is underlined by correspondences of form. In his final monologue, the Student declares:

Jesus Kristus nedsteg till helvetet, det var hans vandring på jorden, till dårhuset, tukthuset, bårhuset jorden.

(9) translates:

Jesus Christ descended into hell—that was his journey on earth, this madhouse, this reformatory, this charnel house the earth.

The sequence "dårhus-tukthus-bårhus" is pregnant in several respects. It contains both rhyme and climax; the repetition of the element "hus" stresses the fact that the house we see before us on the stage symbolizes the world; the verbal metaphors are supported by the visual one. The three words are rendered as follows:

(1) that madhouse, that jail, that morgue, the earth

(2) this madhouse, this jail, this morgue—this earth

(3) this madhouse, this prison, this charnel-house, this earth

(4) this madhouse, this prison, this morgue

(5) this madhouse and morgue of a world

(6) this madhouse, this brothel, this morgue which we call earth

(7) this madhouse, this penal prison, this charnel house that we call the earth

(8) this madhouse, this charnelhouse that we call the earth

(9) this madhouse, this reformatory, this charnel house the earth

As appears from this list, especially the word "tukthus" has presented certain difficulties. Two translators do not reproduce it at all. One breaks the logical sequence by translating it with "brothel", which has quite different connotations; the translator may have been thinking of the Swedish word 'otukt' (fornication). It is less harmful when the other translators have substituted a modern equivalent for the oldfashioned institution mentioned in the original.

It is a weakening of Strindberg's metaphoric expression "bårhuset jorden" when several translators explicate it.

Even when the translations come very close to one another, interesting differences, resulting in different impulses to the actor, may be discerned. A good example is found in the final words of the play, closing the Student's prayer for the Young Lady; in *Spöksonaten* they read:

Du stackars lilla barn, barn av denna villornas, skuldens, lidandets och dödens värld; den eviga växlingens, missräkningarnes och smärtans värld! Himmelens Herre vare dig nådig på färden ...

In the translations they read:

(1) You poor child—you child of a world of illusion, guilt, suffering and death—a world of eternal change, disappointment, and pain—may the Lord of Heaven deal mercifully with you on your journey!

(2) You poor little child, you child of this world of illusion, guilt, suffering, and death; this world of eternal change, disappointment and pain! May the Lord of Heaven have mercy on you in your journey.

(3) You poor little child, child of this world of illusion, guilt, suffering and death, this world of endless change, disappointment, and pain. May the Lord of Heaven be merciful to you upon your journey.

(4) You poor, poor little child—born into a world of illusion, of guilt, of suffering and of death—into a world of eternal change, disappointment and pain! ... May the Lord have mercy upon you in *your* journey!

(5) You poor little child! Child of this world of illusion and guilt and suffering and death—this world of eternal change and disappointment and never-ending pain! May the Lord of Heaven have mercy on you as you journey forth ...

(6) Unhappy child, born into this world of delusion, guilt, suffering and death, this world that is for ever changing, for ever erring, for ever in pain! The Lord of Heaven be merciful to you on your journey.

(7) You poor little child—child of this world of illusion, of sin and suffering and death—this world of never-ending change, of disappointments and pain! May the Father of Heaven be merciful to you on your journey.

(8) My poor, poor child, child of this world of illusion, of guilt, suffering, and of death; this world of eternal change, of disappointment, and of pain. May the Lord of Heaven be merciful to you on your journey.

(9) Poor little child, child of this world of illusions, guilt, suffering, and death, the world of everlasting change, disappointments, and pain! May the Lord of Heaven be merciful to you on your journey ...

An examination reveals that (9), as usual, comes closest to the original, perhaps somewhat at the expense of natural (American) English: the plurals "illusions", "disappointments". The maintenance of *points suspensifs* (...) after the final word is, however, praiseworthy; the sign corresponds to what is being said in the final sentence: that we are dealing with a journey, with something unaccomplished.

When (5) replaces the asyndetic parataxis of the original by parataxis through conjunction ("and guilt and suffering and death"), the line gets a somewhat naïvistic character. (6) presents a translation which in several respects differs from the others. "Unhappy child" sounds somewhat high-flown next to the more intimate "you poor little child", but the expression "born into this world" to a certain extent compensates for this. A completely misplaced tone—and relationship—is established in (4, 8) with their pathetic "poor, poor child".

Of special interest is the final sentence. Strindberg here has a line consisting of three dactyls and two trochees: "Himmelens Herre vare dig nådig på färden . . .". The three dactyls give a harmonious movement to the line corresponding with the idea of a voyage to an isle called the Isle of the Dead but which is in fact the isle of true life. Only two of the translators (2, 5) have created a rhythmic-poetical counterpart of this line which forms a transition to the final soft music.

In a play where so much is written between the words, lines, and speeches, and where the dialogue is so 'musical', even the punctuation marks are of significance (Lindström, 1964*b,* 170ff.). The different signs for silence, for example—*points suspensifs,* one or more dashes, asterisks, the words "*Paus*" (pause) and "*Tystnad*" (silence)—function as indications of the tempo.[7]

Here the translators have taken great liberties with the original. The asterisks are generally omitted; this is quite forgivable since they normally do not indicate silence but entrance or exit. But when the very frequent *points suspensifs* are replaced by full stops, it means that an 'open' line is replaced by a 'closed' one. One example may stand for many:

GUBBEN (*tar upp ett papper*). Om ni läser detta utdrag ur vapenboken, skall ni se att den ätt, vars namn ni bär, har varit utdöd i hundra år!
ÖVERSTEN (*läser*). Jag har visserligen hört sådana rykten, men jag bär namnet efter min far . . . (*Läser.*) Det är rätt; ni har rätt . . . jag är icke adelsman! – Icke ens det! – Då tar jag bort min signetring. – Det är sant, den tillhör er . . . Var så god!

In (3) this passage is translated as follows:

OLD MAN, *producing a document.* If you read this extract from *The Armorial Gazette,* you will see that the family whose name you are using has been extinct for a hundred years.
COLONEL. I have heard rumors to this effect, but I inherited the name from my father. *Reads.* It is true. You are right. I am not a nobleman. Then I must take off my signet ring. It is true, it belongs to you. *Gives it to him.* There you are.

In the Colonel's speech—which concerns us here—an acting direction (the first "*läser*") has been omitted. Instead another, rather superfluos direction has been inserted: "*Gives it to him*". The suggestive line "Icke ens det!" (Not even that!) has been left out. Semicolon has been replaced by comma, *points suspensifs,* dashes and exclamation marks by full stops. Five kinds of punctuation marks in the original have been reduced to two in the translation.

Let us examine the Strindbergian speech. Here the Colonel begins by reading the extract. He starts to defend himself, we may imagine, while still glancing through the beginning of the extract. *Points suspensifs* indicate that the speech is not completed. Why not? Presumably—as the second "*Läser*" indicates—because the Colonel has now come to the heart of the matter, which takes all his attention. Then follows the confession: "Det är rätt, ni har rätt"; it is as though the Colonel must bring home to himself that he has been wrong. Semicolon may at this point represent a substantial pause. Then another pause (...) preceding the conclusion, hard to accept for him and apparently spoken in an agitated tone of voice (the exclamation mark). Then a new pause. The Colonel is thinking. Another conclusion, mystifying to the reader/spectator: "Icke ens det!" (Later we understand that the Colonel here refers to the fact that he is not even the father of the Young Lady, etc.) Pause again (dash): the Colonel is thinking about what he now must do. Then he takes a decision resulting in an action: "Då tar jag bort min signetring." New pause (dash), suggesting that the Colonel has initially planned to put the ring in his pocket; suddenly he recalls that the Old Man has just stated that he, Hummel, owns everything belonging to the Colonel: "Det är sant, den tillhör er ...". *Points suspensifs* here indicate the unwillingness with which the Colonel hands the ring over, until he finally parts with it with a correct "Var så god!".

As we see, Strindberg's punctuation marks function as a kind of directorial signs. To a great extent they help record the Colonel's inner changes. When Strindberg's rich 'partiture' is replaced by a more ascetic one, as in (3), the result is that it becomes far more difficult fo the reader—and for the actor who is to do this part—to imagine what happens inside the Colonel.

We all know how a theatre performance can be spoilt by a tempo lacking nuances due to wrong timing or absence of pauses. It is often during the silence between two speeches or even within one and the same speech that we intensely experience what goes on within and between the characters. The punctuation marks form here an important part of the speeches, especially with writers whose ear is as sensitive as Strindberg's. Few translators seem to realize this.

It may seem as though our examination of how nine translators have turned *Spöksonaten* into English has given a rather negative result. The difficulties have sometimes been insurmountable but often the translators have also proved to be careless and insensitive. It is natural that one concentrates on the unsatisfactory solutions when discussing problems related to translation;

it is the discrepancies between the original text and the translations that signal difficulties, difficulties which are solved in different ways. In all fairness, it should be pointed out that the translations also provide many examples of skillful and imaginative solutions, some of which have been indicated here.

Naturally one translator has often influenced another. Many solutions, both successful and less successful, can be explained in this way. The least influenced by their predecessors are (5) and (6). There is nothing surprising in the fact that a translator studies earlier translations of the same text. What is surprising, with regard to *Spöksonaten*, is that this has been done on a very limited scale. To put it differently: it is surprising to discover that an earlier translator has not infrequently offered a better solution than a later one. Many readers imagine, quite legitimately, that a new translation inevitably means a better translation, a line of thought often suggested by publishers' blurbs.

Most of the translation problems discussed here apply not only to dramatic but also to epic texts. Yet it is obvious that the translation of drama presents special difficulties (Törnqvist, 1978*a*) since the reception of plays (normally) differs from that of novels. Next to the translation proper we may, with regard to drama, speak also of translation in another sense, the translation from book to stage.

It is striking that critics devote far more attention to this second 'translation' than to the translation proper. The reason is obvious. Direction, scenery, acting are elements which the critic can directly comment on. He would be far less inclined to say anything about the translation, unless he knows the original. When confronted with a play translated from a minor language such as Swedish he is not likely to say anything at all about it. Like practically everyone in the audience he must approach the translation in good faith. This is just another way of saying that those who translate from minor languages find themselves in a position different from those translating from English, French and German. Those who translate from minor languages can take enormous liberties with the text without risking very much. In this sense, an Ibsen or a Strindberg is much more vulnerable than a Shakespeare, a Racine or a Goethe.

The situation is clearly documented in Ollén's survey of the stage history of Strindberg's plays. We receive a lot of information about directing, acting and scenery but very little—obviously because the critics have been silent on this point—about the translations used. This is true also of the English and American productions of *Spöksonaten*. An exception to the rule is the following statement concerning a Swiss production of this chamber play in 1952: "The success was to a great extent due to the new translation by Willi Reich which had replaced the old one by Schering" (Ollén, 478). Here, for a moment, the central importance that a drama translation has, or ought to have, is indicated.

Notes

1. INTRODUCTION (pp. 9 ff.)

1. Fortunately such an edition is now under way. Within the next ten years *August Strindbergs Samlade Verk*, in 75 volumes, are scheduled to appear. A French edition, in 9 volumes containing all the plays, has also been scheduled.
2. Critical surveys of the literature on Strindberg are found in Gustafsson (601–609), G. Lindström (1963*a*, 27–51) and Vowles (1962, 256–269).
3. Cf. Weitz' observation that of the four critical procedures—describing, explaining, evaluating, theorizing—"only one, description, is true or false statement" (316).
4. The reason for this is presumably that drama is an 'impure' form, a literary bordercase; an exception to the rule is Brooks/Heilman.
5. For a discussion of various interpretations of 'dramatic structure', see Barry (esp. 25–40) and Levitt (9–23).
6. A moderate, and successful, example of the dynamic approach is found in Northam (1973); see also Törnqvist (1973*b*, 58–69).
7. As Downer (170) points out, "the discovery of the component units remains the first step in the analysis of the total structure of the play".
8. Principles determining act division are discussed in Baker (117–154) and Archer (85–100).
9. This is the rule. Exceptions can of course be found; thus a shift in focus may result in a scene shift; for examples from Shakespeare and Ibsen, see Van Laan (229f.).
10. Essentially the same criterium underlies the concept 'Konfiguration' as used by S. Marcus (287ff.), Link (193) and Pfister (235).
11. It is evident that commentators on drama often refer to 'situations' in a very loose sense totally unrelated to Jansen's precise definition; the homonymic dilemma I have just referred to with regard to 'scene', in other words, appears here again.
12. Moreover, the French division is inconsistent since the entrances/exits of minor characters, such as servants, do not count; yet even such changes may be of significance.
13. Hogendoorn's 'segment' corresponds to my 'sequence', while my 'segment' at least partly corresponds to his 'subsegment'.
14. For an alternative, to my mind less surveyable type of sequence scheme or "Konfigurationsstruktur", see Pfister (237ff.).
15. Cf. Aristotle's recommendation that the structural union of the parts be such that "if any of them is displaced or removed, the whole will be disjointed and disturbed" (Butcher, 35).

2. *FÖRSTA VARNINGEN / THE FIRST WARNING*— AN EFFECTIVE DRAMA (pp. 19 ff.)

1. The terms are borrowed from Brandell (1971, 124ff.).
2. The choice of country can be explained either as part of a natural creative process: Strindberg has utilized impressions from his stay in Bavaria in 1887, or as a strategic move: by placing the action in Germany, the playwright hoped to increase the possibilities of getting the one-acter accepted by German theatres (Ollén, 194ff.).
3. In his novel *En dåres försvarstal / The defense of a madman* (1887) lesbian sexuality, connected with Maria (modelled on Siri von Essen), plays an important part. At one point Axel (Strindberg's alter ego) discovers Maria surrounded by young girls. She "kisses their lips the way tribades kiss one another". One of the young girls is the 15-year old daughter of the landlady.
4. After his divorce from Siri von Essen, the model for Olga, Strindberg's bitterness had been tempered; when composing his play he was not as anxious as before to offend her publicly.

3. IMAGERY IN *FADREN / THE FATHER* (pp. 38 ff.)

1. For discussions of dramatic imagery, see Spurgeon (1935) and Clemen (1951, especially the Introduction).
2. It should be noted that the setting to an increasing degree becomes an image of the Captain's state of mind. Though the scenery remains the same, its symbolic impact changes.
3. For an examination of this theme in *The Father*, see Jacobs (1969) and Brandell (1971, 178ff.).
4. The name of the orderly may also be seen as a

sexual metaphor. In a letter dated January 19, 1887 Strindberg praises Bismarck's Germany, "where patriarchy and virile member are still revered". In a letter, written a month later, he writes: "Have a penis of red sandstone erected on my grave" (*ASB*, VI, 145, 168).

5. Brandell (1971, 186) combines this metaphor with *Hamlet*: "The crime which the Captain smells is the unfaithfulness of his wife, adultery; this is true also of Hamlet, with regard to his mother, but in addition we here deal with a real murder, the assassination of the elder Hamlet. In both cases the protagonist feels hesitant about the reality of the crime."
6. In a letter dated October 17, 1887 Strindberg writes that the Captain faces his fate "wrapping himself in death in these spider's webs which he cannot tear asunder without upsetting the laws of nature" (*ASB*, VI, 282).
7. As Lamm has noted (1924, 281), the strait-jacket is an even more obvious counterpart of Clytemnestra's net.
8. Lagercrantz stresses this circumstrance (a little too much) when he suggests that the Captain's uniform has functioned as a kind of strait-jacket all along: "Laura did not force him into the straitjacket, it was inside himself" (196).
9. Lamm (1924, 282ff.) especially stresses the psychic resemblance between the Captain and the protagonists of Shakespeare's tragedies.
10. For the widening effect of imagery, see Ellis-Fermor (80).

4. SPEECH SITUATIONS IN *FRÖKEN JULIE / MISS JULIE* (pp. 50 ff.)

1. As Gierow (1963, 292ff.) has demonstrated, both pantomimic sequences also provide valuable contributions to the portrayal of Kristin and Jean respectively.
2. We have here an example of Strindberg's habit of ignoring detailed stage directions at the beginning of his plays, whether purposely or not is difficult to ascertain.
3. Similarly, the speech situation in the final sequence is 'colored' by a significant change of costume; in Van Laan's words: "Latter when her father's bell rings, he quickly changes back to his livery even before he replies through the speaking tube. /—/ By means of costume the spectators are shown that Jean is still inherently the servant, that he cannot rise above himself even in his own mind. /—/ But no spectator could safely do without Jean's own spoken realization" (80).
4. Commenting on this situation, Styan rightly points out that "what these particular people say in private works against what a lady and her servant should say in public" (176).
5. It should be noticed that it is Jean, not Julie, who clarifies the Count's superhuman stature—in his final monologue (cf. Törnqvist, 1980*b*, 141).
6. For a discussion of the words of address in the play, see Josephson (148ff.).
7. This situation is not unusual. Iago has more lines than Othello in *Othello*, Antonius and Cassius more lines than Caesar in *Julius Caesar*.
8. Cf. Brainerd/Neufeldt (55) who point out that besides the number of words spoken *by* a character, the number of words spoken *about* him should be taken into account. Alas, it is not possible to be very accurate with regard to this latter category.

5. *DEN STARKARE / THE STRONGER*—A MONODRAMA (pp. 64 ff.)

1. Although Strindberg himself never called *The Stronger* a monodrama, he used the term much later in some letters to his third wife, Harriet Bosse, in a way which suggests that he was thinking of the Scandinavian experimental theatre of the 1880's. "If you were here", he writes her in 1905, "I would write monodramas for you!"From the notes left in the Strindberg archive, we can see that he was outlining monodramas consisting of monologues and pantomimes with music around this time—monodramas, that is, in the 18th century sense of the word (cf. Bergman, 278).
2. For a further discussion of the characteristics of this subgenre, especially with regard to Strindberg, see Törnqvist (1973*c*) and Paul (1976).
3. Paul's standpoint seems, however, determined by the fact that he is only aware of Strindberg's statement in *Politiken*.
4. Cf. *Comrades*, where Abel tells Bertha: "I am a little stronger than you are. Being married seems to have softened you!".
5. Arguing that either woman may be considered the stronger, Swerling (1971, 15f.) draws fairly far-reaching conclusions from this situation: "If the wife is seen to be the 'stronger', then the work is 'comic'—cheaply so: one rival bawling at another. If, as is Strindberg's more covert and ironic meaning, the silent protagonist (of aris-

tocratic dignity before the impotent vituperations) is the victor, then the work is not comic but bitter, not vaudeville but tragic humour." Reading the drama as "a thesis play" (85), Ward insists on Mrs. X's superiority (87), a rather simplistic interpretation.

6. The writer Per Olov Enquist has suggested that the rivalry of the women for the man is a result of Strindberg's wish-thinking, unable as he was to accept a 'lesbian' relationship between his wife Siri and Marie David which would make himself superfluous (Törnqvist, 1977*b*, 198f.).

6. *TILL DAMASKUS I / TO DAMASCUS I*— A DRAMA OF HALF-REALITY (pp. 71 ff.)

1. A reason should be given why I am concerned only with the first part of the trilogy entitled *To Damascus*. Contrary to Børge (77) but in agreement with Brandell (1950, 243 f.), I have chosen to limit myself to this part simply because it forms a complete entity; so far as we can judge Strindberg did not plan any trilogy at the time he finished the first part; *To Damascus I* has also usually been staged as an independent play.
2. Cf. Brandell (1971, 170): "In the first act the conflict is initiated and strengthened; in the second it culminates in a furious fight between two still equal combatants; in the third it is decided, ending with the destruction of the Captain. The phases of the struggle are thus marked by the act endings."
3. It is significant that Strindberg himself hesitated about how to arrange the acts. A ms. page (reproduced in Børge, opposite 80) shows the following act-scene relations: I. 1, II. 2–7, III. 8–9, IV. 10–15, V. 16–17.
4. Cf. Ingmar Bergman's 1970 production of *A Dream Play*, where the Poet was placed on the stage to indicate that the action actually takes place in his mind.
5. Børge (94) regards the Beggar as the Stranger's negative double and the Confessor as his positive one.
6. Dante's importance for Strindberg in *Inferno* and *To Damascus* has been demonstrated by Norman (103ff.).
7. The context and the solemn phrasing recall Jesus' words to his disciples.
8. It is likely that Strindberg got the idea of his constantly crocheting Lady from *Rosmersholm*, where Rebecca keeps crocheting her white shawl (corresponding to the supernatural white horses); when finished, it serves her as bridal gown—and winding-sheet—as she throws herself into the mill pond with Rosmer. Strindberg had devoted an inspired essay to Ibsen's play in 1887. References to the mythological weaving of the Moirai appear, as we have seen, in the play he penned that same year: *The Father*.
9. In the original this untranslatable sentence reads: "Det var satan!", literally: "That was Satan!".
10. Stockenström (316) wants to relate the black and brown colors to the tale about the black penitentiary spirits who thought they were brown.
11. For an indication that the costume had this significance for Strindberg, see Sprinchorn's note (1964, 298).
12. In a drawing, indicating the scenery of the play for the 1900 production, Strindberg, clearly inspired by the biblical story of the cursed mount Ebal and the blessed mount Gerizim (Deuteronomy 11:29), further emphasized the black-and-white pattern by making the mountain behind the blacksmith shop black and that behind the mill white (and furthermore crowned by a church in the distance). See Sylvan (85).
13. The significance of the Christmas rose has been analyzed by Brandell (1950, 240f.) and Stockenström (314f., 530, note 12).
14. For resemblances between *To Damascus I* and Beckett's play, see Swerling (1971, 115ff.).
15. It is interesting to note that *To Damascus I* was written between January 19 and March 6, 1898, that is, about half a year *before* the action of the drama begins. From Strindberg's point of view it was thus a utopian play—a recipe, perhaps, of what he thought he ought to do in the near future, a kind of penance, or, alternatively, a substitute for what he could not force himself to do in real life, a daydream.

7. THE PLOT OF *ERIK XIV* (pp. 96 ff.)

1. Concerning the specific problems related to the writing of historical drama, see Lindenberger and Törnqvist (1980*a*).
2. Lamm seems influenced by Strindberg himself, who in a letter dated August 5, 1899 (quoted in *SS*, XXXI, 406f.) points out that *Master Olof*, *Gustav Vasa* and *Erik XIV* constitute a trilogy. Five days later, however, he is willing to have both *Gustav Vasa* and *Erik XIV* produced as independent plays (*ASB*, XIII, 180).
3. The terminology partly agrees with that of G.

Lindström (1969, 52, 77) and Kayser (77). To the concepts 'plot' and 'fable' I have added 'story', the reason being that a comparison between the story and the plot of a play must be considered a meaningful undertaking, while a comparison between its fable and plot seems meaningless, since the concepts do not cover the same material.

4. Steene is correct in stating that "throughout the entire play all the events, with the exception of Göran's love story, are arranged primarily with a view to the effect they will have or the light they may throw on the king's personality" (1971, 133). In fact, even Göran's love story, as we shall see, indirectly throws light on Erik.
5. In his essay on *Hamlet* (*SS*, L, 75). Strindberg speaks of Gyllenstjerna's "complete lack of character and reliability". Sjöstedt's attempt (110) to turn him into "the most upright character in the play" seems misplaced. Even Johnson's description, obviously colored by our knowledge of the historical Gyllenstjerna, appears too mild (1959, 259, 332).
6. In one of the ms. notes for the play, Max is explicitly referred to as Karin's "fiancé". In that case Karin is legally allied to Max and Erik cannot marry her. The following notation then becomes comprehensible: "Göran decides that Karin should be queen; when all hope abroad is gone; also in order to suppress nobility. Therefore Max is drowned."
7. Agda's infidelity, Johnson argues (1963, 126), deprives Göran of "the power to act and even to doubt that there is any point in acting". But this is contradicted by Göran's attempt later in the play to clear up the mess Erik has caused. The resigned pronouncement Johnson quotes in support of his argument appears very late in the play (seq. 82) and seems inspired by Göran's premonitions that the game will soon be lost.
8. The choice of the name Agda may have been determined by the fact that Erik XIV had a mistress by that name before he met Karin.
9. Vogelweith (177), on the other hand, juxtaposes the two love relationships, although he denies that Göran's adoration concerns Agda.

8. THE OPENING OF *DÖDSDANSEN I / THE DANCE OF DEATH I* (pp. 119 ff.)

1. Like the final play title, several of the rejected titles indicate the central role of death in the play: "The struggle against death", "Dance macabre", "Preparation for death".
2. Lamm draws a simplified picture of the situation, when he claims that Alice's "only pathos consists in her hatred of the husband" and that her only desire is "to see him dead" (1926, 134).
3. One may think here of the garden of Eden, of Hamlet's "unweeded garden", and of Candide's decision to "cultiver notre jardin". Cf. also Caesar in *To Damascus I,* who "wanders about the garden, putting nature to rights".
4. Cf. the Stranger in *To Damascus I*, who is 'punished' by discovering that his fellow-men are actually better than he had imagined; the same goes for Hummel in *The Ghost Sonata*. In all his post-Inferno dramas of penance Strindberg adheres to a fundamental hubris-nemesis pattern; this is true also of *The Dance of Death I*.
5. This is in accordance with the view of H. Lindström (1976, 74), who rightly opposes Lamm's opinion that at the end of the play we have the same situation as at the beginning (1926, 136).
6. Like other pastimes, the card-playing may also be seen as an expression of a secular attitude which Edgar is soon to renounce. At the beginning of Act IV he sacrifices, in H. Lindström's words (1976, 72), "the symbols of life and material existence: the pack of cards, the whiskey bottles, the cigar boxes /—/. One is reminded of a similar ritual: the great auto-da-fé shortly before the end of *A Dream Play*".
7. Cf. Johnson (1971*b*, 120): "The lively, enthusiastic dance performed in grotesque contrast to the deadly and boring environment serves as an effective parallel to the medieval dance in which the living try to escape from thoughts of their own mortality. Just as the medieval dance ends in certain death, the captain's dance ends with his own collapse.
   In a much broader and figurative sense, the twenty-five years have been a dance of death."
8. Both Jolivet (278f.) and H. Lindström (1976, 70f.) are of the opinion that Edgar dies from the stroke and then goes on 'living' as a ghost. But if this is true, it is difficult to see the significance of the play ending.

9. THE COHERENCE OF *ETT DRÖMSPEL / A DREAM PLAY* (pp. 147 ff.)

1. The most relevant example, in this context, is the statement made in the diary after the completion of the play: "The world has come into existence only through Sin,—if in fact it exists

at all—for it is really only a dream picture,* a phantom and the ascetic's allotted task is to destroy it. But this task conflicts with the love impulse, and the sum total of it all is a ceaseless wavering between sensual orgies and the anguish of repentance:
This would seem to be the key to the riddle of the world.
* Consequently my Dream Play is a picture of life" (*OD*, 152).

2. It is characteristic that the only part lacking in dream elements is the *Prolog im Himmel*.
3. Her absence in this scene, however, is noteworthy. It is not Indra's Daughter who is the dreamer of the play; it is the recipient—if we accept the idea that we can dream of people who dream. For a discussion of the problems related to this question, see Lunin (182ff.). As Pfister points out (297), the idea of the recipient as dreamer appears as early as in *A Midsummer Night's Dream*, but here more as an after-thought (Puck's Epilogue) and without the consequences inherent in Strindberg's drama.
4. By general agreement, the castle represents the World (or Life). With its ability to grow and its "seven walls", it resembles a bulb with its seven scales, corresponding to "the earth with its seven layers" (*A Blue Book I*, *SS*, XLVI, 352). In *The Ghost Sonata*, similarly, the hyacinth is seen as a counterpart of the universe:
"The bulb is the earth, which rests in the water or lies in the dust; now the stalk shoots up, straight as the earth's axis, and at the top sit six-pointed starflowers. /—/ So it's a copy of the cosmos."
Figuratively speaking, Scenes 2–14 are set inside the castle, while Scene 1 (arrival) and 15 (leave-taking) are set outside it.
5. In the notes for a planned production of *To Damascus*, Strindberg lists the attributes related to Calvary, including St. Veronica's veil with Christ's face on it; a drawing is added (facsimile, Falck, 324).—The Doorkeeper recalls the Lady in *To Damascus*, who not only keeps crocheting but also wears a veil.
6. That Strindberg was inclined to regard this attitude as sinful appears from many remarks around this time, for example the following on Hamlet:

   He wants to know what one is not permitted to know; and because of arrogantly wanting to know God's secrets which have a right to remain secrets, Hamlet is punished by the kind of madness called skepticism, which leads to absolute uncertainty, and out of which the individual can be saved only by faith: childish faith whic through the sacrifice called obedience one ge as a sort of Christmas-gift wisdom, the absolu certainty that surpasses understanding" (*SS*, 100).

7. Unlike Børge who stresses the metaphysic implication of the second Fall, Thomsen (9 distinguishes between a metaphysical Fall (the Prologue) and an ethical one (in Scene 8).
8. The castle referred to here is thus not the grow ing castle as is often assumed.
9. The fish, of course, is a well-known symbol Christ; this also explains the Daughter's and th Billposter's concern with it.
10. Both images appear in *A Blue Book II*, where the piece called "King Lear's Wife", Strindbe quotes from Shakespeare's play:

    "Down from the waist they are centaurs,
    Though women all above:
    But to the girdle do the gods inherit.
    Beneath is all the fiend's; there's hell, there darkness

    He then gives a botanical equivalent: "Goo and evil, with her roots in the dirt and h flower in the light, the most beautiful grafted the most ugly, /—/ that is how Shakespea depicts woman /—/" (*SS*, XLVII, 757ff.). Wh is stated here about one of the sexes applies *A Dream Play* to both.
11. It is characteristic that one color is specified *"sulphur yellow"*—cf. the *"sulphur vapors"* in th Foulstrand scene—to distinguish clearly the ye low hollyhocks from the golden bud.
12. In the notes for a planned production of *Dream Play*, Strindberg equates the bl monkshood with "the deceptive Hope" (Falc 272). He seems to take the view here th even the hope for a happier hereafter is delusion. More relevant with regard to the en of *A Dream Play* is another interpretation, ful borne out by the play: the hope that this ear will ever become a paradise (the blue monk hood covering the ground) is a delusion.

10. THE WEB OF *BRÄNDA TOMTEN* / *THE BURNED HOUSE* (pp. 163ff.)

1. As in the other chamber plays, Strindberg a stains from any designation of the (two) parts presumably in order to underline the (music unity of these plays. However, for practic reasons we need a designation. Commentato have variously referred to the parts as 'mov ments', 'acts' and 'scenes'. The first term, d

rived from the analogy between chamber play and chamber music, will be discussed in connection with *The Ghost Sonata* (see p. 187 f.). 'Act' implies that *The Burned House* is a two-act play, 'scene' that it is a one-acter. Since the latter is characterized by limited playing time, no intermissions and a strict adherence to the three unities (Schnetz; Szondi, 92), it is obvious that all the chamber plays are border cases, hybrids. Since Strindberg himself indicates that the parts most closely correspond to acts (*SS,* XLV, 281, 345) and since these plays have often been performed with intermissions, I shall refer to these units as 'acts'.

2. Elmquist's view (46f.) is not satisfactory; he writes: "The piece has, among other things, the great and conspicuous flaw that it does not present any solution to the dramatic conflict indicated in the opening scenes: who has set fire to the house and why? These questions are never answered, simply because Strindberg gradually loses interest in them and follows other tracks." Elmquist's phrasing reveals that he is thinking only in terms of arson. As we shall see, Strindberg hardly follows other tracks at the end of the play; at most we may speak of a widening and deepening of the problems symbolized by the fire.
   My opinion also differs from those of Blom-Edström (278) and Berendsohn (536). According to the former, the problem of the fire is finally solved "through the unexpected explanation: the fire was accidental". According to the latter, we finally learn that the Dyer was the incendiary.
   In agreement with my own view—and somewhat in conflict with her own—Blom-Edström claims that Strindberg "has not wanted to explain the cause of the fire. On the contrary: his description shows symbolically how everyone and no one is to blame in an existence where all fates are of necessity entangled".
3. The statement is, however, somewhat categorical. As Stockenström (123) has demonstrated, inferno and purgatory were to Strindberg identical concepts, since he saw life on earth as an inferno "in relation to a pre-existence, from which man was born to reconcile his guilt through suffering".
4. It seems probable that there is a connection, already in the Bible, between the "fig leaves" of Adam and Eve and the fig tree in the New Testament which consists "merely of leaves". —For the autobiographical background of the apple tree (actually a plum tree), see *SS*, LIV, 466f.
5. More dubious is C. D. Marcus' view that "der Held is das Volk selbst" (413); although the collective plays an important role, it is rather as antagonist than as protagonist.
6. Cf. Diebold: "Alles war gefärbt im Hause des Färbers, Ehebruch, Brandstiftung, Uneheliche Vaterschaft, Zuchthäuslerei, Scheintod—hohangesehene Schmugglerfamilie! Doch daneben beim Gärtner: Osterlilien, Narzissen Tulpen und Seidelbast—ein Frühling für die Jungen" (205).
7. Lamm (1926, 389) is blind to the significance of the family symbol. "One does not understand", he writes, "why this 'stranger' necessarily must be related to everyone he meets. The play would have been much better, if he arrived as a total stranger and judged them without having his own finger in the pie." The situation sketched here by Lamm—the righteous sitting in judgement over the rest—strikes me as uninteresting in its simple moralism. The point of the play is precisely that the Stranger, too, has a finger in the pie and that he is only gradually inclined to admit that he is not a true 'stranger'.
8. This interpretation differs from G. Lindström's view (1966, 61) that the Stonecutter is unequivocally informed concerning the question of paternity.
9. When asked by his German translator, Emil Schering, why the bishop's funeral is mentioned several times at the beginning, although it does not later seem to be of any significance in the play, Strindberg answered, in a letter dated April 24, 1907, that "the bishop's funeral is merely background scenery creating mood; possibly it means something I cannot remember any more; perhaps 'an undeserved halo', signifying the worthlessness of everything, the glorification of worthlessness" (*ASB*, XV, 364).
10. The connection with Ismael, the son of a servant, is here obvious (cf. *SS*, XXIX, 280).

11. *SEIN* AND *SCHEIN* IN *SPÖKSONATEN* / *THE GHOST SONATA* (pp. 181 ff.)

1. According to Vowles (1967, 176), the three instruments correspond to the three leading parts in the play. The Young Lady is the violin, the Student the cello, and Hummel the piano. But Vowles does not develop this idea; the fact that Hummel is absent in Act III does not support his argument.
2. One is reminded of the contrasting couple Edgar-Edmund in *King Lear*.

3. This interpretation is in disagreement with Berendsohn (541), who regards the Mummy's madness as simulated.
4. This according to the text. What one would expect is, of course, that it is the dead Consul's bed clothes that are being aired on the balcony, and that the celestial combination of colors has to do both with his and, prospectively, with the Young Lady's departure from life.
5. The longhand draft of the play clearly shows that the Cook, who significantly is not found in the list of *dramatis personae*, has been added to the play at a late stage (cf. Törnqvist, 1973*e*, 31). For the biographical background, see *OD* (1977, 251).
6. For a comparison between *Hamlet* and *The Ghost Sonata*, see Törnqvist (1965). Equally important is the affinity with *Faust* (Törnqvist, 1979*b*).
7. In the annotations for the play this symbolism is quite explicit: "He must pass through the room of ordeals ...".
8. This according to the stage directions of Act III. The stage directions of Act II present another picture; here the hyacinth room seems to border on the hall and the green room to the left.
9. Cf. Gina's relationship to director Werle in Ibsen's *The Wild Duck*.
10. In that case his situation is similar to that of doctor Rank in *A Doll's House* and of Osvald in *Ghosts*.
11. In the longhand draft, Strindberg has originally written: "... and a virgin with hereditary or acquired ..." (*SS*, XLV, 345).
12. Under the heading "Factors", Strindberg mentions in his annotations for the play: "The State of Innocence = the Tree of Knowledge /—/ the Marble statue."

12. THEME AND STRUCTURE OF *PELIKANEN / THE PELICAN* (pp. 207 ff.)

1. Brustein (106) has drawn attention to the resemblance between the plot of *The Pelican* and that of Aeschylus' *Coephoroe*: "Frederick and Gerda, the two dispossessed children, are Orestes and Electra, swearing vengeance on their mother for the 'murder' of their father. The Aegisthus /—/ is Axel, the mother's second husband [*sic*] and co-conspirator."
2. Diebold fittingly refers to the three parts as "Miniaturakte" (206).
3. In Olof Molander's 1922 production there were, for example, two intermissions, in Ingmar Bergman's 1945 production none.—Berend sohn here again emphasizes the chamber pla aspect and, rather dubiously, sees the thre parts as three musical movements. To War similarly, the play is a "sonata" with the move ments "largo", "allegro", "presto" (263).
4. The ages of the characters are mentioned in ms. list of the *dramatis personae*. Elise is 45, Ax 23.
5. One of the ms. annotations from this peric reads: "He murders her with words." Th phrase suits not only Fredrik-Elise but als Hamlet-Gertrud, Hamlet-Ophelia and the Stu dent-the Young Lady (in *The Ghost Sonata*).
6. Cf. Strindberg's ms. annotation: "The mother killed. On the chaise longue outside the bed room." Another annotation reads: "The moth on the chaise longue; is plucked alive." He the retributive pattern is applied to the pelica motif: having abstained from sacrificing hersel the mother is sacrificed.
7. Cf. the Gentleman in *Storm*, Strindberg's fir chamber play: "I can't leave; I'm bound to th apartment by memories."
8. Cf. in this respect *The Dance of Death I*, t Szondi (96) a prime existentialist example the attempt to save the dramatic aspect by fo cing people together in a narrow space.
9. The basis for this idea is found in the red sp appearing on the breast of the pelican durir the brooding period.
10. It is in this connection interesting to note th the pelican has also been regarded as a symb of resurrection: according to popular belief, th bird so lovingly presses her children to h breast that they stifle—after which the moth revives them with her own blood.

13. THE MODERNITY OF STRINDBERGIA DRAMA (pp. 216 ff.)

1. Dietrich, similarly, is of the opinion that "d modernen Traditionen unserer Zeit beganne schon zu Ende des 19. Jahrhunderts mit Ibse Strindberg, Tolstój, Čéchov, Shaw, Benavent dem frühen Hauptmann, Hofmannsthal, Ma terlinck, Wedekind und dem erst jet eigentlich entdeckten enfant terrible des Par ser Fin de siècle Jarry" (17).
2. The periodization is based on Strindberg's re ligious crisis in the mid-nineties resulting in th autobiographical novel *Inferno* (1897).
3. The two groups of plays exemplify Perger's di tinction between 'Einortsdrama' and 'B

wegungsdrama'. In the former group we deal with, in Klotz' terminology, 'Ausschnitt als Ganzes: das geschlossene Drama', in the latter with 'Das ganze in Auschnitten: das offene Drama'.

APPENDIX. TRANSLATING STRINDBERGIAN DRAMA. *SPÖKSONATEN* IN ENGLISH (pp. 220ff.)

1. Problems related to the translation of Strindberg's plays are discussed by Swerling (1971, 1972), Bjurström, and Mattson.
2. The translation appearing under the title '*Miss Julie*' and '*The Ghost Sonata*' (introd. Aziz Soliman), Cairo, n.d. (preface dated Aug. 1967), 59-112, is Elizabeth Sprigge's.
3. (9) implies that he has used this edition by mentioning it in his "Bibliographic and Biographic Notes".
4. For an analysis of the translations of "The Song of the Sun", see Törnqvist (1976*b*, 16ff.).
5. During rehearsals of *Spöksonaten,* autumn 1972, Ingmar Bergman declared that although this was his third production of the play he had never understood these lines (Törnqvist, 1973*d*, 8).
6. It is of course possible—and I here especially think of (9)—that another translation than King James has been used.
7. It should be pointed out that the difference between Landquist's version of the play and Strindberg's longhand draft in this respect is considerable (Törnqvist, 1973*e,* 29).

Strindberg's Plays

For plays not published in English the title is in roman.

Date of composition	*Swedish title*	*English title*
1869	*Fritänkaren*	The Freethinker
1869	*Det sjunkande Hellas*	The Sinking Hellas
1870	*Hermione*	Hermione
1870	*I Rom*	In Rome
1871	*Den fredlöse*	*The Outcast*, *The Outlaw*
1872	*Mäster Olof* (prosa)	*Master Olof* (prose)
1875–76	*Mäster Olof* (vers)	Master Olof (verse)
1876–77	*Anno fyrtioåtta*	Anno Forty-eight
1879–80	*Gillets hemlighet*	The Secret of the Guild
1882	*Lycko-Pers resa*	*Lucky Pehr*, *Lucky Peter's Travels*, *Lucky Per's Journey*
1882	*Herr Bengts hustru*	Sir Bengt's Wife
1886	*Marodörer*	Marauders
1887	*Kamraterna*	*Comrades*
1887	*Fadren*	*The Father*
1888	*Fröken Julie*	*Countess Julia, Countess Julie, Miss Julia, Miss Julie, Lady Julie*
1888	*Fordringsägare*	*The Creditor*, *Creditors*
1888	*Den starkare*	*The Stronger, The Stronger Woman*
1889	*Paria*	*Pariah*
1889	*Hemsöborna*	The Natives of Hemsö
1889	*Samum*	*Simoon*
1891–92	*Himmelrikets nycklar*	*The Keys of Heaven*
1892	*Första varningen*	*The First Warning*
1892	*Debet och kredit*	*Debit and Credit*
1892	*Inför döden*	*Facing Death*, *In the Face of Death*
1892	*Moderskärlek*	*Motherlove*, *Motherly Love*
1892	*Leka med elden*	*Playing with Fire*
1892	*Bandet*	*The Link*, *The Bond*
1898	*Till Damaskus I–II*	*To Damascus*, *The Road to Damascus*
1898	*Advent*	*Advent*
1899	*Brott och brott*	*There Are Crimes and Crimes*, *Crime and Crime, Crimes and Crimes*
1899	*Folkungasagan*	*The Saga of the Folkungs*
1899	*Gustav Vasa*	*Gustavus Vasa*, *Gustav Vasa*
1899	*Erik XIV*	*Erik XIV*, *Erik the Fourteenth*
1899–1900	*Gustav Adolf*	*Gustav Adolf*

1900	*Midsommar*	*Midsummer*
1900	*Påsk*	*Easter*
1900	*Dödsdansen I–II*	*The Dance of Death I–II*
1900–1901	*Kronbruden*	*The Bridal Crown, The Virgin Bride, The Crownbride*
1901	*Svanevit*	*Swanwhite*
1901	*Karl XII*	*Charles XII*
1901	*Till Damaskus III*	*To Damascus III*
1901	*Engelbrekt*	*Engelbrekt*
1901	*Kristina*	*Queen Christina*
1901	*Ett drömspel*	*The Dream Play, A Dream Play*
1902	*Gustav III*	*Gustav III*
1902	*Holländarn*	The Dutchman
1903	*Näktergalen i Wittenberg*	*The Nightingale of Wittenberg*
1903	*Genom öknar till arvland, eller Moses*	*Moses, Through Deserts to Ancestral Lands*
1903	*Hellas, eller Sokrates*	*Hellas*
1903	*Lammet och vilddjuret, eller Kristus*	*The Lamb and the Beast*
1907	*Oväder*	*The Storm, The Thunderstorm, Storm Weather, Storm, Stormy Weather*
1907	*Brända tomten*	*After the Fire, The Burned House, The House That Burned*
1907	*Spöksonaten*	*The Spook Sonata, The Ghost Sonata*
1907	*Toten-Insel*	*Isle of the Dead*
1907	*Pelikanen*	*The Pelican*
1908	*Siste riddaren*	*The Last of the Knights*
1908	*Abu Casems tofflor*	Abu Casem's Slippers
1908	*Riksföreståndaren*	*The Regent*
1908	*Bjälbojarlen*	*Earl Birger of Bjälbo*
1908	*Svarta handsken*	*The Black Glove*
1909	*Stora landsvägen*	*The Great Highway*

Strindberg's Plays in English Translation

(in Order of Appearance)

1899 *The Father*, tr. N. Erichsen. London.

1906 *Three One-Act Plays (The Outcast, Simoon, Debit and Credit),* tr. (from German) Mary Harned, *Poet Lore*, XVII, Autumn.

1909 *Swanwhite*, tr. F. J. Ziegler. Philadelphia.

1910 *The Creditor*, tr. F. J. Ziegler. Philadelphia.

1910 *Motherlove*, tr. F. J. Ziegler. Philadelphia.

1911 *Facing Death*, tr. O. M. Johnson. Easton, Pa.

1912 *Countess Julia*, tr. C. Recht. Philadelphia.

1912 *Easter and Stories (Easter)*, tr. Velma S. Howard. Cincinnati.

1912 *Lucky Pehr*, tr. Velma S. Howard. Cincinnati.

1912 *There Are Crimes and Crimes*, tr. Edwin Björkman. New York.

1912–14 *Plays*, tr. Edith and Warner Oland, 3 vols. (I: *The Father*, *Countess Julie, The Outlaw, The Stronger*. II: *Comrades, Facing Death, Pariah, Easter*. III: *Swanwhite, Advent, The Storm*). Boston/London.

1912–16 *Plays by August Strindberg*, tr. Edwin Björkman, 5 vols. (I: *The Dream Play, The Link, The Dance of Death I–II*. II: *There Are Crimes and Crimes, Miss Julia, The Stronger, Creditors, Pariah*. III: *Swanwhite, Simoon, Debit and Credit, Advent, The Thunderstorm, After the Fire.* IV: *The Bridal Crown, The Spook Sonata, The First Warning, Gustavus Vasa*. V: *The Father, The Black Glove, The Pelican, Moses*). New York.

1913 *Advent*, tr. C. Field. London.

1913 *To Damascus. A Dream Trilogy in Three Parts*, tr. Sam E. Davidson. Boston.

1914 *Comrades*, tr. H. B. Samuel. London.

1914 *The Creditor*, tr. H. B. Samuel. London.

1914 *Pariah, Simoon. Two Plays by August Strindberg*, tr. H. B. Samuel. London.

1915 *The Father*, tr. N. Erichsen. In: Thomas H. Dickinson (ed.), *Chief Contemporary Dramatists*. Boston.

1915 *Master Olof*, tr. Edwin Björkman. New York.

1918 *Miss Julie and Other Plays (Miss Julie, The Creditor, The Stronger Woman, Motherly Love, Pariah, Simoon*), no translator indicated. *Modern Library Series.* New York.

1929 *Easter and Other Plays (Easter, The Dance of Death, The Ghost Sonata, A Dream Play),* tr. E. Classen, C. D. Locock, Erik Palmstierna and James Bernard Fagan. London.

1930 *Lucky Peter's Travels and Other Plays (Lucky Peter's Travels, The Father, Lady Julie, Playing with Fire, The Bond),* tr. E. Classen, C. D. Locock, Elizabeth Sprigge and Claude Napier. London.

1931 *Master Olof and Other Plays (Master Olof, Gustav Vasa, Erik XIV, The Saga of the Folkungs*), tr. C. D. Locock and Joan Bulman. London.

1939 *To Damascus. A Trilogy*, tr. Graham Rawson. London.
1945 *The Great Highway*, tr. Arvid Paulson.
1949 *Easter*, tr. Elizabeth Sprigge. London.
1949 *Eight Famous Plays by Strindberg (The Link, The Father, Miss Julia, The Stronger, There Are Crimes and Crimes, Gustavus Vasa, The Dance of Death, The Spook Sonata)*, tr. Edwin Björkman and N. Erichsen. New York/London.
1951 *The Ghost Sonata*, tr. Elizabeth Sprigge. In: Eric Bentley (ed.), *The Play. A Critical Anthology*. New York.
1954 *The Great Highway*, tr. Arvid Paulson. In: *Modern Scandinavian Plays*. New York.
1955 *Queen Christina, Charles XII, Gustav III*, tr. Walter Johnson. Seattle.
1955 *Six Plays of Strindberg (The Father, Miss Julie, The Stronger, Easter, A Dream Play, The Ghost Sonata)*, tr. Elizabeth Sprigge. Garden City, N. Y.
1956 *The Last of the Knights, The Regent, Earl Birger of Bjälbo*, tr. Walter Johnson. Seattle.
1957 *Gustav Adolf*, tr. Walter Johnson. Seattle.
1958 *Three Plays by August Strindberg (The Father, Miss Julia, Easter)*, tr. Peter Watts. London.
1959 *The Saga of the Folkungs, Engelbrekt*, tr. Walter Johnson. Seattle.
1959 *The Vasa Trilogy (Master Olof, Gustav Vasa, Erik XIV)*, tr. Walter Johnson. Seattle.
1960 *Five Plays of Strindberg (Creditors, Crime and Crime, The Dance of Death, Swanwhite, The Great Highway)*, tr. Elizabeth Sprigge. Garden City, N. Y.
1960 *The Road to Damascus*, tr. Graham Rawson. New York.
1960 *Miss Julie and Other Plays (Miss Julie, Creditors, The Stronger, The Ghost Sonata)*, tr. Max Faber. London.
1960 *The Pelican*, tr. Evert Sprinchorn. In: *Tulane Drama Review*, 4.
1960 *Seven Plays by August Strindberg (The Father, Miss Julie, Comrades, The Stronger, The Bond, Crimes and Crimes, Easter)*, tr. Arvid Paulson. New York.
1962 *Isle of the Dead*, tr. R. Vowles. In: *Modern Drama*, 3.
1963 *Twelve Plays (The Father, Miss Julie, Creditors, The Stronger, The Bond, Crime and Crime, Easter, The Dance of Death, Swanwhite, A Dream Play, The Ghost Sonata, The Great Highway)*, tr. Elizabeth Sprigge. London.
1963 *Playing with Fire*, tr. Michael Meyer. London.
1964 *The Father, A Dream Play*, tr. and ed. Valborg Anderson. New York.
1964 *The Plays*, Vol. I *(The Father, Miss Julie, Creditors, The Stronger, Playing with Fire, Erik the Fourteenth, Storm, The Ghost Sonata)*, tr. Michael Meyer. London.
1964 *To Damascus*, Part I, tr. Evert Sprinchorn. In: Evert Sprinchorn (ed.), *The Genius of the Scandinavian Theater.* New York.
1965 *Eight Expressionist Plays (Lucky Per's Journey, The Keys of Heaven, To Damascus I–III, A Dream Play, The Great Highway, The Ghost Sonata)*, tr. Arvid Paulson. New York.
1966 *A Dream Play and The Ghost Sonata*, tr. Carl Richard Mueller. San Francisco.
1966 *The Dance of Death*, tr. Norman Ginsburg. In: C. Trewin (ed.), *Plays of the Year*. London.
1969 *Strindberg's One-Act Plays (The Outlaw, Miss Julie, Creditors, The Stronger, Pariah, Simoon, The First Warning, Debit and Credit, In the Face of Death, Motherlove, Playing with fire, The Bond, The Pelican)*, tr. Arvid Paulson. New York.

1970 *Pre-Inferno Plays (The Father, Lady Julie, Creditors, The Stronger, The Bond)*, tr. Walter Johnson. Seattle.

1970 *World Historical Plays (The Nightingale of Wittenberg, Through Deserts to Ancestral Lands, Hellas, The Lamb and the Beast)*, tr. Arvid Paulson. New York.

1973 *A Dream Play*. Adapted by Ingmar Bergman, tr. Michael Meyer. Stockholm.

1973 *A Dream Play and Four Chamber Plays (A Dream Play, Stormy Weather, The House That Burned, The Ghost Sonata, The Pelican)*, tr. Walter Johnson. Seattle.

1975 *The Plays*, Vol. II (*To Damascus I–III, Easter, The Dance of Death I–II, The Virgin Bride, A Dream Play*), tr. Michael Meyer. London.

1975 *Three Experimental Plays (Miss Julie, The Stronger, A Dream Play)*, tr. F. R. Southerington. Charlottesville.

1976 *The Dance of Death*, tr. Arvid Paulson. New York.

1976 *Dramas of Testimony (The Dance of Death I–II, Advent, Easter, There Are Crimes and Crimes)*, tr. Walter Johnson. Seattle.

1979 *Plays of Confession and Therapy (To Damascus I–III)*, tr. Walter Johnson. Seattle.

1981 *Apologia and Two Folk Plays (The Great Highway, The Crownbride, Swanwhite)*, tr. Walter Johnson. Seattle.

Bibliography

Adamov, A. 1955. *August Strindberg, dramaturge*. Paris.

Archer, W. (1912) 1960. *Play-making. A Manual of Craftsmanship*. New York.

Baker, G. P. (1919) 1947. *Dramatic Technique*. Boston.

Bandy, S. C. 1968. "Strindberg's Biblical Sources for *The Ghost Sonata*." *Scandinavian Studies*, XL.

Barry, J. G. 1970. *Dramatic Structure. The Shaping of Experience*. Berkeley.

Bayerdörfer, H.-P. 1976. "Eindringlinge, Marionetten, Automaten. Symbolistische Dramatik und die Anfänge des modernen Theaters." *Jahrbuch der deutschen Schillergesellschaft*, XX. Stuttgart.

Beckerman, B. 1970. *Dynamics of Drama. Theory and Method of Analysis*. New York.

Bennich-Björkman, B. 1971. "Fyrväpplingen och korset. Om symbolmeningen i Strindbergs Ett drömspel." In: G. and S. Bergsten (eds.), *Lyrik i tid och otid. Lyrikanalytiska studier tillägnade Gunnar Tideström*. Lund.

Bentley, E. (1946) 1955. *The Playwright as Thinker. A Study of the Modern Theatre*. New York.

Berendsohn, W. 1962. *August Strindbergs skärgårds- och Stockholmsskildringar*. Stockholm.

Bergman, G. M. 1966. *Den moderna teaterns genombrott 1890–1925*. Stockholm.

Bjurström, C. G. 1974. "Bokstav och ande." *Svensk Litteraturtidskrift*, 4.

Blom-Edström, V. 1954. "Vävsymbolen hos Rydberg, Selma Lagerlöf och Strindberg." *Göteborgsstudier i litteraturhistoria tillägnade Sverker Ek*. Göteborg.

Brainerd, B./Neufeldt, V. 1974. "On Marcus' Methods for the Analysis of the Strategy of a Play." *Poetics*, X.

Brandell, G. 1950. *Strindbergs Infernokris*. Stockholm. Engl. tr.: *Strindberg in Inferno*. Cambridge, Mass., 1974*a*.

Brandell, G. 1971. *Drama i tre avsnitt*. Stockholm.

Brandell, G. 1974*b*. *Svensk litteratur 1870–1970*, I. Stockholm.

Brooks, C./Heilman, R. (1945) 1961. *Understanding Drama*. New York.

Brustein, R. 1964. *The Theatre of Revolt*. Boston.

Bull, F./Koht, H./Seip, D. A. (eds.) 1928–57. *Henrik Ibsen. Samlede Verker*, I–XXI. Oslo.

Butcher, S. H. (1894) 1951. *Aristotle's Theory of Poetry and Fine Art*. New York.

Børge, V. 1942. *Strindbergs mystiske Teater. Æstetisk-dramaturgiske Analyser med særlig Hensyntagen til Drömspelet*. København.

Carlson, H. G. 1979. *Strindberg och myterna*. Stockholm.

Clemen, W. (1936) 1951. *The Development of Shakespeare's Imagery*. Cambridge, Mass.

Dahlström, C. E. W. L. 1930. *Strindberg's Dramatic Expressionism*. Ann Arbor.

Delblanc, S. 1968. "Kärlekens föda. Ett motiv i Strindbergs kammarspel." In: E. Törnqvist (ed.), *Drama och teater*. Stockholm.

Delblanc, S. 1979. *Stormhatten. Tre Strindbergsstudier*. Stockholm.

Diebold, B. 1928. *Anarchie im Drama*. Leipzig.

Dietrich, M. 1974. *Das moderne Drama. Strömungen, Gestalten, Motive*. Stuttgart.

Downer, A. 1955. *The Art of the Play*. Princeton.

Dyfverman, H. (1949) 1969. *Dramats teknik*. Stockholm.
Ellis-Fermor, U. (1945) 1964. *The Frontiers of Drama*. London.
Elmquist, C. J. 1949. *Strindbergs kammerspil*. København.
Falck, A. 1935. *Fem år med Strindberg*. Stockholm.
Freytag, G. 1863. *Die Technik des Dramas*. Leipzig.
Fraenkl, P. 1966. *Strindbergs dramatiske fantasi i Spöksonaten. En stildramaturgisk undersøkelse*. Oslo.
Gassner, J. 1965. *Directions in Modern Theatre and Drama*. New York.
Gierow, C. O. 1963. "Det franska pantomimintresset under 1800-talet såsom bakgrund till Fröken Julie." In: *Dramaten 175 år. Studier i svensk scenkonst*. Stockholm.
Gierow, C. O. 1967. *Documentation-évocation. Le Climat littéraire et théâtral en France des années 1880 et 'Mademoiselle Julie' de Strindberg*. Stockholm.
Gravier, M. 1949. *Strindberg et le théâtre moderne* I. *L'Allemagne*. Paris.
Hagsten, A. 1951. *Den unge Strindberg. Studier kring Tjänstekvinnans son och ungdomsverken*. Lund.
Hogendoorn, W. 1976. *Lezen en zien spelen. Een studie over simultaneïteit in het drama*. Leiden.
Holm, I. 1969. *Drama på scen*. Stockholm.
Ingarden, R. 1931. *Das literarische Kunstwerk*. Halle.
Jacobs, B. 1969*a*. "Introduction." In: *Strindberg's One-Act Plays*, tr. A. Paulson. New York.
Jacobs, B. 1969*b*. "Psychic Murder and Characterization in Strindberg's *The Father*." *Scandinavica*, 1.
Jansen, S. 1968. "Esquisse d'une théorie de la forme dramatique." *Langages*, XII.
Johnson, W. 1959. "Introduction" to *Erik XIV*. *The Vasa Trilogy*, tr. W. Johnson. Seattle.
Johnson, W. 1963. *Strindberg and the Historical Drama*. Seattle.
Johnson, W. 1971*a*. "'A Dream Play': Plans and Fulfilment." *Scandinavica, 2*.
Johnson, W. 1971*b*. "Strindberg and the Danse Macabre." In: O. Reinert (ed.), *Strindberg. A Collection of Critical Essays*. Englewood Cliffs.
Johnson, W. 1976. *August Strindberg*. Boston.
Jolivet, A. 1931. *Le théâtre de Strindberg*. Paris.
Josephson, L. 1965. *Strindbergs drama Fröken Julie*. Stockholm.
Kayser, W. (1948) 1969 *Das sprachliche Kunstwerk*. Bern/München.
Kjellin, G. 1971. "Spöksonaten." In: Kjellin G./Ramnefalk M.-L., *Modern dramatik*. Stockholm.
Klotz, V. 1960. *Geschlossene und offene Form im Drama*. München.
Kärnell, K.-Å. 1962. *Strindbergs bildspråk. En studie i prosastil*. Stockholm.
Lagercrantz, O. 1979. *August Strindberg*. Stockholm.
Lamm, M. 1924–26. *Strindbergs dramer,* I–II. Stockholm.
Lamm, M. 1940–42. *August Strindberg*, I–II. Stockholm.
Lamm, M. 1948. *Det moderna dramat*. Stockholm. Engl. tr.: *Modern Drama*. New York, 1973.
Larthomas, P. 1972. *Le langage dramatique. Sa nature. Ses procédes*. Paris.
Leifer, L. 1960. "Den lutrende ild." *Samlaren*, LXXXI.
Levitt, P. H. 1971. *A Structural Approach to the Analysis of Drama*. The Hague.
Lindenberger, H. 1975. *Historical Drama. The Relation of Literature and Reality*. Chicago.
Lindström, G. 1962. "Drama i d-moll." *Studiekamraten*.
Lindström, G. 1963*a*. "Strindberg Studies 1915–1962." *Scandinavica*, 1.

Lindström, G. 1963*b*. "Kommentar." In: A. Strindberg, *Spöksonaten*. Lund.
Lindström, G. 1964*a*. "Inledning." In: A. Strindberg, *Till Damaskus*. Lund.
Lindström, G. 1964*b* "Dialog och bildspråk i Strindbergs kammarspel." In: G. Lindström (ed.) *Strindbergs språk och stil*. Lund.
Lindström, G. 1966. "Strindberg's Chamber Play, Opus 2, 'After the Fire'." In: C. R. Smedmark (ed.), *Essays on Strindberg*. Stockholm.
Lindström, G. 1969. *Att läsa dramatik*. Lund.
Lindström, H. 1952. *Hjärnornas kamp. Psykologiska idéer och motiv i Strindbergs åttiotalsdiktning*. Uppsala.
Lindström, H. 1976. "Vad händer i Dödsdansen?" In: J. Stenkvist (ed.), *Från Snoilsky till Sonnevi. Litteraturvetenskapliga studier tillägnade Gunnar Brandell*. Stockholm.
Lindström, H. 1979. "Mosaiken i Spöksonaten." *Svensk Litteraturtidskrift*, 3.
Link, J. 1975. "Zur Theorie der Matrizierbarkeit dramatische Konfigurationen." In: A. van Kesteren/H. Schmid (eds.), *Moderne Dramentheorie*. Kronberg.
Lucas, F. L. 1962. *Ibsen and Strindberg*. London.
Lunin, H. 1962. *Strindbergs Dramen*. Emsdetten.
Madsen, B. G. 1962. *Strindberg's Naturalistic Theatre. It's Relation to French Naturalism*. København.
Marcus, C. D. 1918. *August Strindbergs Dramatik*. München.
Marcus, S. 1973. *Mathematische Poetik*. Frankfurt.
Mattsson, M. 1974. "Strindberg's *Miss Julie* in English: The Value of Literature in Translation." *Scandinavica*, 2.
McFarlane, J. W. 1960–75. *The Oxford Ibsen*, I–VIII. Oxford.
Müssener, H. 1965. *August Strindberg, "Ein Traumspiel". Struktur- und Stilstudien*. Meisenheim am Glan.
Norman, N. 1964. "Strindberg och Dante." *Svensk Litteraturtidskrift*, 3.
Northam, J. 1966. "Strindberg's Spook Sonata." In: C. R. Smedmark (ed.), *Essays on Strindberg*. Stockholm.
Northam, J. 1973. *Ibsen. A Critical Study*. Cambridge.
Ollén, G. (1948) 1961. *Strindbergs dramatik*. Stockholm.
Paul, F. 1976. "Strindberg og monodramaet." *Edda*, 5.
Paul, F. 1979. *August Strindberg*. Stuttgart.
Perger, A. 1952. *Grundlagen der Dramaturgie*. Graz.
Pfister, M. 1977. *Das Drama*. München.
Pilick, E. 1969. *Strindbergs Kammerspiele. Ein Beitrag zur Dramaturgie des intimen Dramas*. Köln.
Rinman, S. 1957. "Strindberg." In: *Ny illustrerad svensk litteraturhistoria*, IV. Stockholm.
Rothwell, B. 1966. "The Chamber Plays." In: C. R. Smedmark (ed.), *Essays on Strindberg*. Stockholm.
Schérer, J. 1959. *La dramaturgie classique en France*. Paris.
Schnetz, D. 1967. *Der moderne Einakter. Eine poetologische Untersuchung*. Bern.
Shipley, J. T. (ed.) 1960. *Dictionary of World Literature*. Paterson, N. J.
Sjöstedt, N. Å. 1963. "Strindbergs Erik XIV." *Modersmålslärarnas förenings årsskrift*.
Smedmark, C. R. 1952. *Mäster Olof och Röda rummet*. Stockholm.
Smedmark, C. R. 1970. "Inledning till Den starkare, Paria och Samum." "Inledning till Debet och kredit, Första varningen, Inför döden och Moderskärlek." In: *August Strindbergs dramer*, IV, ed. C. R. Smedmark. Stockholm.
Sokel, W. H. 1963. "Introduction." In: *An Anthology of German Expressionist Drama*, ed. W. H. Sokel. Garden City, N. Y.

Sourieau, E. 1950. *Les deux cent mille situations dramatiques*. Paris.
Sprinchorn, E. 1962*a* "Introduction." In: August Strindberg, *The Chamber Plays*, tr. E. Sprinchorn, Seabury Quinn, Jr., K. Petersen. New York.
Sprinchorn, E. 1962*b*. "The Logic of *A Dream Play*." *Modern Drama*, 3.
Sprinchorn, E. (ed.) 1964. *The Genius of the Scandinavian Theater*. New York.
Spurgeon, C. F. E. 1935. *Shakespeare's Imagery and What It Tells Us*. Cambridge.
Steene, B. 1971. "Shakespearean Elements in Historical Plays of Strindberg." In: O. Reinert (ed.), *Strindberg. A Collection of Critical Essays*. Englewood Cliffs.
Steene, B. 1973. *The Greatest Fire. A Study of August Strindberg*. Carbondale/Edwardsville.
Stockenström, G. 1972. *Ismael i öknen. Strindberg som mystiker*. Uppsala.
Strindberg, A. 1912–21. *Samlade skrifter* (*SS*), I–LV, ed. J. Landquist. Stockholm.
Strindberg, A. 1918–19. *Samlade otryckta skrifter (SOS)*, I–II. Stockholm.
Strindberg, A. 1962–70. *August Strindbergs dramer* (*ASD*), ed. C. R. Smedmark. Stockholm.
Strindberg, A. 1948–76. *August Strindbergs brev* (*ASB*), I–XV, ed. T. Eklund. Stockholm.
Strindberg, A. 1977. *Ockulta dagboken* (*OD*), Stockholm.
Styan, J. L. (1960) 1967. *Elements of Drama*. Cambridge.
Swerling, A. 1971 *Strindberg's Impact in France 1920–1960*. Cambridge.
Swerling, A. 1972. "Frenchifying Strindberg—a literary hoax?" *Svensk Litteraturtidskrift*, 4.
Sylvan, G. 1948. "August Strindberg som målare." *Dikt och konst. Tidskrift för konstvetenskap*. Stockholm.
Szondi, P. (1956) 1970. *Theorie des modernen Dramas (1880–1950)*. Frankfurt am Main.
Tomaševskij, B. 1971. *Teorija Literatury*. Letchworth.
Thomsen, E. 1943 "Bidrag til Tolkningen af 'Ett Drömspel'." *Orbis Litterarum*, I.
Törnqvist, E. 1965. "Hamlet och Spöksonaten." *Meddelanden från Strindbergssällskapet*, 37. Engl. tr.: "*Hamlet* and *The Ghost Sonata*". *Drama Survey*, 1–2, 1968–69.
Törnqvist, E. 1970*a*. "Sein und Schein in Strindbergs 'Spooksonate'." *Maatstaf*, 10.
Törnqvist, E. 1970*b*. "Strindberg's *The Stronger*." *Scandinavian Studies*, 3.
Törnqvist, E. 1973*a*. "Bildspråket i Strindbergs Fadren." *Meddelanden från Strindbergssällskapet*, 51–52.
Törnqvist, E. 1973*b*. *Svenska dramastrukturer* (esp. "August Strindberg: *Första varningen* (1893)"). Stockholm.
Törnqvist, E. 1973*c*. "Monodrama: Term and Reality." In: *Essays on Drama and Theatre. Liber Amicorum Benjamin Hunningher*. Amsterdam.
Törnqvist, E. 1973*d*. "Ingmar Bergman Directs Strindberg's 'Ghost Sonata'." *Theatre Quarterly*, July–Sept.
Törnqvist, E. 1973*e*. *Bergman och Strindberg. Spöksonaten – drama och iscensättning. Dramaten 1973*. Stockholm.
Törnqvist, E. 1975. "Strindberg and the Drama of Half-reality. An Analysis of To Damascus I." *Strindberg and Modern Theatre*. Stockholm.
Törnqvist, E. 1976*a*. "Strindbergs syn på Fröken Julie." *Värld och vetande*, 4.
Törnqvist, E. 1976*b*. "Att översätta Strindberg. Spöksonaten på engelska." *Svensk Litteraturtidskrift*, 2.
Törnqvist, E. 1977*a*. "Intrigen i Strindbergs Erik XIV." *Svensklärarföreningens årsskrift*. Stockholm.
Törnqvist, E. 1977*b*. "Scenens Strindberg och verklighetens. Per Olov Enquists *Tribadernas natt* (1975) som dokumentärt drama." In: *Literature and Reality. Creatio*

versus Mimesis. Problems of Realism in Modern Nordic Literature, ed. A. Bolckmans. Ghent.

Törnqvist, E. 1978*a*. "Ett dramatiskt dilemma." *Svensk Litteraturtidskrift*, 2.

Törnqvist, E. 1978*b*. "Första turen i Dödsdansen." *Svensk Litteraturtidskrift*, 3.

Törnqvist, E. 1978*c*. "Inledningssekvensen i Dödsdansen 1." *Tidskrift för litteraturvetenskap*, 4.

Törnqvist, E. 1979*a*. "Talsituationerna i *Fröken Julie*." Värld och vetande, 1.

Törnqvist, E. 1979*b*. "*Faust* and *The Ghost Sonata*." *Strindberg und die deutschsprachigen Länder. Beiträge zur nordischen Philologie*, 8. Basel/Stuttgart.

Törnqvist, E. 1980*a*. "De bewerking van de realiteit: het historie-drama." *Scenarium*, IV.

Törnqvist, E. 1980*b*. "Der Schluss in *Fröken Julie*." *Skandinavistik*, 2.

Valency, M. 1963. *The Flower and the Castle. An Introduction to Modern Drama*. New York.

Van Kesteren, A. 1975. "Der Stand der modernen Dramentheorie." A. van Kesteren/H. Schmid (eds.) *Moderne Dramentheorie*. Kronberg.

Van der Kun, J. I. M. (1938) 1970. *Handelingsaspecten in het drama*. Amsterdam.

Van Laan, Th. F. 1970. *The Idiom of Drama*. Ithaka.

Ward, J. 1980. *The Social and Religious Plays of Strindberg*. London.

Weitz, M. 1966. *Hamlet and the Philosophy of Literary Criticism*. Cleveland/New York.

Vogelweith, G. 1972. *Le psychothéâtre de Strindberg*. Paris.

Vowles, R. 1962. "A Cook's Tour of Strindberg Scholarship." *Modern Drama*, 3.

Vowles, R. 1967. "Strindberg and Beethoven." In: G. Svanfeldt (ed.), *Växelverkan mellan skönlitteraturen och andra konstarter*. Uppsala.